Food, Wine
&
Friends

FOOD, WINE & FRIENDS

Robert Carrier

BOOK CLUB ASSOCIATES
London

This edition published 1980 by
Book Club Associates
by arrangement with
Sidgwick and Jackson Limited
Copyright © 1980 Robert Carrier

Designed by Gillian Allan and Ray Hyden

Printed in Great Britain by
W. S. Cowell Limited of Ipswich

To my favourite ladies Eileen Dickson, Ailsa Garland, Psyche Pirie and Doris Shaw – who over the years have shared so much with me – my grateful thanks.

Contents

Food, Wine & Friends– How it all Began

I have a confession to make. I am as gregarious as I am greedy. Or should I put it the other way around? In any case, it is irrefutable: I love the good things of life – good food, fine wine and lovely people.

Of course, I also like reading and gardening, listening to music and lazing on hot, sunny beaches. And of course I'm a workaholic, always planning three more projects when I should be finishing two that were promised for yesterday. But I still find time for my very special pleasures: food, wine and friends. What more can anyone ask? Particularly when all three can be brought together in an exciting new project: a series of 24 half-hour cooking shows on the 'box' called, of all things,' Food, Wine & Friends'.

When I first planned my work-in/live-in kitchen at Hintlesham, I never dreamed that one day it would be the setting for a new series of television programmes. All I really wanted was one big workroom where I could express my own brand of comfortable non-conformity. I wanted it to be a studio, a dining room, a place where I could paint if I wanted to, and a place to cook in all the time where my friends could be with me while I was at it. A really comfortable common room, in fact. But as *uncommon* a room as I could make it, for my twentieth-century version is at one and the same time a living room, a dining room and a kitchen. And I've added one important new element: the door opens directly on to a large terrace and vegetable garden which becomes a sort of annex to the house, a place to prepare vegetables as well as pick them.

I've been on television many times in America and Australia, and invariably they have asked me to cook on the show. I don't mind cooking in public. I actually enjoy it. But I always found at the last minute that there was no proper knife or large frying pan available, and I was stuck with transporting huge quantities of kitchen equipment across these very large continents to make sure I had everything I required.

Here at last was the opportunity to do it all in the comfort of my own home. No carrying half-cooked dishes miles to cold, draughty studios where the ovens don't work; no last-minute shopping for fresh foodstuffs (the restaurant kitchen and vegetable garden are right next door) and no frantic search for 'props' (the entire house is full of bowls, platters and dishes of every description). I jumped at the chance to talk about food and wine in my own home, cook in my own kitchen, use vegetables and herbs from my own garden and share the fun with

This book is really the story of a man in love with a house. The house – four-hundred-year-old Hintlesham Hall in Suffolk – is more than just my home. Restaurant, headquarters for the Robert Carrier Dining Club and home of my recently created New School of Cooking, Hintlesham provides the perfect setting for 'Food, Wine & Friends'.

Cloris Leachman, movie star and food buff, lends her own kind of zany fun to the series when she discusses one of her favourite subjects – nutrition.

Barry Levinson and the 'food man' enjoy a break in filming in the Blue Kitchen at Hintlesham.

friends who came from all over the world to join me in the series to talk about their favourite foods.

There were three ideas behind this new series: (1) to teach the basic techniques of good cooking, not just recipes. (2) To take the *mystique* out of buying and enjoying wines by talking to the growers, the bottlers and the *négociants* on their own home grounds in the wine-growing regions of France, Italy and Germany, and (3), to share with friends from all over the world my favourite recipes and cooking techniques.

John Cleese learns how to make a Béarnaise sauce; how to ruin it (heaven forbid!) and then how to save it again (with nothing more than an ice cube!). The beautiful Italian *diva*, Valentina Cortese, first tastes the excitements of Elizabeth I's favourite herb, 'sweet' rocket, and pasta with black truffles, and tells me about putting vodka in her own pasta sauce. (These Italians!) Liv Ullman, one of Ingmar Bergman's brightest stars and one of the truly great actresses in the world, with her daughter Linn, learns all about Japanese noodles and many other appetizers. Burgess Meredith instructs us on American wines, and Petula Clark, Hugh Johnson, Joanna Lumley, Paul Bocuse, Joseph Cotten, Bianca Jagger, and many others, bring their own lustre and knowledge to the series.

Working on the show was great fun. Naturally, there had to be follow-up dishes created to be ready for the many times we had to shoot. Stig Henriksen and Nigel Rolfe, my two head cooks at Hintlesham, were the assistants here, and Mohamed el Klahi, Polly Planner and Jackie Cottee helped with the ordering of foodstuffs, the typing of manuscripts and the correcting of proofs. My thanks to all of them. And to Janet Levinson who created my 'wardrobe' with her wonderful selection of cashmere sweaters for the series (I'm still wearing them!); to Patrick Dromgoole, the imaginative and courageous head of HTV, who commissioned the series and had the doubtful pleasure of footing the bills; and to Sebastian Robinson, my director, who gently guided me through a whole new world of video cameras, trackings, dubbings and scripts. He put up patiently with my many suggestions (only punishing me once when he made me walk up a huge hill in Italy, talking into a sound mike the whole, interminable, gasping way) and with my four-letter words (each and every time I fluffed some very important line). But my greatest thanks of all go to my producer, the man who thought up the whole idea, who nursed me through the gruelling two months of filming, and who piloted me through France, Italy and Germany, suggesting ways which would make the presentation of the fine foods and wines on the programme both more meaningful and more down-to-earth: Barry Levinson.

Lovely Liv Ullman in a pensive mood.

A book to complete the series

Obviously we needed a book to complete the picture so that you can follow the recipes more easily. This is it. Whether or not you see all the programmes, this book tells the whole story of each of the recipes demonstrated, plus many more on the same theme. Appetizers and first courses; making soups and sauces; open-fire grilling and pan-grilling; roasting; deep-frying and pan-frying; steaming; casseroles; cooking *en papillote* and *au gratin*; making cakes, sweets and puddings; and emergency shelf meals for unexpected guests.

And then there are the photographs: still photographers Stuart Sadd and Rod Ebdon were on hand to record moments with the guest stars; John Stewart came over from America to photograph many of the dishes for me, and Michael Boys, James Mortimer, Roy Rich and John Miller in England and Jack Nisberg in Paris each took a hand with the others. All in all there are 130 beautiful colour photographs of food, wine and friends in this book. It is a very visual book, one that I hope will bring us pleasure for years to come.

Guest star Burgess Meredith (he has one of the finest cellars in California) and I discuss the relative merits of French and American wines. Floor manager takes note.

*Nasturtium leaves and basil set the
scene for a light-hearted appetizer
from the South of France. (Recipe,
page 17)*

The Story of a Garden

Once you grow your own tomatoes, the chances are you will never again buy the tough-skinned bullets passed off under that name at the local super-market. But at least you can get tomatoes there; the same cannot always be said for salsify, sorrel, fresh new potatoes and peas, or fresh herbs.

That is why growing vegetables in the eighteenth-century manner – in small plots decoratively edged with colourful herb and flower borders – is the great new craze for all cooks with a back garden to play with.

And this sort of gardening is easy, too. Only four years ago, my eighteenth-century kitchen garden at Hintlesham Hall was the grim setting for the best nettle and boulder crop in East Anglia. Today, after a year of preparation – clearing the area of rocks, roots and shrubs, activating and feeding the soil and even irrigating the sub strata with folded-up cardboard boxes to facilitate drainage – the garden is the pleasure-ground that you see now.

The crop and border in each bed have been specially chosen for the most exciting combinations of colours and shapes; dark green wild strawberry plants with a border of silver grey cotton lavender; cool green curly lettuces edged with serried rows of blue-green chives; and cascading 'wigwams' of green beans teamed with bright orange-flowered nasturtiums.

Guests who lunch or dine at Hintlesham come and walk through this garden, and are allowed to pick any amount of herbs. One favourite is French tarragon, which grows wonderfully in the garden both as a main crop and as a border plant. I use this pungent herb in salads, chicken and veal recipes, and for fish sauces.

Another favourite herb is *roquette*, which Queen Elizabeth I called 'sweet rocket'. It has a dark-green, spiky leaf with a peppery flavour that is almost meaty. I like to put whole sprigs of it in salad with tarragon, green and purple basil, flat-leaved Italian parsley, feathery fennel and lemon-scented *pourprier*. *Pourprier*, or purslane as it was called in old herbals, has a fat succulent leaf, giving great body and interest to 'sallet' in the old English way.

Above *Once a grim setting for the best nettle and boulder crop in East Anglia, the eighteenth-century kitchen garden is a pleasure-ground of ordered parterres separated by herb-bordered walks that make gardening simple for lazy gardeners like me.*

Plants are seeded in nearby greenhouses in small batches before being transferred to the kitchen garden. We sow a row or two of each variety, then wait a week and sow again. The seedlings are then transplanted at intervals, providing a succession of tasty young crops throughout the summer.

Far left *Head gardeners George Trinder and Mark Nunn are responsible for the day-to-day running of the greenhouses, gardens and grounds.*

Near left *Terrine de Saumon Persille is a fresh-tasting terrine of salmon and chopped smoked salmon and hard-boiled eggs, and herbs from the garden. (Recipe, page 16)*

Cooking with herbs

Fresh herbs from the garden add much to good cooking: rosemary goes wonderfully well with roast lamb when combined with a little finely chopped garlic and crumbled bay leaf. Sage is marvellous with pork in the Provençal manner. Just cut slits in the deep fat of the roast and tuck a little sliver of garlic, a leaf or two of sage and a tiny sprig of rosemary in each incision.

I recently visited the Troigros brothers' famous restaurant in Royanne. There I had the most marvellous sole dish that I've ever tasted: the sole had been sautéed in butter, covered in fresh breadcrumbs and baked until the crumbs were golden; the fish was served in a sauce of thick *crème fraîche* liberally spiked with freshly chopped chives.

Les Farcies aux Herbes

Ingredients

Butter
½ oz (15g) plain flour
¼ pint (1½ dl) milk
2 oz (50g) Gruyère cheese, freshly grated
Salt and freshly ground black pepper
Freshly grated nutmeg
¼ lb (100g) button mushrooms
1 tablespoon lemon juice
1 level teaspoon chopped fresh tarragon leaves
½ level teaspoon dried oregano
4 small brioches, or rolls

1 Make a thick white sauce with ½ oz (15 g) butter, flour and milk. Beat in cheese smoothly over a low heat and season to taste with salt and freshly ground black pepper, and freshly grated nutmeg.

2 Trim mushroom stems but leave them intact. Wash and wipe mushrooms clean and slice very thinly lengthwise. Brush a few of the most attractive mushroom slices with a little lemon juice to prevent discoloration and put them aside for garnish.

3 Sauté remaining sliced mushrooms gently in ½ oz (15 g) butter for 3–4 minutes, sprinkling them with remaining lemon juice. Add to sauce, together with fresh tarragon and dried oregano, and season to taste.

4 Preheat oven to moderate (350°F/180°C/Mark 4).

5 Remove tops from brioches or rolls, and scoop out centres to leave firm cases about ¼ inch (½ cm) thick.

6 Fill brioches, or rolls, with mushroom sauce and arrange them in an ovenproof dish. Garnish each brioche, or roll, with reserved mushroom slices; replace top and brush with a little melted butter. Heat through in preheated oven for 10–15 minutes, or until very hot. Serve immediately.

Serves 4

Terrine de Saumon Persille *(Illustration, page 14)*

Ingredients

6 11-inch (27½ cm) strips lightly poached salmon
8 heaped teaspoons powdered gelatine
2 pints (1.1 litres) well-flavoured fish stock (see page 26)
Salt and freshly ground black pepper
Diced whites of 4 hard-boiled eggs
4–6 oz (100–175g) diced smoked salmon
1 bunch parsley, chopped

1 To make aspic: dissolve gelatine in 8 tablespoons hot water and add to fish stock. Season with salt and freshly ground black pepper, to taste. Blend in diced egg white, diced smoked salmon and chopped parsley and allow aspic to set until it is syrupy, stirring from time to time.

2 To assemble terrine: cover bottom of rectangular terrine (11¾ × 3¼ inches [29 × 8 cm]) with a thin layer of aspic; allow to set in refrigerator; arrange 2 strips of poached salmon on top of aspic, leaving space between strips; cover salmon with aspic; return to refrigerator to set as above; place another 2 strips of poached salmon on top of aspic; cover with aspic; allow to set; place remaining 2 strips of fresh salmon on top. Fill terrine with remaining aspic.

3 Place terrine in refrigerator and chill overnight or until set. Serve with cucumber cream (see page 63).

Note: keep aspic syrupy while aspic-filled terrine sets in refrigerator by immersing bowl containing aspic in a larger bowl of warm water.

Fifine's Tomato Salad *(Illustration, page 12)*

1 Wash tomatoes and cut in half horizontally. Arrange tomato halves, cut side up, on a serving dish and season generously with salt and freshly ground black pepper.

2 Sprinkle each tomato half with finely chopped *echalote rose* (or finely chopped onion or spring onions). Mix fresh herbs together and sprinkle each tomato half with a thick green layer of chopped herbs.

3 Make a well-flavoured French dressing (3 parts olive oil to 1 part wine vinegar, Dijon mustard and salt and freshly ground black pepper, to taste). Dribble 2-3 tablespoons dressing over each tomato half.

Serves 4

Ingredients
4 large tomatoes
Salt and freshly ground black pepper
8 level tablespoons finely chopped echalote rose, or finely chopped onion or spring onions
4 level tablespoons finely chopped tarragon leaves
4 level tablespoons finely chopped basil leaves
4 level tablespoons finely chopped parsley
Olive oil
Wine vinegar
Dijon mustard

Italian Herb Pancakes

1 To make crêpes: sift flour and salt into a mixing bowl. Beat egg and add to dry ingredients. Mix in milk and melted butter or oil gradually to avoid lumps. Strain through a fine sieve; add finely chopped basil and leave batter to stand for at least 2 hours before cooking the crêpes. Batter should be as thin as single cream. Add a little water if too thick.

2 For each crêpe, spoon about 2 tablespoons batter into heated pan, swirling pan to allow batter to cover entire surface thinly. Brush a piece of butter on or around edge of hot pan with the point of a knife and cook over a medium heat until just golden, but not brown (about 1 minute each side). Repeat until all crêpes are cooked, stacking them on a plate as they are ready. The mixture makes 8-12 golden crêpes.

3 To make filling: wash watercress and lettuce. Drain. Remove stalks and yellowed leaves from watercress. Remove outer leaves from lettuce. Chop coarsely. Combine chopped watercress and lettuce with chopped fresh herbs and sauté in 2 level tablespoons butter. Season with salt and freshly ground black pepper, to taste. Press dry and then add ricotta, or cottage cheese, together with beaten eggs, freshly grated Parmesan cheese, cream and nutmeg, to taste.

4 Spread each crêpe generously with filling. Roll pancakes and put them in a well-buttered rectangular baking dish. Chill until 1 hour before using.

5 When ready to serve: brush each pancake with melted butter; sprinkle with freshly grated Parmesan cheese and bake for 20 minutes in a moderate oven (350°F/180°C/Mark 4). Serve with a well-flavoured tomato sauce.

Serves 4-6

Ingredients
CRÊPES
3 level tablespoons flour
¼ level teaspoon salt
1 egg
7 fluid oz (2 dl) milk
1 tablespoon melted butter, or oil
6 level tablespoons finely chopped fresh basil
Butter or oil, for cooking

FILLING
1 bunch watercress
1 head lettuce
2 level tablespoons chopped tarragon
2 level tablespoons chopped chives
Butter
Salt and freshly ground black pepper
½ lb (225g) ricotta cheese, or cottage cheese
3 eggs, lightly beaten
1-2 oz (25-50g) freshly grated Parmesan cheese
6 tablespoons double cream
freshly grated nutmeg
½ pint (3 dl) well-flavoured tomato sauce (see page 58)

Cooking with spices

Four thousand years before the birth of Christ, in the Valley of the Indus, the people of what is now known as Pakistan were grinding mustard seeds with fennel and cumin seeds to flavour sophisticated stews of meats and poultry. They knew how to grind their grain into flour; made use of ovens to bake their breads and meats; and cultivated melons and dates, coconuts and bananas, pomegranates and, perhaps, even lemons and limes. Sheep, goats, buffalo, pigs, elephants and camels were all common species, and the Indian jungle fowl – later to become the world's chicken – was already domesticated.

It was this same remarkable people who first invented the mortar and pestle to grind spices and blend them into exciting flavouring compounds that changed culinary history. And it was they who first collected the little green berries, dried them in the sun, and ground them to produce pepper, the aromatic spice that one day would be deemed as valuable as gold.

Whenever I see the beautiful, sharp acid yellow of mustard fields growing alongside the roads in East Anglia, I think back to the twin cities of Harappa and Mohenjodaro, which have influenced so greatly what we eat today.

Mustard seed – either ground or whole – was later used by the ancient Greeks and Romans, who sprinkled it on to cooked dishes much as we now use salt and pepper to season our foods. Indeed, the Roman legions liked this pungent herb so much that they carried mustard seeds with them wherever they went. It is thanks to them that mustard is such an important culinary crop in Britain today.

There are recipes calling for the use of mustard in the earliest recorded cookbooks from ancient Greece and Rome. But it was not until centuries later that mustard became the prime agent in preparations of honey and vinegar, or *verjuice*, as we call it now. In France particularly, mustard mixing became such a fad in the eighteenth century that the crushed seeds were blended with a common variety of foods, including capers, rose water, honey and anchovies.

English mustard – a plain dry powder – is mixed with cold water (not hot water

Mustard seeds – either ground or whole – were used by the ancient Greeks and Romans, who sprinkled them on to cooked dishes much as we use salt and pepper. The Roman legions liked this pungent herb so much that they carried mustard seeds with them wherever they went. It is thanks to them that mustard is such an important culinary crop in France and England today.

Opposite page *A field of mustard in France.*

Above *Antique mustard-pots in a mustard shop in Dijon.*

Left *Seventeenth-century mustard-jar from Dijon.*

or vinegar, which tend to make mustard less flavourful and bitter) and left for 10 minutes to develop its typical flavour. It is a clean and pungent seasoning, the perfect accompaniment to roast beef, grilled beef steaks, pork chops and hot or cold boiled ham.

Dry mustard is wonderful with baked ham. Just add 1 level teaspoon to glaze. Combine with olive oil to spread over steak before grilling. Add to coating mixture for croquettes or fried chicken. Add to baked macaroni and cheese. It is very good in casseroles of ham, turkey and seafood, croquettes and baked beans.

Add dry mustard to a French dressing, you'll find it helps the emulsifying process. It is also a necessity for mayonnaise (for the same reason). Add to tuna, crab, lobster and salmon salads, to macaroni and ham salads and to potato salads.

Dry mustard is excellent to spark up cream sauces and cheese sauces. Mix with butter and lemon juice, to taste, to dress cooked cabbage, broccoli and Brussels sprouts.

Add a tablespoon of whole mustard seeds to poaching liquid for spiced shrimps and prawns or spiced meats. Mustard seeds are an essential ingredient of cucumber pickles, vegetable relishes, chutney, pickled onions and pickled lemons.

Add 1 level teaspoon mustard seeds to cole slaw. Add to mixed vegetable salads and potato salads. They also provide good flavour change for French dressing.

Arabian Kefta

Ingredients

1½ lb (675g) lamb, from leg
½ lb (225g) lamb fat,
½ Spanish onion, finely chopped
6–8 mint leaves, finely chopped
6–8 sprigs parsley, finely chopped
½ level teaspoon dried marjoram
Salt and fresh black pepper
¼ level teaspoon each powdered cumin, cayenne pepper and paprika
1 generous pinch of two or more of the following: powdered nutmeg, cinnamon, cloves, ginger and cardamom
Butter

KEFTA SAUCE

1 lb (450g) tomatoes, peeled, seeded and chopped
½ Spanish onion, finely chopped
2 level tablespoons finely chopped parsley
1 clove garlic, finely chopped
4 tablespoons olive oil
½ pint (3 dl) water
Paprika
Cayenne pepper
Salt

1 To made *kefta* sauce: combine ingredients (sauce should be very highly flavoured) and simmer for 1 hour, uncovered.

2 Put lamb, lamb fat and Spanish onion through the finest blade of your mincer 3 times.

3 Combine mixture in a large mixing bowl with finely chopped mint leaves and parsley, marjoram and salt and freshly ground black pepper and spices, to taste. Mix well. The *kefta* mixture should be very highly flavoured.

4 Form *kefta* mixture into little balls the size of a marble and poach gently in water for 10 minutes. Then sauté gently in butter until lightly browned.

5 Finally, simmer in *kefta* sauce for at least 10 minutes before serving. Serve *kefta* in sauce or on a bed of rice with sauce apart.

Serves 6–8

Choosing wines in restaurants

When in doubt about the wine to order with your meal, it is always a good idea to consult the captain or wine-waiter, telling him the type of wine you prefer (dry, light, full-bodied, rich) and the price range you would like to consider (inexpensive, medium-priced or an exceptional bottle for a special occasion). The wine-waiter's job is to serve a wine that will please you. But, as he does not know your palate, it is up to you to make your preferences known.

In deciding whether to accept or reject a bottle of wine ordered in a wine bar or restaurant, it is well to keep the restaurant's obligation in mind: to serve a wine that is in sound condition.

Cumin seed, ginger, cinnamon, cayenne pepper and paprika are the five magical spices of Arabian cooking. Use them to add interest to stews, terrines and mixed vegetables and to spike Spiced Grilled Hamburgers and Arabian Kefta.

Spiced Grilled Hamburgers

1 Combine minced rump steak, chopped beef marrow, finely chopped onion and parsley, spices and salt and freshly ground black pepper, to taste. Form mixture into 8 patties.

2 Brush patties with melted butter and grill for 4 to 5 minutes on each side.

Serves 4

Ingredients

2 lb (900g) rump steak, minced

6 level tablespoons chopped beef marrow

4 level tablespoons finely chopped onion

4 level tablespoons finely chopped parsley

½ level teaspoon powdered cumin

¼ level teaspoon powdered paprika

¼ level teaspoon powdered cayenne pepper

Salt and freshly ground black pepper

4 tablespoons melted butter

Tasting wines in restaurants

Once the wine has been selected, the wine-waiter will open the bottle and pour out a sample for your opinion before he fills the glasses at the table. And here it is important to remember that your goal in tasting the wine is to verify its soundness and condition, not to decide whether or not you like the wine in question.

So (1) take the glass gently by the stem and (2) roll the wine around the glass lightly to release its bouquet and to show its quality; then (3) bring the glass to your nose to inhale its bouquet; and finally (4) taste the wine. Lastly, make your menu known to the wine-waiter.

Madras Chicken Curry

Ingredients

4 tablespoons ghee or clarified butter
1 chicken (about 3 lb (1.4 kg))
2 Spanish onions, chopped
2 cloves garlic, chopped
2 tart green apples, peeled, cored and coarsely chopped
2 bananas, peeled and sliced
2 level tablespoons Special Curry Blend (see below)
4 level tablespoons raisins
2 level tablespoons mango chutney, chopped
¾ pint (4 dl) chicken stock
Salt and freshly ground black pepper
Ground ginger
Cayenne pepper
Juice of ½ lemon

1 Cut chicken into 8 serving pieces and sauté pieces in *ghee* or clarified butter in a large, thick bottomed-frying pan until golden. Transfer to a heatproof casserole.

2 Sauté the chopped onions, garlic and apples in the remaining fats until onions begin to turn colour. Stir in sliced bananas and sauté for a few minutes more. Add ingredients with a slotted spoon to the chicken pieces in the heatproof casserole.

3 Stir the Special Curry Blend into the fat remaining in the pan, adding a little more *ghee* or clarified butter if necessary, and cook for 5 minutes, stirring from time to time, being careful not to let it burn.

4 Stir in raisins, mango chutney and chicken stock. Pour this mixture over chicken pieces. Chicken stock should just cover chicken. Add more, if necessary.

5 Cook, covered, for ½ hour, then taste sauce – adding salt and freshly ground black pepper, ginger and cayenne pepper, to taste. Continue to simmer curry, uncovered, until the chicken is tender and the sauce is thick. Stir in lemon juice just before serving.

Serves 4–6

Special Curry Blend

Ingredients

4 level tablespoons coriander seed
3 level tablespoons cumin seed
2 level teaspoons mustard seed
2 level teaspoons fenugreek seed
2 level tablespoons ground cinnamon
3 level tablespoons ground black peppercorns
2 level teaspoons ground nutmeg
1 level teaspoon ground cloves
1 level teaspoon ground cardamom seeds
1 level tablespoon ground turmeric seeds
1 level tablespoon ground ginger
1 level tablespoon cayenne pepper

1 Put the coriander, cumin, mustard and *fenugreek* seeds into a thick iron-bottomed frying pan and toast over a medium flame until the mustard seeds pop. Do not allow spices to burn.

2 Cool spices and then grind them and combine with the remaining ingredients.

3 Put through a fine sieve and store in an air-tight jar until ready for use.

Indian Rice

Indian rice is always carefully rinsed and drained, and cooked in a large container with boiling salted water in the proportions three of water to one of rice. The rice is then drained, flavoured with carefully ground spices – a mixture of equal parts of ground cinnamon, cardamom and mace – and tossed with *ghee* (Indian clarified butter). Or try the following variations:

Finely chop ½ Spanish onion and sauté it, stirring constantly in 4 level tablespoons of butter or *ghee* until the onion is transparent. Remove the onion with a slotted spoon and reserve for later use. Add 6 level tablespoons each of cashew nuts and sultanas to the pan and sauté for a few minutes more. Then add ½ level teaspoon each of fennel seeds, cumin seeds, mustard seeds and powdered turmeric to the pan. Stir in 2 level tablespoons butter or *ghee* and sauté spices, stirring, for two minutes more. When ready to serve, combine sautéed onion, nuts, sultanas and spice mixture and heat through. Then add drained rice and toss gently over a low heat until rice is hot. Serve immediately. In Southern India, freshly grated coconut is added to the nuts and sultanas.

Jamaican Curry

1 Grind peppercorns, ginger root, coriander seeds, bay leaves, dried red peppers and cardamom seeds in a mortar. Add 1 level tablespoon curry powder, freshly grated nutmeg and salt, to taste.

2 Cut lamb into 1–1½ inch (3–4 cm) cubes, or chicken into serving pieces, and rub ground spices well into each piece. Leave for at least 4 hours.

3 Sauté prepared lamb or chicken pieces in olive oil and butter in a heatproof casserole until golden; remove lamb or chicken. Sauté chopped onion and garlic in remaining fat until transparent; add diced green pepper and chopped tomato and continue cooking until vegetables are soft.

4 Return lamb or chicken pieces to casserole; add any ground spices that remain with the cinnamon stick, lemon peel and lemon juice, thyme and chicken stock; stir well and simmer gently, covered, for 1 hour. Add remaining curry powder and continue to cook for 10 to 15 minutes, or until lamb or chicken is tender.

Serves 4

Ingredients
1 shoulder of lamb (3–4 lb (1.4–2 kg)) or 1 roasting chicken (about 3 lb (1.4 kg))
Black peppercorns
1 small piece ginger root (or ¼ level teaspoon powdered ginger)
½ level teaspoon coriander seeds
2 bay leaves
2 dried hot red peppers
4 cardamom seeds
3 level tablespoons curry powder
⅛ level teaspoon freshly grated nutmeg
Salt
2 tablespoons olive oil
2 level tablespoons butter
1 Spanish onion, finely chopped
1 large clove garlic, finely chopped
1 small green pepper, diced
2–4 tomatoes, chopped
1 stick cinnamon
Grated peel of 1 lemon
Juice of ½ lemon
1 sprig thyme (or ¼ level teaspoon powdered thyme)
¾ pint (4 dl) chicken stock

Spicy Rice Casserole

I often serve Jamaican Chicken Curry at outdoor parties on the lawn. It is an expansive dish, that doubles or triples easily for large parties. With it, I usually serve a delicious Spicy Rice Casserole. To make Spicy Rice: sauté ½ Spanish onion, thinly sliced, in 6 level tablespoons butter in a large heatproof casserole until the onion is transparent and soft. Add 12 oz (350g) washed and drained rice to the casserole and stir until rice begins to turn golden. Then stir in 2 bay leaves, 4 cloves, 6 cardamom pods and 6 allspice berries (all lightly crushed), 1-inch (3 cm) stick of cinnamon and ½ level teaspoon powdered turmeric. Add 1 pint (6 dl) chicken stock; stir once to dislodge any grains stuck to the bottom of the casserole; cover casserole and simmer until rice is tender.

Roast Sliced Sirloin with Aromatic Mayonnaise

1 Sear beef on all sides in hot melted bacon fat or butter, or a combination of the two.

2 Transfer meat to a roasting pan, fat side up; sprinkle generously with salt and freshly ground black pepper and crumbled rosemary and roast in a preheated hot oven (450°F/230°C/Mark 8) for about 25 minutes for rare beef, longer if you prefer it more thoroughly cooked, adding 4 tablespoons warm water or red wine to the pan after the first 15 minutes.

3 Remove beef from oven and allow to cool; then cover meat loosely and chill overnight in refrigerator.

4 Slice beef thinly and arrange slices on a serving dish. Delicious served with chilled aromatic mayonnaise (made by combining mayonnaise with freshly grated horseradish and cayenne).

Ingredients
1½ lb (675g) trimmed sirloin steak, in 1 piece
4 tablespoons hot melted bacon fat, or butter
Salt and fresh black pepper
Crumbled rosemary
4 tablespoons warm water, or red wine
Mayonnaise (see page 63)
1–2 level tablespoons freshly grated horseradish
Cayenne pepper

Cooking with Wine

Y ou will find that cooking with wine is as easy as opening the bottle and taking a sip. If, like some of my friends, you are a little inhibited in your use of this magic cook's aid, think of it as just another ingredient like butter, olive oil, fresh herbs or cream.

'Take 2-3 lb (900–1.3kg) of an inexpensive cut of meat. Cut into $1\frac{1}{2}$–$1\frac{3}{4}$ inch ($3\frac{1}{2}$–$4\frac{1}{2}$ cm) slices; dust the pieces generously with flour, salt and freshly ground black pepper and sauté in equal quantities of olive oil and butter until the meat is browned on all sides. Simmer some coarsely chopped onion and garlic in the same combination of fats; combine vegetables and meat; add strips of orange peel which you have dried in the oven, 2 cloves, 2 bay leaves and a reduction of red wine. Cover the casserole and simmer gently over the lowest of heats, until the meat is meltingly tender and the vegetables and wine dissolve into a smooth, richly flavoured sauce.'

This easy casserole recipe probably originated centuries ago on the sun-washed hillsides of southern France, when the natives of the region were learning how to cultivate the local grapes to make wine. The casserole was undoubtedly cooked in the ashes. Today the task is easier, but all the magic 'constants' remain.

Slow, even cooking

All casseroles – vegetables as well as meats, poultry, fish and game – respond wonderfully well to 'low heat' cookery. Over the many years that I have been experimenting with heat I have gradually lowered the temperature at which I like to cook stews, daubes, ragoûts and casseroles to 225°F/110°C/Mark $\frac{1}{4}$ or 275°F/140°C/Mark 1, and when cooking this type of dish on top of the stove I always use an asbestos or wire mat to help keep the cooking down to a very faint, barely perceptible simmer. It is a good idea, the first few times you follow this method of cooking, to check up on your casserole frequently. Thermostats vary, and you may find you have to adjust the setting slightly to keep the casserole at this low 'barely simmering' point. And always make sure that you bring the ingredients up to a bubble on top of the stove before you put the casserole in the oven.

Reduction

Wine 'reduced' to a quarter of the original quantity by a fast boil over a high heat is one of the best ways of adding savour to a casserole. Professional cooks often use this method of seasoning to intensify the depth of flavour of their wine dishes.

Opposite page *Red Wine Marinade for fish and meats. (Recipe, page 27)*

Below *Raw ingredients for a classic Boeuf à la Bourguignonne. (Recipe, page 31)*

I like to reduce stock in the same manner, adding a combination of two separate reductions to the dish at the last minute to give hidden depth and interest to a ragoût of meat, poultry or game. Try combining separate reductions of fish stock and dry white wine to add excitement to a fish soup, casserole or fish-based cream or velouté sauce.

Small quantities of wine can make a great difference to your cooking

1 Add 2 tablespoons dry white wine to your usual salad dressing; add a little finely chopped spring onion, onion or garlic and mix with sliced, boiled new potatoes for a delicious potato salad. Always remember to toss the potato slices with the dressing when potatoes are still warm.

2 Combine 6 tablespoons each olive oil and dry white wine with 2 crumbled bay leaves, a little finely chopped onion and parsley, and salt and freshly ground black pepper, to taste. Use to marinate brochettes of lamb, chicken or fish before grilling.

3 Combine 1 glass red wine with 2 cloves crushed garlic, ¼ level teaspoon dried marjoram or thyme (or a combination of the two), ¼ chicken stock cube and freshly ground black pepper, to taste. Reduce these ingredients over a high heat to half the original quantity and use this aromatic sauce with a little butter swirled in to baste lamb, veal or chicken.

4 Always add 2 or more tablespoons red wine just before serving a casserole of meat or game which you have marinated or simmered in red wine. You will find it helps the flavour of the finished dish.

5 Try adding a tablespoon or two of dry sherry or Madeira and a tablespoon of Worcestershire sauce to your steak and kidney pie just before serving.

You will find recipes for wine-simmered dishes on the following pages, and then again, on pages 131-137.

White Wine Fish Stock (Fumet de Poisson)

Ingredients

2 lb (900g) fish heads and
   bones
1 Spanish onion, sliced
4 carrots, sliced
2 stalks celery, sliced
4 tablespoons olive oil
1½ pints (9 dl) dry white wine
Dash of dried fennel
4 parsley sprigs
2 bay leaves
Salt and freshly ground
   black pepper

1 Chop fish heads and bones into pieces about 3 inches (7½ cm) long. Combine chopped bones and sliced vegetables in a large heatproof casserole and sauté in olive oil, stirring constantly, until vegetables begin to take on colour. Add dry white wine and 1½ pints (9 dl) water and bring to the boil.

2 Skim surface of stock. Add fennel, parsley and bay leaves. Simmer for 2 hours.

3 Strain stock through a fine sieve lined with muslin. Season with salt and freshly ground black pepper, to taste.

White Wine Cooked Marinade

(For fish or chicken)

Ingredients

1½ pints (9 dl) dry white wine
1½ pints (9 dl) water
1 Spanish onion, sliced
4 carrots, sliced
2 stalks celery, sliced
Dash of dried fennel
4 parsley sprigs
1 bay leaf
Salt and freshly ground
   black pepper

Combine marinade ingredients in a large casserole. Bring gently to the boil; skim impurities from surface; lower heat and simmer for 20 minutes. Cool.

Red Wine Marinade

(For fish, poultry or meat)

Ingredients

1 bottle full-bodied red wine
2 Spanish onions, thinly
   sliced
2 large carrots, thinly sliced
2 stalks celery, thinly sliced
1 clove garlic, peeled
2 sprigs parsley
1 sprig thyme
1 bay leaf
2 tablespoons olive oil

Combine marinade ingredients in a large bowl and mix well. Cover bowl tightly with foil and leave overnight in a cool place.

Poached Fillets of Sole in White Wine

1 Season sole fillets with salt and freshly ground black pepper and place in a flameproof, shallow casserole or gratin dish.

2 Mix dry white wine and vermouth with 6 tablespoons melted butter and tomato purée and pour over fish. Add finely chopped onion; bring to the boil; reduce heat to a simmer and cook fish gently for 5 minutes or until fish is just tender.

3 While fish is cooking, sauté mushrooms in 2 tablespoons melted butter and a little lemon juice over a low heat for 10 minutes.

4 Remove sole fillets from casserole with a perforated spoon and place on a heated serving dish. Cover and keep hot.

5 Strain sauce into a clean saucepan; add mushrooms and their juices to sauce and heat through.

6 Beat cream and egg yolks together in a small bowl; add to contents of pan. Reheat gently, stirring constantly, until sauce has thickened slightly. Do not allow sauce to reach boiling point or it may curdle. Season to taste with salt and freshly ground black pepper and a little more lemon juice or vermouth, if desired.

7 Pour sauce over sole fillets; sprinkle with finely chopped parsley and serve hot, garnished with lemon slices.

Ingredients

2 sole, weighing about 1½ lb
   (675g) each, filleted
Salt and freshly ground black
   pepper
6 tablespoons dry white wine
2 tablespoons dry vermouth
Butter
2 level teaspoons tomato
   purée
½ Spanish onion, finely
   chopped
20 small button mushrooms
Lemon juice
¼ pint (1½ dl) double cream
2 egg yolks
Finely chopped parsley
Thin lemon slices

Serves 4

Preceding pages Jack Nisberg's evocative photographs of a wine harvest in France underline the work and care that go into even the simplest bottle of French wine.

Wines of California

Wine has been produced in California since the early nineteenth century. In the old days, Californian wines were imitative in that they were named after well-known European wines, without really approaching them in flavour, bouquet or finesse. But today, Californian vintners are far more sophisticated in their approach to fine wines and broader markets. Wines are now named after grape varietals – grapes such as the *Riesling* which produces the greatest wines of Alsace, the Rhine and Mosel; the *Pinot noir*, responsible for red Burgundies; the *Chardonnay*, from which all the great white wines of Burgundy are produced; and *Zinfandel*, a grape of Italian or Swiss origin, that is unique to California.

Of course, the wine industry in California is still a young industry, searching for its identity. But California's wines have been winning medals in Wine Olympics against the products of the world's most experienced wine-makers. Californian wine – the state's new gold – has come of age.

Fillets of Trout in Lettuce Packets

Ingredients

4 fresh trout, skinned and filleted
8 large green lettuce leaves
Salt
Freshly ground black pepper
Butter
$\frac{1}{4}$ chicken stock cube
Dry white wine
2 level tablespoons finely chopped onion
2 level tablespoons finely chopped mushroom stalks

HERBED BREADCRUMB STUFFING

$\frac{1}{4}$ lb (100g) fresh breadcrumbs mixed with 1 level tablespoon each finely chopped parsley, tarragon and chives

FISH VELOUTÉ SAUCE

1 level tablespoon butter
1 level tablespoon flour
Bones, heads and trimmings of trout
Salt and freshly ground black pepper
$\frac{1}{4}$ Spanish onion, finely chopped
$\frac{1}{2}$ chicken stock cube
1 level tablespoon tomato purée
$\frac{1}{4}$ pint ($1\frac{1}{2}$ dl) double cream

1 Place lettuce leaves (I use dark Cos for colour) in a large saucepan of boiling salted water for a few seconds to make them flexible. Remove lettuce leaves and place in bowl of cold water until ready to use. When lettuce leaves are cool enough to handle spread them out on a kitchen towel to dry.

2 Preheat your oven to moderate (375°F/190°C/Mark 5).

3 Season trout fillets on both sides with salt and freshly ground black pepper and sauté in butter on both sides for about 1 minute each side or until they start to colour. Remove from pan.

4 Cut a rectangle from each fillet about $2\frac{1}{2}$–3 inches (6–$7\frac{1}{2}$ cm) long, making 8 rectangles altogether. (Save remaining trout trimmings for sauce.) Place 1 trout segment on a lettuce leaf, spread with a quarter of herbed breadcrumb mixture; top with second trout segment, and make a packet with a second lettuce leaf, tucking in the ends, so that it all holds together neatly without any need for tying. Make 3 other lettuce leaf packets in the same way.

5 To make fish velouté sauce: melt butter in the top of a double saucepan; add flour and cook for a few minutes to form pale roux. Add 1 pint (6 dl) fish stock (made from bones, and trimmings of trout heads), salt and freshly ground black pepper, and cook, stirring vigorously with a whisk until well blended. Add finely chopped onion, chicken stock cube and tomato purée; reduce heat and simmer gently, stirring occasionally and skimming from time to time, until the sauce is reduced to half the original quantity. Strain through a fine sieve. Stir in double cream; correct seasoning; keep warm.

6 To bake trout fillets: place the trout packets in a baking dish large enough to contain them side by side, without touching. Crumble $\frac{1}{2}$ chicken stock cube into $\frac{1}{2}$ pint (3 dl) dry white wine; pour over fillets and sprinkle them with finely chopped onion and mushroom stalks.

7 Set the pan in preheated oven and leave it for about 10 minutes, depending on the thickness of the fillets. Lift the packets on to 4 heated individual dishes and keep warm.

8 Add trout trimmings to juices in the baking pan; add a splash of dry white wine and boil the liquid over a high heat to reduce it until it is almost a glaze. Stir into sauce. Taste and adjust seasonings and heat to serving temperature. Pour sauce around each fish packet and serve immediately.

Serves 4

Turbot in Champagne

1 Melt half the butter in a large shallow saucepan with olive oil; sauté finely chopped shallots until transparent; add sliced mushrooms and continue cooking until tender. Remove.

2 Add remaining butter to pan and sauté turbot fillets until lightly coloured. Add sautéed mushrooms and onions, fish stock and half the champagne, adding more if necessary barely to cover the turbot fillets. Season to taste with salt and white pepper and simmer very slowly for a few minutes until tender. Remove turbot fillets to a serving dish and keep warm.

3 Add cream to the liquid in the pan; let simmer without boiling until cream is warm.

4 Mix cornflour with a small amount of water, add to sauce and cook, stirring constantly, over a very low heat, until sauce is smooth and rich.

5 When ready to serve, pour in remaining champagne, stir and mix with the sauce until warm. If you prefer a thicker sauce, use less champagne. Pour over turbot fillets and serve immediately.

Serves 4

Ingredients
4 turbot fillets, boned and skinned
¼ lb (100g) butter
2 tablespoons olive oil
2 shallots, finely chopped
¼ lb (100g) button mushrooms, sliced
6 tablespoons fish stock made from fish trimmings
½ quarter bottle of champagne
Salt and white pepper
¼ pint (1½ dl) double cream
1 level tablespoon cornflour

Boeuf à la Bourguignonne *(Illustration, page 25)*

1 Cut beef into large cubes; remove fat and roll cubes in flour. Heat 2 tablespoons olive oil and 2 tablespoons butter in a large frying pan and sauté diced salt pork until crisp and brown. Remove pork from pan and transfer to a large earthenware casserole. Brown meat well on all sides in remaining fat, season to taste with salt and pepper and moisten with warmed Cognac. Ignite Cognac; let the flame burn away and add meat to casserole.

2 Coarsely chop carrots, leek, shallots, onion and garlic, and cook vegetables in fat remaining in frying pan, stirring occasionally, until they are lightly browned, adding a little more butter and olive oil, if necessary.

3 Transfer vegetables to the casserole with the meat; add the calf's foot and bouquet garni. Pour over all but 4 tablespoons of the wine, and just enough hot water or good beef stock to cover contents of the casserole.

4 Cover and cook in a cool oven (225°F /110°C/Mark ¼) for 1½ to 2 hours.

5 Remove fat from sauce; stir in, bit by bit, 1 level tablespoon butter worked with 1 level tablespoon flour; cover; continue to cook gently in the oven for about 2 hours or longer.

6 Brown onions in 1 level tablespoon butter in a saucepan with a little sugar. Add 4 tablespoons red wine, cover and cook over a low flame until onions are almost tender. Keep warm. Sauté mushroom caps in remaining oil and butter and a little lemon juice. Keep warm.

7 When meat is tender, remove calf's foot and bouquet garni; correct seasoning; add onions and mushroom caps and sprinkle lavishly with finely-chopped parsley.

Serves 4–6

Note: like many wine-based dishes, *boeuf à la bourguignonne* is better when re-heated and served on the following day.

Ingredients
3 lb (1.3 kg) topside or top rump of beef
Flour
4 tablespoons olive oil
Butter
¼ lb (100g) diced salt pork
Salt
Freshly ground black pepper
4 tablespoons warmed Cognac
2 carrots
1 leek
4 shallots
1 Spanish onion
1 clove garlic
1 calf's foot, split (optional)
1 bouquet garni
½ bottle red Burgundy
Beef stock or water, to cover
1 level tablespoon flour
18 button onions
12 button mushrooms
Sugar
Lemon juice
Chopped parsley

Below *Artichokes with Walnut Dressing, an appetizer star-turn, photographed among the artichokes at Hintlesham. (Recipe, page 38)*

Below right *Nasturtium Leaves and Sliced Cucumber makes a fresh-tasting summer appetizer when dressed with a a well-flavoured vinaigrette. (Recipe, page 39)*

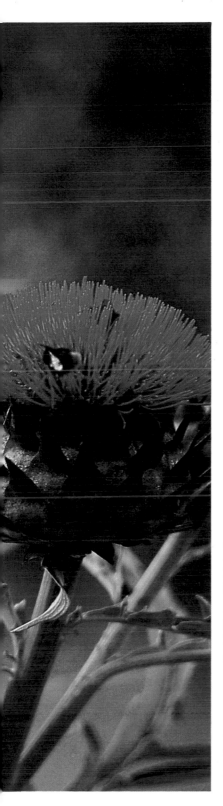

Appetizer Salads, Pâtés and Terrines

French 'composition salads' - *salades composées* - make wonderful first course or luncheon salads for spring and summer meals. The procedure is simple: just toss the elements of your choice, raw or cooked, in a well-flavoured vinaigrette dressing (1 part wine vinegar or lemon juice to 3 parts olive oil, $\frac{1}{4}$ level teaspoon Dijon mustard and salt and freshly ground black pepper, to taste); add chopped fresh herbs or flavour with finely chopped onion, shallot, garlic or crumbled cooked bacon.

Salade Italienne
Lettuce leaves, crisp rings of fennel, sprigs of fresh fennel and stuffed green olives. Vinaigrette dressing.

Salade Mexicaine
Cos lettuce leaves, canned corn kernels and red pepper strips. Vinaigrette dressing flavoured with mustard and finely chopped parsley or chives.

Salade Japonaise
Lettuce leaves and sprigs of watercress, garnished with radishes cut into flower shapes. Vinaigrette dressing flavoured with finely chopped garlic and soy sauce.

Salade Fermière

Lettuce leaves (Salad Bowl) and sprigs of watercress, garnished with tomato wedges and quartered hard-boiled eggs. Vinaigrette dressing flavoured with mustard and chopped onion.

Salade Provençale

Lettuce leaves and barely cooked cauliflowerets, garnished with black olives and anchovy strips. Vinaigrette dressing flavoured with mustard and finely chopped garlic.

Salade Gitane

Chick peas, lentils and *haricots blancs*, soaked overnight and then cooked separately in water until just tender (you'll need three separate pans); each tossed, separately, while still warm, in a vinaigrette dressing flavoured with chopped onion and anchovies. Garnish with tomato wedges and black olives.

Salade Tricolore

Lettuce leaves and thin strips of barely cooked carrot and celery tossed in a well-flavoured vinaigrette dressing with strips of raw green and red cabbage.

Salade Paysanne

Lettuce leaves, sliced mushroom and diced Swiss cheese, tossed in a well-flavoured vinaigrette dressing. Garnish with walnut halves and crumbled cooked bacon.

Salade Jardinière

Lettuce leaves (Salad Bowl), cooked green beans, carrot strips and raw cucumber strips. Vinaigrette dressing. Garnish, if desired, with nasturtiums.

Tomato and Egg Salad

Ingredients

4 ripe tomatoes
4 hard-boiled eggs
6-8 tablespoons olive oil
2-3 tablespoons wine vinegar
Salt and freshly ground black pepper
2 level tablespoons finely chopped parsley
2 level tablespoons finely chopped onion

1 Wipe tomatoes clean and slice crosswise into even slices.

2 Shell eggs and slice crosswise into even slices.

3 Place slices of egg and tomato in a large flat hors-d'oeuvre dish; mix olive oil, wine vinegar and salt and freshly ground black pepper, to taste, and pour over salad.

4 Sprinkle egg slices with finely chopped parsley and tomato slices with finely chopped onion.

Serves 4

Green Beans Salad

Ingredients

1½ lb (675g) young green beans
Salt
2-3 tablespoons wine vinegar
½ level teaspoon Dijon mustard
6-8 tablespoons olive oil
Freshly ground black pepper
Lettuce leaves
2 level tablespoons finely chopped onion
2 level tablespoons finely chopped parsley

1 Top and tail green beans and cook them in boiling salted water until they are barely tender.

2 Drain and toss immediately while still warm in a French dressing made from wine vinegar, Dijon mustard, olive oil and salt and freshly ground black pepper, to taste. Chill.

3 When ready to serve, line a salad bowl or rectangular hors d'oeuvre dish with lettuce leaves; arrange green bean salad in the centre of the dish and sprinkle with finely chopped onion and parsley.

Serves 4 - 6

34

Saffron Rice Salad

1 Dissolve saffron, cumin and cayenne pepper in dry white wine and chicken stock, and combine in a large saucepan with rice, coarsely chopped onion, and salt, to taste.

2 Cover pan and simmer until all the liquid is absorbed and the rice is tender. Add some more liquid if necessary.

3 Drain well and toss with dressing. Stir in diced peppers, black olives and anchovy fillets. Allow to cool. Add more olive oil, wine vinegar or seasonings, if necessary.

Serves 4 - 6

Ingredients

½ level teaspoon powdered saffron

¼ level teaspoon powdered cumin

¼ level teaspoon cayenne pepper

6 tablespoons dry white wine

1 pint (6 dl) hot chicken stock

¾ lb (350g) Italian rice for risotto

1 Spanish onion, coarsely chopped

Salt

½ green pepper, seeded and cut into squares

½ red pepper, seeded and cut into squares

6 black olives, pitted and coarsely chopped

3 anchovy fillets, cut into squares

DRESSING

2-3 tablespoons wine vinegar

½ level teaspoon Dijon mustard

6-8 tablespoons olive oil

2 level tablespoons finely chopped parsley

Salt and freshly ground black pepper

Red Wines of Bordeaux

Bordeaux is one of the richest wine growing areas of all France. The estates of wine-producing companies here are called *châteaux*. But a *château* in the Bordeaux wine trade is not necessarily what we think of as a *château*; it can be a castle, of course, but it can also be a stately home, an imposing farm house or just a simple farm.

If you stop at any crossroads in this wine-growing area, you are almost certain to be within a stone's throw of some of the greatest red wines in the world; the Bordeaux classified growth of Château Haut-Brion, Château Lafite-Rothschild, Château Latour, Château Margaux and Château Mouton-Rothschild.

Why is it that this particular area of France boasts so many prestigious wines? The answer lies in the soil. The dry, pebbly, rocky soil of Bordeaux, which could not even produce a carrot successfully, does grow some of the greatest vines, producing the finest wines in the world. Here in this small area, 10% of all wines of France are produced, and 30% of all the really top-rated wines of France.

There are over 30,000 vineyards in this small area. It would be impossible for each of these vineyards to market their own wines, so over the years a new species of wine merchant, the *négociant*, has come into being. It is the *négociant* who buys the wine from the different vineyard owners either in the bottle or in larger quantities in the wood.

There are many famous *négociants* in Bordeaux: Calvet, Cordier, Alexis Lechine and Barton & Guestier, to name some of the better known.

Wine Labels

There are five different labels to define different types of Bordeaux wine: (1) *château*-bottled, where the wine has been put in bottles at the *château*; (2) wine purchased from the *châteaux* and bottled by the *négociant*. The greatest part of the business of *négociant-eleveurs* is blended generic wine. A generic wine is (3) commune or regional wine that comes from a defined area, Bordeaux, St-Julien, Bordeaux Supérieur, etc., selected carefully and blended each year from wines from the vineyards of the region. When the *négociant* is pleased with the type of blended wine that has been tasted with success by his customers year after year, he gives (4) a *monopole* or trade mark name. The last type of label (5) is a varietal label for wines made only of one type of grape, like a Gamay. By French law, varietal wines must come from a specific area and there must be 100% of the same type of grape in the vine.

Liv Ullman and daughter Linn enjoy a selection of cooked and raw appetizers in the Blue Kitchen at Hintlesham.

Inset *The hit of the tasting? Japanese Noodles: so easy to make and yet so deliciously different! (Recipe, page 39)*

Roman Vegetables

Ingredients

4 small courgettes
2 stalks celery
¼ lb (100g) green beans
4 small carrots, scraped and
    cut into eighths
12 button mushrooms
12 button onions
½ head cauliflower
1 green pepper
2 red peppers
1 small aubergine
¼ pint (1½ dl) olive oil
2 cloves garlic, quartered
2 bay leaves
Salt and freshly ground black
    pepper
4 tablespoons dry white wine
4 tablespoons wine vinegar
¼ pint (1½ dl) tomato ketchup
2 tablespoons sugar
12 stuffed olives
Lemon juice (optional)
Lettuce leaves and finely
    chopped parsley, to
    garnish

1 Cut courgettes into ¼-inch (½ cm) slices. Cut celery, green beans and carrot sticks into 1-inch (2½ cm) segments. Wash mushrooms and trim stems. Peel onions. Trim cauliflower and break into flowerets. Remove stems, pith and seeds from green and red peppers and cut them into thick chunks. Cut unpeeled aubergine into slices ¼-inch (½-cm) thick; then cut each slice into quarters.

2 Heat the olive oil in a large thick-bottomed casserole; add vegetables, quartered garlic and bay leaves, and season generously with salt and freshly ground black pepper. Cover casserole and simmer vegetables gently over a low heat until the vegetables are tender, but still quite crisp.

3 Combine dry white wine, wine vinegar, tomato ketchup and sugar; stir into casserole; add stuffed olives and continue to cook gently for another 10 minutes.

4 Remove casserole from the heat and allow vegetables to come to room temperature. Mix well and chill until ready to serve. Correct seasoning, adding a little lemon juice and a little more salt and freshly ground black pepper, if desired.

5 To serve: place crisply cooked vegetables on lettuce leaves and sprinkle with finely chopped parsley.

Serves 4 - 6

Artichokes with Walnut Dressing *(Illustration, page 32)*

Ingredients

4 artichokes
Salt
Juice of ½ lemon
Freshly ground black pepper
Finely chopped fresh herbs

WALNUT DRESSING

¼ pint (1½ dl) double cream
Salt and freshly ground black
    pepper
Walnut oil
Lemon juice

1 Remove the tough outer leaves of artichokes and trim tops of inner leaves. Trim the base and stem of each artichoke with a sharp knife. Cook until tender (30–40 minutes) in a large quantity of boiling salted water, to which you have added the juice of ½ lemon. Artichokes are cooked when a leaf pulls out easily. Turn artichokes upside down to drain.

2 Remove inner leaves of cooked artichokes, leaving a decorative outer ring of 2 or 3 leaves to form a cup around the heart of each artichoke. Season with salt and freshly ground black pepper, and chill in the refrigerator.

3 To make walnut dressing: whip double cream until stiff; flavour with salt and freshly ground black pepper, walnut oil and lemon juice to taste.

4 Just before serving: pile artichoke hearts with whipped walnut cream filling and sprinkle with finely chopped herbs.

Serves 4

To Choose and Store Artichokes

When buying artichokes, look out for ones that are fresh and heavy for their size, with supple, tightly closed leaves. Stiff, dry leaves and an 'overblown' appearance generally indicate that the artichoke will be tough and woody.

The size of an artichoke is no indication to its quality, but small ones are better for pickling, medium-sized and large ones for serving whole as an appetizer, or in dishes where only the heart is called for.

Artichokes can be stored in the refrigerator, tightly covered to preserve their moisture.

Cucumber and Nasturtium Leaf Salad

(Illustration, page 33)

1 Peel and slice cucumber thinly. Wash nasturtium leaves; remove stems and drain.

2 Combine mustard and vinegar in a bowl and stir until well blended. Add olive oil, and salt and freshly ground black pepper, to taste. Blend well. Stir in tarragon.

3 When ready to serve, combine cucumber and nasturtium leaves in a salad bowl; add vinaigrette dressing and toss well. Garnish with nasturtium flowers, if desired.

Serves 4 - 6

Ingredients
1 cucumber
36 small nasturtium leaves
1 level teaspoon Dijon mustard
2 tablespoons wine vinegar
6 tablespoons olive oil
Salt and freshly ground black
   pepper
2 level tablespoons finely
   chopped fresh tarragon
6 nasturtium flowers
   (optional)

Tomato and Mozzarella Cheese Appetizer Salad

1 Place 2 lettuce leaves on each salad plate. Arrange 2 slices of *mozzarella* and 3 slices tomato on each plate. Garnish each serving with 2 black olives and 2 anchovy fillets.

2 Sprinkle cheese and tomatoes with a little freshly crushed coriander seeds and finely chopped fresh marjoram. Dribble over 2 to 3 tablespoons vinaigrette sauce.

Serves 4

Ingredients
8 lettuce leaves
8 slices mozzarella cheese
12 slices ripe tomato
8 black olives
8 anchovy fillets
Freshly crushed coriander
   seeds
Finely chopped fresh
   marjoram
Well-flavoured vinaigrette
   sauce (see page 33)

Japanese Noodles *(Illustration, page 36)*

1 Place dried mushrooms in a small bowl and add 1½ pints (9 dl) boiling water to cover. Let mushrooms steep in water until soft. Squeeze dry. Add 1 tablespoon each sesame oil and soy sauce. Mix well.

2 Bring 1½ pints (9 dl) water to the boil. Add contents of 2 packets *Udon* noodles to water, together with the contents of small seasoning packets (found in each packet of noodles). Stir until noodles are separated. Cook noodles for 2 minutes in all.

3 Drain noodles and transfer to a large bowl. Add marinated mushrooms and 1 tablespoon each sesame oil, soy sauce and vegetable oil. Stir well and allow noodles to cool.

4 Sprinkle chopped coriander or parsley over the Japanese noodles and serve cold in an hors-d'oeuvre dish as one of a selection of cold hors-d'oeuvres.

Serves 4 - 6

Ingredients
2 packets Japanese Udon
   noodles
1 packet dried Chinese
   mushrooms
2 tablespoons sesame oil
2 tablespoons soy sauce
1 tablespoon vegetable oil
2 tablespoons chopped fresh
   coriander or parsley

Pâtés and Terrines

When I was very young, pâtés always meant the extremely rich *pâté de foie gras* that we often used to have as a special occasion feast at Christmas. These expensive pâtés – made in France from the livers of specially fattened geese, usually studded with truffles, and eaten with hot, crisp slices of toast and farm-house butter – were a sensuous treat that the whole family used to look forward to from year to year.

Now that I have been cooking my own pâtés for years, a pâté can mean almost anything that contains a mixture of ground meats, or poultry or game; the mix is 'softened' in flavour with a little ground pork and veal, and then studded with strips of ham, tongue, poultry or game.

One of my favourite pâtés is a delicious green herb pâté, studded for texture

and colour contrast with diced tongue, diced ham, diced bacon, a little diced pork fat and some diced chicken livers sautéed in butter.

I first made *pâté aux herbes* (see page 42) in St Tropez. I had visited a tiny restaurant in upper Provence, and enjoyed a very gutsy herb and ham pâté that I tasted there. Deciding to make it at home, I simmered some fresh leaves of spinach and *blette* in a little butter. I added a little finely chopped pork to the mix, with cream and egg yolks for extra richness. Then the problem was how to recreate the wonderfully herby flavour of the original. It was time to experiment. Did it have thyme in it? Yes, it did have thyme. A little more thyme, a little rosemary, and a little sage. Now perhaps the flavour was a little *too* rich, so I softened it with a little added cream. Cooking is really like painting . . . all the flavours and aromatics that we use in our daily cooking are like the colours on an artist's palette:

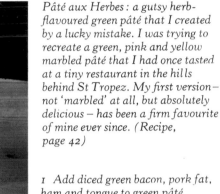

Pâté aux Herbes: a gutsy herb-flavoured green pâté that I created by a lucky mistake. I was trying to recreate a green, pink and yellow marbled pâté that I had once tasted at a tiny restaurant in the hills behind St Tropez. My first version – not 'marbled' at all, but absolutely delicious – has been a firm favourite of mine ever since. (Recipe, page 42)

1 Add diced green bacon, pork fat, ham and tongue to green pâté mixture.

2 Line bottom and sides of an ovenproof terrine with thin strips of pounded pork fat to 'moisturize', pâté as it cooks.

3 Fill terrine with pâté mixture; and fold over overlapping strips of pork fat to seal terrine.

41

Cold Parsleyed Ham *(Illustration, page 45)*

(A simpler version of the French classic Jambon Persille de Bourgogne)

Ingredients

2 lb (900g) cooked ham (cut in 1 piece)
1 pint (6 dl) well-flavoured chicken stock
¼ pint (1½ dl) dry white wine
Freshly ground black pepper
Nutmeg
Finely chopped fresh parsley
2 level tablespoons powdered gelatine
1-2 tablespoons tarragon vinegar

1 Cut ham into cubes. Bring chicken stock and dry white wine gently to the boil; add ham cubes and freshly ground black pepper and nutmeg, to taste. (No salt. The ham is salty enough.) Lower heat and simmer ham in this stock very gently for 5 minutes.

2 Drain, reserving stock, and place ham cubes loosely in a wet glass bowl which you have dusted thickly with finely chopped parsley.

3 Soften gelatine in a little water. Stir into stock; add 6-8 tablespoons parsley and tarragon vinegar. Allow to cool until syrupy, then pour over diced ham. If there is not enough liquid to cover ham, add a little more dry white wine, to cover. Allow to set for 12 hours in the refrigerator before unmoulding.

Serves 6 - 8

Pâté aux Herbes *(Illustrations, pages 40 and 41)*

Ingredients

1 lb (450g) lean pork
Butter
1 Spanish onion, finely chopped
1 lb (450g) fresh or ¼ lb (100g) frozen leaf spinach
¼ lb (100g) cooked ham
¼ lb (100g) green bacon
¼ lb (100g) pork fat
¼ lb (100g) cooked ox tongue
2 cloves garlic, finely chopped
2 level tablespoons finely chopped basil
2 level tablespoons finely chopped parsley
2 level tablespoons finely chopped chervil
24 spikes rosemary, finely chopped
4 eggs, beaten
Salt and freshly ground black pepper
Cayenne pepper
Freshly grated nutmeg
6 oz (175g) chicken livers
¼ pint (1½ dl) double cream
2 level tablespoons powdered gelatine
Thin strips of pounded pork fat
Gherkins

1 Cut the pork into small cubes; place in blender or food processor and blend until minced. Melt 2 level tablespoons butter in a large frying pan; add finely chopped onion and sauté, stirring constantly, until it is transparent. Add spinach and continue to cook, stirring, until spinach has wilted (if fresh). Remove onions and spinach and chop coarsely. Add onion and spinach mixture to pork and blend again. Transfer mixture to a large bowl.

2 Dice ham, green bacon, pork fat and ox tongue and add to green pâté mixture. Then add finely chopped garlic and fresh herbs. (If you use dried herbs, use only half the quantities.)

3 Stir in the beaten eggs and add salt and freshly ground black pepper, cayenne pepper and nutmeg, to taste.

4 Cut chicken livers into dice and sauté in 2 level tablespoons butter until golden.

5 Stir in cream and powdered gelatine, which you have dissolved in a little water, and mix well. Add to pâté mix-ture and mix well. The raw pâté will now be a nice, loose, spoonable mixture ready for cooking.

6 Line the bottom and sides of an ovenproof terrine with thin strips of pounded pork fat. (*Note:* you can ask your butcher to do this for you. But I warn you, don't ask him on a busy Saturday morning when the shop is crowded.) Spoon pâté mixture into terrine; cover with thin strips of pounded pork fat and cook in a slow oven (325°F/170°C/Mark 3) for ½ hour. Lower heat to 300°F/150°C/Mark 2 and cook for another 30–40 minutes.

7 Remove from oven to cool, pressing excess juices out of the terrine with a board, or the back of a spoon. Serve cold, cut into slices, with gherkins.

Note: to remove pâté from terrine, place terrine in a pan of hot water for a minute or two, then insert a sharp pointed knife all around pâté, loosening it from the sides of the terrine. Turn terrine upside down over serving plate, and the pâté will slide out easily.

Serves 8-10

Hedgehog Pâté *(Illustration, page 44)*

1 Combine cubed ham and ham fat in bowl of electric blender or food processor and blend until mixture is like a coarse pâté.

2 Add chopped onion and garlic, Dijon mustard, wine vinegar, anchovy paste, ground nutmeg and ground black pepper, ginger, ground cloves and dried thyme or oregano. Blend again until mixture is smooth. Taste and correct seasoning, adding a little more of any of the above aromatics and spices, if necessary.

3 Pack mixture into a large bowl; cover and refrigerate for 2 days to allow flavours to amalgamate.

4 To form hedgehog: mound mixture on a flat serving dish and then, using a spatula, shape into a smooth oval, bringing the front of hedgehog into a sharp point to represent the 'head' (see photo). Brush hedgehog with liquid aspic to give it a translucent look; stud with toasted slivered almonds for 'spikes', bits of black olive or truffle for 'nose', and currants for 'eyes'.

5 Chill in refrigerator until ready to serve. Serve with hot toast and chilled butter.

Ingredients
1¼ lb (550g) cooked ham, cut into cubes
¼ lb (100g) firm fat from cooked ham, cut into cubes
½ Spanish onion, chopped
1 small clove garlic, chopped
2 level teaspoons Dijon mustard
1 tablespoon wine vinegar
½ level teaspoon anchovy paste
½ level teaspoon ground nutmeg
¼ level teaspoon each ground black pepper, ginger, ground cloves and dried thyme or oregano
¼ pint (1½ dl) liquid aspic, cooled until it is syrupy
Toasted slivered almonds
2 currants
Bits of black olive or truffle

Italian Veal Pâté with Tuna

1 Have your butcher bone and tie a piece of leg of veal.

2 Cut anchovy fillets into small pieces; pierce holes in surface of meat with a sharp knife or skewer and insert pieces of anchovy fillet and garlic into the holes. Top meat with bay leaves, inserting them under strings. Place rolled meat in a flameproof casserole with sliced onions, carrots and celery, parsley, cloves and salt and freshly ground black pepper, to taste. Pour in dry white wine and add just enough water to cover meat (or use water only); bring slowly to the boil, turn down heat, cover casserole, and simmer veal for 1½–2 hours. When veal is tender, remove strings and/or skewers and allow it to cool in stock.

3 To make tuna fish sauce: pound tuna fish, anchovy fillets and capers with lemon juice and freshly ground black pepper until smooth. Combine with mayonnaise in electric blender and blend (adding a little veal stock if too thick) until the sauce is smooth and creamy.

4 When meat is cold, remove it from stock (reserve stock); dice thickly and place in a bowl; pour over tuna fish sauce; cover bowl and let the meat marinate in the sauce overnight.

5 Blend veal and half the sauce in a blender or food processor to a smooth paste, adding a little reserved meat stock if mixture seems too dry. Soak 4 leaves gelatine in 6 tablespoons cold water, until limp, then heat to dissolve. Add to veal and tuna mixture and blend again. Correct seasoning and pour into individual soufflé moulds to set.

6 To serve: turn individual veal pâtés out of moulds. Arrange lattice work of thin strips of anchovy on each pâté and garnish with sliced stuffed olives. Brush each pâté with melted aspic two or three times. Serve with remaining tuna fish sauce.

Ingredients
1 piece leg of veal (2 lb (900g) when boned and trimmed)
6 anchovy fillets
2 cloves garlic, slivered
Several bay leaves
2 Spanish onions, sliced
4 carrots, sliced
2 stalks celery, sliced
2 sprigs parsley
2 cloves
Salt and fresh black pepper
½ pint (3 dl) dry white wine
4 leaves gelatine

TUNA FISH SAUCE
6 oz (175g) tuna fish
6 anchovy fillets
1 teaspoon capers
2 tablespoons lemon juice
Freshly ground black pepper
¼ pint (1½ dl) well-flavoured mayonnaise (see page 63)

GARNISH
Anchovy fillets, cut into thin strips
Stuffed olives, sliced
Aspic, to glaze

Gravad Mackerel

1 Combine sugar, salt, coarsely ground black pepper and saltpetre (the latter is not essential, but if obtainable from chemist should be used to improve colour of dish) and rub mackerel pieces on all sides with this spice mixture.

2 Line the bottom of an earthenware or porcelain terrine or pâté dish with sprigs of fresh dill. Place 1 piece of mackerel on this, skin side down, and sprinkle generously with spice mixture; add more sprigs fresh dill; top with second piece of mackerel, skin side up. Place a board cut to fit terrine on top; weight it with a weight and refrigerate for 48 hours.

3 When ready to serve: slice *gravad* mackerel across the grain into very thin slices and serve as an unusual first course with black bread, unsalted butter and a wedge or two of lemon. The uncooked mackerel will have a fine flavour.

Ingredients

2 even-sized pieces fresh
  mackerel, bone removed
  (about 1 lb (450g) each)
8 level tablespoons sugar
10 level tablespoons salt
1 level tablespoon coarsely
  ground black pepper
½ level teaspoon saltpetre
Fresh dill

Opposite page *A truffle for a nose, two dried currants for eyes and carefully tailored almonds for a coat: this hedgehog is for eating. (Recipe for Hedgehog Pâté, page 43)*

Left *Cold Parsleyed Ham, a delicious combination of poached ham and finely chopped parsley in wine-flavoured aspic. (Recipe, page 42)*

Rillettes d'Anguilles aux Petits Légumes

Ingredients

1 lb (450g) fresh smoked eel, middle cut
1 fresh smoked trout
¼ pint (1½ dl) double cream
Salt and freshly ground black pepper
Lemon juice

GARNISH

4 small radishes, thinly sliced
2 slices cooked beetroot, diced
1 medium carrot, cooked until just firm, thinly sliced
Tiny sprigs curly endive or corn salad
Well-flavoured vinaigrette dressing (see page 33)
Finely chopped fresh herbs

1 Skin and fillet eel and trout.

2 Combine the trout and one-third of the eel in a blender or food processor; add cream and salt and freshly ground black pepper, to taste, and blend until smooth. Add lemon juice.

3 Cut remaining eel into thin strips about the size of matchsticks and fold gently into eel and trout mixture.

4 To serve: shape *rillettes* mixture into 4–6 oval shapes using 2 tablespoons dipped in hot water (*Note*: shapes should resemble 'eggs') and serve on individual plates. Garnish each plate with a ring of sliced radishes, diced beetroot, carrot rounds and sprigs of curly endive or corn salad. Dribble vinaigrette dressing over salad greens and vegetables. Sprinkle each *rillettes* 'egg' with finely chopped fresh herbs.

Note: do not use frozen eel or trout because they produce too much moisture.

Serves 4 - 6

Fondant de Volailles

Ingredients

1 large capon (about 3½ lb (1.6 kg))
½ pint (3 dl) dry sherry
2 tablespoons cognac
6-8 tablespoons Noilly Prat
2 tablespoons port
4 sprigs thyme
1 bay leaf
4 sprigs parsley
4 shallots, finely chopped
2 carrots, finely chopped
¼ Spanish onion, finely chopped
2 cloves garlic
1 coffeespoon peppercorns
½ lb (225g) pork fat
½ lb (225g) loin of pork
2 level tablespoons coarse salt
Freshly ground black pepper
½ lb (225g) shoulder of pork, diced
½ lb (225g) foie gras
1 oz (25g) pistachio nuts
Thin strips pork fat
Diced foie gras
Dough (made of flour, water and salt)

1 Skin capon and remove meat from bones, leaving breasts whole.

2 Combine sherry, cognac, Noilly Prat, port, herbs, finely chopped shallots, carrots and onion with garlic and peppercorns in a large porcelain bowl. Add chicken pieces and marinate in this mixture for at least 12 hours.

3 Dice pork fat and loin of pork and combine with coarse salt and freshly ground black pepper, to taste. Leave in the refrigerator for 6 hours, so that meat does not change colour during cooking. Pass through the finest blade of your mincer.

4 Place chicken pieces in a roasting pan with diced shoulder of pork and roast in a hot oven (450°F/230°C/Mark 8) for 4–5 minutes, or until meat has coloured slightly. Then strain marinade juices over meat and continue to cook for 5 minutes more.

5 Remove chicken breasts and pass the remaining chicken pieces and pork shoulder, with juices, through the finest blade of your mincer, blending in *foie gras* at the same time. Combine minced pork and pork fat with chicken mixture; stir in pistachio nuts and place pâté mixture in refrigerator to 'relax' for 2–3 hours.

6 When ready to cook pâté: line a large terrine or pâté mould with thin strips of pork fat; fill a quarter full with pâté mixture; scatter diced *foie gras* over this; cover with a layer of pâté mixture and place marinated chicken breasts on this. Repeat alternate layers of pâté mixture and diced *foie gras*, ending with pâté mixture. Top with thin strips of pork fat; cover terrine and seal edges with a dough made of flour, water and salt so that no moisture escapes. Place terrine in a pan of boiling water and bake in a preheated cool oven (225–250°F/110–130°C/Mark ¼-½) for 1 hour. Keep pâté in refrigerator for 2 days before serving.

Italian Wines
Chianti

Chianti, the home of what is probably the most famous wine bottle in the world, is located in the middle of the Tuscan hills. It is a beautiful sight to come across grape vines in perfectly regimented rows, nestled against wooded slopes and little silver rows of olive trees.

The ordinary red wines of Chianti, in the *fiaschi* bottles, are meant to be enjoyed right away. This fresh tasting, fruity wine is almost clear in its consistency and has a slight sparkling effect which the Italians call *frisante*.

The secret of Chianti is the fact that they use four types of grapes to make this individualistic wine. First, there is the *Sangiovese* grape, and, according to the laws laid down in 1963, *Sangiovese* must account for 50% to 70% of the volume of Chianti. Then, there is a small-grained green grape called *Malvasia di Chianti* that makes up 10% of the volume. *Canaiola nero* makes up a further 10% to 20%. A rich dark purple grape, *Canaiola nero* gives some of the colour necessary to the wine. The fourth variety is a white, tart-flavoured grape called *Treviano Tuscano*, which counts for 10% to 20% of the volume. At Rocca del Marche, where we filmed, they add one more grape – 2% to 3% of *Colorino*, an almost black grape – for its rich dark colour.

Sounds complicated? Not really, because the wine producers of the region grow their grapes to these percentages. The correct percentage of their vines is given over to this grape, so they pick field by field to the exact percentages.

They are very proud of their wines in Chianti – Chianti Classico and Chianti Riserva. Chianti Classico comes from the central region of Chianti, which has the best slopes and produces the best grapes. A Chianti Classico can also be a *riserva*. *Riserva* means reserve, and the wine has had to mature longer in oak or wood before it can be bottled. A Chianti Classico Riserva is at its best when 10 years old: a really noble wine.

Chianti Classico is bottled in Bordeaux-type wine bottles as well as in the straw-covered *fiaschi*. Always look for the black rooster label on each bottle: it is the insignia of the consortium of wine producers of Chianti Classico – about 700 of them, who produce 90% of all Chianti Classico – and the sign of the little black rooster is a guarantee of quality.

Barolo

Barolo is the heaviest and richest of the red wines of Italy, and one of the few that really matures well. In fact, it is not advisable to drink Barolo until it is at least 3 to 5 years old. And some Barolo wines are even better when they are 10 to 12 years old. Barolo is a wonderfully full-bodied wine, perfect to drink with *stuffato*, and good with game.

Valpolicella

They have been making Valpolicella wine in the Verona hills ever since the fifth century BC. The recipes have been handed down from father to son with the same careful tending of the vines, the harvesting and fermenting of the grapes to give a rich ruby red wine with a soft delicious bouquet. But today the artisan approach to wine-making in this region has changed. Now it's big business, with huge modern vats and completely scientific installations, that shows just how important wine-making has become in Italy today.

Home-made stocks — chicken and beef — are the twin basics of good cooking. Keep strained stocks in stoppered jars in the refrigerator; every 5–7 days bring stocks to the boil, cool and return to refrigerator. (Recipes for stocks and soups begin on page 51)

Magic with Stocks and Soups

In the world of good food, nothing offers greater variety for nourishing meals than soup. Fresh-tasting, clear soups are the new fashion in France today, piled high with slivers of chicken and beef and a mosaic of crisp vegetables, or with plump slices of gently poached seafood and a fine *julienne* of crisp vegetables for flavour and colour contrast. I like, too, the great peasant soups of French and Italian country cooking – one-dish dinners in fact – made of lentils and pork or game; *haricots blancs,* goose and garlic, or chick peas, chicken and Spanish sausage.

Today, many of us have gardens of our own once more, and through the summer months we have learned to enjoy delicious soups made from home-grown vegetables. The new trick is to handle such vegetables almost like seasonings, in a clear meat, poultry or fish-based broth, spiked with a little dry white wine and tomato and given a last-minute pinch of fresh herbs for extra savour. Or to purée them with a little well-flavoured stock and double cream and blend them so skilfully that, while you don't taste any one vegetable individually, the result is a triumph of country flavours.

And remember: excellent soups and stocks can be made quite simply and economically from leftovers. Bones, scraps and carcasses, vegetable tops and leaves, even vegetable peelings and trimmings of meat, poultry or game, can find their way into the soup pot to add flavour and nourishment to a meal.

Basic stocks
Stock – the liquid into which the juice and flavour of various nutritive substances have been drawn by means of long, slow cooking – serves as a foundation for most soups, stews, gravies and sauces.

Stock can be made from various ingredients; and although meat and bones, cooked or uncooked, flavoured with vegetables, are the usual basics, poultry, game or fish combined with vegetables, and even vegetables alone, may all be utilized for this purpose.

Stock especially meat stock – should always be made the day before it is to be used, as best results can be obtained only by long, slow cooking. And it is only when the stock is cold that the fat can be easily skimmed off the surface.

49

Flavouring the stock

Do not let the flavour of the vegetables overpower the flavour of the meats used in a meat, poultry or game stock; one flavour must not predominate over another. Onions, shallots, carrots, turnips and celery are the vegetables generally used, but leeks, tomatoes, parsnips and mushrooms may also be used for the darker stocks.

Vegetables are usually diced or left whole for stocks. They must not be allowed to cook too long in the stock, for after a certain time they tend to absorb flavours instead of adding to them. If a large quantity of meat is used and the stock is likely to cook for many hours, the vegetables should not be put in at the beginning of the cooking time, or they should be lifted out before the stock has finished cooking. Stock vegetables may be served as a separate vegetable dish on their own, or made into a vegetable purée, with a little butter and cream added.

Different kinds of stock

Brown stock
Beef, beef bones and vegetables, with sometimes a little veal or some chicken or game bones added for extra flavour.

White stock
White meat such as veal, rabbit, chicken or mutton, and vegetables, with sometimes a calf's foot added for extra flavour.

Fish stock
Fish or fish trimmings with vegetables, and sometimes shellfish trimmings added for extra flavour (see page 76).

Game stock
Game, or game bones and trimmings, and vegetables.

Vegetable stock
This is made from vegetables alone, either dried or fresh or a mixture of the two. For vegetarian soups and dishes.

Glaze
A stock which is so much reduced in quantity that it forms an almost solid substance when cold. It is a means of preserving any surplus stock.

Different kinds of soups

Clear soups or consommés
are made from stocks as above, but clarified by adding beaten egg white and crushed egg shells to the stock and bringing it to the boil. The impurities in the soup adhere to the egg white and shell mass and can then be strained out through a fine muslin.

Broths
differ from clear soups in that they are unclarified. The meat or poultry or game with which they are made is served either in the soup or after it as a separate course. A broth is usually garnished with rice or barley and diced vegetables.

Thickened soups
can be made of fish, meat or vegetables. They generally have some stock as their basis. The soups are thickened with flour, arrowroot, cornflour, tapioca or sago. In some of the richer soups, a combination of eggs and cream is used.

Purées
are perhaps the simplest and most economical kind of soup. They can be made of almost any vegetable, either fresh or dried, and of meat, game and fish. They sometimes have farinaceous substances such as rice, barley or macaroni added. A small amount of diced butter is often added at the very last moment.

Rich Chicken Stock

1 Put the fowl in a large stockpot, with the veal knuckle for its extra gelatine content, and cover with 6 pints (3.4 litres) cold water. Add salt, to taste, and peppercorns, and bring slowly to the boil. Skim any impurities from the top of the liquid, then reduce the heat and simmer, with the liquid barely bubbling, for at least 1 hour. You will notice that the stock will begin to get cloudy. These are the essences being released from the chicken. As these bubble gently to the surface, skim them off to remove all impurities from the stock. This is one of the most important parts of soup-making, strange as it may seem, because it is so simple. Yet this is what makes the difference between a clear stock and a cloudy stock.

2 Add sliced leeks, carrots, onion, tomatoes and celery, bouquet garni, 1 mashed garlic and chicken stock cube, and continue to simmer very gently for 1½ – 2 hours longer, or until the chicken is cooked through.

3 Remove fat, correct seasoning and then strain the stock through a fine sieve, or a piece of muslin in a colander. Cool the stock and store in the refrigerator for further use.

Makes 3 pints

Ingredients
1 fine, fat boiling fowl (about 4-5 lb (1.8-2.2kg)), complete with neck, feet and giblets for added flavour
1 large veal knuckle
Salt
6-8 peppercorns
2 leeks, sliced
3 large carrots, sliced
1 Spanish onion, sliced
2 tomatoes, seeded and sliced
4 stalks celery, sliced
1 bouquet garni (2 sprigs parsley, 2 sprigs thyme and 1 bay leaf)
1 clove garlic, mashed with the point of a knife
1 chicken stock cube

Rich Beef Stock

1 Ask your butcher to remove the meat from the shin (or neck) of beef and shin of veal, and to chop the bones up into large chunks.

2 Preheat oven to very hot (475°F/ 240°C/Mark 9).

3 Trim any excess fat from the meat.

4 Put beef and veal bones, and ham bone, if available, in a roasting tin. Add roughly chopped onions and carrots and thickly sliced leeks and celery, and dot with dripping.

5 Roast bones and vegetables in the oven for 40–45 minutes, turning occasionally, until richly browned.

6 Scrape contents of roasting tin into a large saucepan, casserole or stockpot. Add boned meat, ham (if used), mushroom stalks or trimmings and soft tomatoes.

7 Add ½ pint (3 dl) cold water to roasting tin; bring it to the boil, scraping bottom and sides of tin with a wooden spoon to dislodge all the crusty bits and sediment stuck there. Pour over vegetables, then add 5½ pints (3.1 litres) cold water.

8 Place pan over a low heat and bring to the boil. Allow foam to settle into a scum on the surface; skim it off with a slotted spoon, then add a little salt (not too much – remember stock will reduce), which will draw out more scum. Skim again.

9 When all the scum has been drawn out of the meat and bones, throw in herbs, bay leaf, clove and black peppercorns, and leave stock to simmer gently for 3 hours.

10 Strain stock through a fine sieve into a large bowl and allow to cool before skimming off fat. Store until ready to be used.

Note: meat can be eaten with coarse salt and freshly ground black pepper, or combined with fresh vegetables to make another, less rich, portion of stock.

Makes 3 pints

Ingredients
3 lb (1.3 kg) shin or neck of beef on the bone (see Step 1)
1 lb (450g) shin of veal on the bone (see Step 1)
1 small ham bone (about ½ lb (225g)) or ¼ lb (100g) lean ham
2 Spanish onions, roughly chopped
3 large carrots, roughly chopped
2 leeks, thickly sliced
3-4 stalks celery, thickly sliced
2 oz (50g) beef dripping
A few mushroom stalks or trimmings
2-3 soft over-ripe tomatoes
Salt
3 sprigs parsley
1 sprig thyme or a pinch of dried thyme
1 bay leaf
1 clove
9 black peppercorns

Summer Tomato Soup. This uncooked tomato soup is garnished with diced cooked ham, raw cucumber and fresh herbs for flavour and texture appeal. (Recipe, page 55)

Cream of Spinach Soup

Ingredients

2 lb (900g) fresh spinach or 1 lb (450g) frozen chopped spinach
4 level tablespoons butter
½ pint (3 dl) double cream
½–¾ pint (3–4½ dl) chicken stock (see page 51)
Juice of ½ lemon
Salt and freshly ground black pepper
Finely chopped hard-boiled egg, to garnish

1 If using fresh spinach, wash leaves in several changes of cold water, nipping off any tough stems and discarding yellowed leaves. Drain well in a colander, pressing out excess moisture, and chop roughly.

2 Melt butter in a heavy saucepan; add spinach, either fresh or still in a frozen block, and simmer gently, stirring occasionally, for 8–10 minutes, or until spinach is soft.

3 Purée spinach in an electric blender. Pour back into rinsed out pan.

4 Stir in cream and dilute to taste with chicken stock, using ½ pint (3 dl) if you want a very thick, rich soup; ¾ pint (4½ dl) for a lighter consistency. Heat through over a moderate heat, stirring.

5 Season to taste with a little lemon juice and salt and freshly ground black pepper, and serve hot, each portion garnished with a sprinkling of chopped hard-boiled egg.

Serves 6

Chinese Seafood Soup

1 Make a light fish stock by cooking bones and trimmings of sole, sliced onion and carrot and chicken stock cube in 2 pints (1.1 litres) water until vegetables are tender. Strain, reserving liquid.

2 Slice each fillet of sole in half lengthwise; tie each strip loosely into a knot; poach knotted fish strips in enough fish stock to cover until just tender.

3 Sauté halved mushrooms in vegetable oil until just tender; add prawns and stir for 1 minute. Add dry white wine and remove from heat.

4 Cook vermicelli or thin spaghetti in boiling salted water until tender but not mushy. Drain.

5 Add sole, mushrooms and prawns to stock; bring to the boil; add curly endive or young spinach leaves and heat through.

6 To serve: place a coil of hot cooked vermicelli or spaghetti in the bottom of each small Chinese bowl, and then ladle soup, vegetables and seafood over. Top with bean sprouts, if desired, and serve with chopsticks and a Chinese porcelain spoon.

Serves 4

Ingredients
1 small sole, filleted
Bones and trimmings from sole
½ onion, sliced
4 slices of carrot
1 chicken stock cube
8 button mushrooms, halved
1 tablespoon vegetable oil
8 frozen prawns, defrosted
1 glass dry white wine
Vermicelli (or thin spaghetti)
Salt
Curly endive or young spinach leaves
Bean sprouts (optional)

Seafood Saffron Soup

1 Combine sliced onions and potatoes with milk and chicken stock cube, and cook gently until potatoes are soft. Blend in electric blender and then strain through a fine sieve.

2 Poach fish in salted water until just tender. Drain; remove the bones from the pieces of fish and keep warm.

3 Place the strained mixture over a low heat; add cream and saffron (and a little turmeric for extra colour, if desired), and bring to the boil. Simmer for 5 minutes; add the pieces of fish; correct seasoning and heat through.

4 Serve soup hot, with a piece of fish in each plate, and 2 croutons of fried bread.

Serves 4

Ingredients
1½ lb (675 g) halibut, flounder or sole
½ lb (225g) onions, sliced
½ lb (225g) potatoes, sliced
¾ pint (4dl) milk
1 chicken stock cube
Salt
1 pint (6 dl) double cream
½ level teaspoon saffron
Freshly ground black pepper
8 croutons

Seafood Saffron Soup.

Chinese Seafood Soup.

Cream of Watercress Soup

Ingredients

4 tablespoons butter
2 tablespoons olive oil
1 Spanish onion, finely chopped
1 clove garlic, finely chopped
½ lb (225g) potatoes, peeled and thinly sliced
Salt and freshly ground black pepper
1½ bunches watercress
½ pint (3 dl) milk
½ pint (3 dl) chicken stock (see page 51)
¼ pint (1½ dl) single cream
2 egg yolks

1 Heat butter and olive oil until butter is melted in a large, heavy saucepan, and sauté finely chopped onion and garlic over a moderate heat until transparent but not coloured.

2 Add sliced potatoes; sprinkle with salt and freshly ground black pepper and cover with ½ pint (3 dl) water. Bring to the boil; reduce heat and simmer until potatoes are almost tender, 5–7 minutes.

3 Wash watercress carefully. Separate stems from leaves. Put about a quarter of the best leaves aside for garnish. Chop stems coarsely and add them to the simmering pan, together with remaining leaves.

4 Stir in milk and chicken stock. Bring to the boil and simmer for 15–20 minutes, or until all the vegetables are very soft.

5 Rub soup through a fine wire sieve, or purée in an electric blender. Pour back into the rinsed out saucepan; correct seasoning if necessary and reheat gently.

6 Blend cream with egg yolks. Pour into the heating soup and continue to cook, stirring continuously, until soup thickens slightly. Do not allow soup to boil once the egg yolks have been added, or they will scramble and ruin its appearance.

7 Shred reserved watercress leaves, sprinkle them over the soup and serve immediately.

Serves 6

Vichyssoise

Ingredients

6 large leeks
4 level tablespoons butter
4 medium potatoes
1½ pints (9 dl) chicken stock (see page 51)
Salt and freshly ground black pepper
Finely grated nutmeg
½ pint (3 dl) double cream
Finely chopped chives

1 Cut the green tops from the leeks and cut the white parts into 1-inch (2½-cm) lengths.

2 Sauté the white parts gently in butter until soft. Do not allow to brown.

3 Peel and slice potatoes and add to leeks, together with chicken stock and salt and freshly ground black pepper and finely grated nutmeg, to taste, and simmer until vegetables are cooked.

4 Force the vegetables and stock through a fine sieve, or blend in an electric blender until smooth. Chill.

5 Just before serving, add cream and serve sprinkled with chives.

Serves 4 - 6

Green Consommé

Ingredients

3 pints (1.75 litres) well-flavoured beef stock (see page 51)
1 ripe avocado pear
Lemon juice
6 level tablespoons diced cooked green beans
6 level tablespoons frozen peas
Salt and white pepper
Tabasco

1 Peel, stone and dice avocado pear. Strain lemon juice over diced avocado and toss well in lemon juice to preserve colour.

2 Add diced cooked green beans and frozen peas to avocado. Flavour vegetables with salt and white pepper and toss again so that flavours permeate vegetables.

3 Bring beef stock gently to the boil. Skim, if necessary, and season with a drop or two of Tabasco.

4 When ready to serve: add prepared vegetables and bring soup to the boil again.

Serves 6 – 8

Provençal Vegetable Soup with Pistou

1 Soak dried haricot beans in water overnight. Drain.

2 Simmer beans in beef stock until tender. Drain.

3 To make soup: put French beans, cut in ½-inch (1-cm) slices, sliced baby marrows, carrots, potatoes and leeks, into 4 pints (2–3 litres) boiling water. Season with salt and freshly ground black pepper and let them cook fairly quickly.

4 When vegetables are cooked, add prepared haricot beans; add *pistou* sauce and cook gently for 5 minutes more. Serve this hearty soup with grated Parmesan cheese.

Serves 6 - 8

Ingredients

1 lb (450g) dried haricot beans
2½ pints (1.2 litres) beef stock (see page 51)
1 lb (450g) French beans
2 baby marrows, sliced
4 medium-sized carrots, sliced
2 potatoes, sliced
2 leeks, sliced
Salt and freshly ground black pepper
Grated Parmesan cheese

Pistou Sauce

1 Mash garlic cloves in a mortar; remove leaves from fresh basil and add to garlic. Mash with pestle until well blended.

2 Beat olive oil into this sauce very gradually; then add grated Parmesan cheese and pound until richly coloured sauce is well-blended.

Note: this highly-flavoured sauce is also delicious with hard boiled eggs, poached fish, or to flavour mayonnaise or a fish salad.

Ingredients

8 large cloves garlic
12 sprigs fresh basil
6–8 tablespoons olive oil
8 level tablespoons grated Parmesan cheese

Summer Tomato Soup *(Illustration, page 52)*

1 Quarter tomatoes and blend to a purée in an electric blender; put purée through a fine sieve.

2 Stir in lemon juice and rind, sugar, grated onion and salt, to taste. Chill.

3 Just before serving, add chilled double cream; mix well; pour into a bowl and garnish with diced ham, cucumber and finely chopped parsley.

Serve 4 – 6

Ingredients

2½ lb (1.1 kg) ripe tomatoes
Juice and finely grated rind of 1 lemon
4 level teaspoons castor sugar
1-1½ level tablespoons grated onion
Salt
½ pint (3 dl) double cream, chilled
½ lb (225g) ham, cut into ¼-inch (½ cm) dice
½ lb (225g) cucumber, peeled, seeded and cut into ¼-inch (½ cm) dice
4 level tablespoons finely chopped parsley

Gazpacho – iced Spanish soup

According to Brillat Savarin, a woman who can't make soup should not be allowed to marry. The Spanish solved this ticklish problem early in their history with *gazpacho,* a chilled summer soup that requires absolutely no cooking.

To make *gazpacho*: blend 6 tomatoes and 1 garlic clove in electric blender; add 1 to 2 tablespoons juice from a finely grated onion, and ½ cucumber, peeled, seeded and cut into cubes, to mixture and blend again. Strain into a large tureen or serving bowl and chill.

Just before serving, blend 6 tablespoons olive oil, 4 tablespoons lemon juice and ¾ pint (4 dl) chilled tomato juice; add to puréed vegetables, mix well and season with salt and cayenne pepper, to taste.

Serve *gazpacho* with individual bowls of raw vegetables – diced tomatoes, onion, cucumber and green pepper – and fried garlic-flavoured *croûtons*. Guests help themselves to a little of each.

Try the basic recipe for *gazpacho* and then ring the changes by stirring in 2 to 4 level tablespoons of fresh breadcrumbs, or a little well-flavoured mayonnaise, finely ground almonds or the beaten yolk of an egg. Or add a little gelatine and serve it slightly jelled.

New Ways with Sauces

In French cooking, the word sauce means any liquid or semi-liquid that complements a dish – the lightly thickened gravy that inevitably accompanies the Sunday roast; the cream sauce for a steamed cauliflower; the melted butter and lemon dressing for a grilled or poached fish; and the many salad dressings with which we are all familiar – from a simple vinaigrette sauce to a mustard and lemon-flavoured mayonnaise.

In other words, sauces – no matter how simple – are important in cooking.

But don't make the mistake of thinking that sauces should always be thick and rich. The modern thought in France is to use as little flour in cooking as possible – this makes the sauce more delicate in flavour, more suave in texture and more easily assimilated by the digestive system.

The heart of every sauce is its flavoursome stock, which is made by reducing home-made meat, poultry or fish broth to a concentrated essence, before adding it to the sauce. The liquid ingredient of the sauce – whether it is home-made beef stock, stock made from veal, fish or poultry, or more simply milk or cream – is most important to the final quality and flavour of your finished sauce.

In French cooking terminology, reduction is a magic word. Magic only because this terribly simple process (it just means cooking stocks over a high heat to reduce them to a third or quarter of their original quantity before adding them to the sauce) gives such intensity of flavour to the finished sauce.

It is no secret that French chefs use more liquid in their sauces – almost twice as much – and consequently cook them longer than do most other cooks; and, as a result of this concentration and blending of flavours, their sauces are more suave, more transparent, and consequently more delicious.

The secret of easy sauce-making, therefore, is the careful reduction of your sauce by slow simmering over a low heat, leaving the sauce thicker in consistency, smoother in texture and more concentrated in flavour.

Stuffed Fillets of Sole with Prawns,
Sauce Hollandaise. (Recipe,
page 81)

A flavoursome sauce trio. (Sauce
recipes begin on page 59)

To strain sauce

Always strain all sauces before serving, except, of course, those which have chopped ingredients in them. A conical strainer is best, as it is easier to direct the flow of the liquid. For a finer sauce, line the strainer with a clean cloth to give a smooth, glossy appearance.

To add butter to a sauce

French chefs often incorporate finely diced butter into a sauce just before serving. The butter is usually whisked into the strained sauce with a wire whisk after the sauce has been taken off the heat. This makes the sauce thicker and more flavoursome. Do not return the sauce to the heat after the butter has been whisked into it, or it will separate and become fatty.

To keep sauces warm

When a sauce has to stand for some time before serving, place the saucepan containing it in a larger one with hot, not boiling, water, or in a bain-marie, and cover the saucepan to prevent a skin forming. With thicker sauces, a spoonful of liquid – water, stock or milk – or melted butter may be run over the top. Just before serving, whisk this protective covering into the sauce.

White sauces

Are you frightened of making sauces? Many of my friends tell me they are, and I don't really know why, for making a classic French sauce is very easy. Sauce Béchamel, for instance, the classic white sauce of French cooking, goes way back in culinary history to the time of Louis XIV of France. It is the Marquis de Béchamel, Louis' Maître d'Hôtel who ran the royal palace at Versailles, who has been given the credit for creating this sauce. At any rate, it was named after him because he was a famous gourmet. Cooks of the time were apt to name their dishes after their patron whether or not he himself actually created it.

In the days of the Marquis de Béchamel, the sauce was more complicated than it is now. The original sauce Béchamel combined a partridge, ham, chicken and perhaps a guinea fowl to flavour the rich, creamed sauce we know today.

Variations on the Béchamel theme

Add a touch of mustard and a tablespoon of capers and you have a mustard and caper sauce. Then add a little finely chopped fresh herbs and you have a terrific sauce for eggs, fish and even poached lamb.

Stir a little tomato purée, either fresh or canned, into the basic sauce to give it a pale blush, flavour it with a little Madeira or brandy and add a touch of cream to make it just that much richer. You'll find this a very subtle sauce for poached fish, boiled eggs and steamed vegetables.

Or, for another, more exotic variation, add a little lobster butter to the above sauce. Lobster butter is easily prepared from cooked lobster shells, pounded in a mortar and then simmered in ¼ lb (100g) butter with a bay leaf, a ½ onion, a little bit of garlic, some tomato purée and some brandy. Chill the sauce in the refrigerator and then just skim off the top of your juices and you have lobster butter. So don't throw away those lobster shells. Keep them in the fridge to give a wonderful buttery richness to your sauces for poached fish.

Professional cooks use a spoonful of *glace de viande* (see page 62) to swirl into the pan juices of cooked meats to create a deliciously limpid sauce in a twinkling. This cook's aid keeps indefinitely in a stoppered jar in the refrigerator, and is well worth the trouble and expense involved. Use only a teaspoon or two with an equal quantity of lemon juice to create a delicious sauce from the pan juices of grilled or pan-fried steaks, chops, liver or kidneys. I like, too, to whisk a bit into melted butter with almonds or pine nuts before tossing this simple sauce with

To keep sauces

Velouté, brown and tomato sauces, like stocks, can be kept in covered jars in the refrigerator for 1 week. Seal jars by pouring a little melted fat over the sauce. If you want to keep your sauces longer, bring to the boil after 7 days and return to the refrigerator in a clean covered jar.

Sauces containing milk, cream or eggs should be stored in the refrigerator for only 1 or 2 days.

cooked noodles or rice as an accompaniment to meat, fish or poultry. And it is an invaluable 'strengthener' for beef and game soups and consommés.

Butter always contains a little milk which, when brought to a high heat, is apt to make a sauce 'gritty' or slightly discoloured. I usually clarify butter before using it for the more delicate sauces by melting it in a small, thick-bottomed, enamelled saucepan over a very low heat. The butter foams, and the foam falls gently to the bottom of the saucepan, leaving the clarified butter as clear as oil. Be careful when you decant this transparent liquid not to disturb any of the white sediment at the bottom. Use as directed.

Basic Sauce Béchamel

1 In a thick-bottomed saucepan, or in the top of a double saucepan, melt 2 level tablespoons butter and cook onion in it over a low heat until transparent. Stir in flour and cook for a few minutes, stirring constantly, until mixture cooks through but does not take on colour.

2 Add hot milk and cook, stirring constantly, until the mixture is thick and smooth.

3 In another saucepan, simmer finely chopped lean veal or ham in 1 level tablespoon butter over a very low heat.

Season with thyme, bay leaf, white peppercorns and grated nutmeg. Cook for 5 minutes, stirring to keep veal or ham from over-browning.

4 Add meat to the sauce and cook over hot water for 45 minutes to 1 hour, stirring occasionally. When reduced to the proper consistency (two-thirds of the original quantity), strain sauce through a fine sieve into a bowl, pressing meat and onion well to extract all the liquid. Cover surface of sauce with tiny pieces of butter to keep film from forming.

Ingredients
Butter
½ onion, minced
2 level tablespoons flour
1 pint (6 dl) hot milk
2 level tablespoons lean veal
  or ham, finely chopped
1 small sprig thyme
½ bay leaf
White peppercorns
Freshly grated nutmeg

Mornay Sauce

1 In a thick-bottomed saucepan, or in the top of a double saucepan, melt 2 level tablespoons butter and cook onion in it over a low heat until transparent. Stir in flour and cook for a few minutes, stirring constantly, until mixture cooks through but does not take on colour.

2 Add hot milk and cook, stirring constantly, until the mixture is thick and smooth.

3 In another saucepan, simmer finely chopped lean veal or ham in 1 level tablespoon butter over a very low heat. Season with thyme, bay leaf, white peppercorns and grated nutmeg. Cook for 5 minutes, stirring to keep veal from browning.

4 Add veal to the sauce and cook over hot water for 45 minutes to 1 hour, stirring occasionally. When reduced to the proper consistency (two-thirds of the original quantity), strain sauce through a fine sieve into a bowl, pressing meat and onion well to extract all the liquid.

5 Mix slightly beaten egg yolks with a little cream and combine with sauce. Cook, stirring constantly, until it just reaches boiling point; add 2 level tablespoons butter and grated cheese. Cover surface of sauce with tiny pieces of butter to keep film from forming.

Ingredients
Butter
½ onion, minced
2 level tablespoons flour
1 pint (6 dl) hot milk
2 level tablespoons lean veal
  or ham, finely chopped
1 small sprig thyme
½ bay leaf
White peppercorns
Freshly grated nutmeg
2 egg yolks, slightly beaten
Cream
2-3 level tablespoons grated
  cheese (Parmesan cheese
  or Swiss cheese)

Parsley Sauce

Ingredients

1 level tablespoon butter
1 level tablespoon flour
½ pint (3 dl) milk
2 level tablespoons finely
    chopped parsley
Salt and white pepper
Lemon juice

1 Melt butter in the top of a double saucepan; stir in the flour and mix with a wooden spoon until smooth. Cook for a few minutes over water but do not allow roux to colour.

2 Add milk, heated to boiling point, and cook, stirring constantly, until boiling. Add finely chopped parsley, season to taste with salt and white pepper, and simmer for 2-3 minutes longer.

3 Just before serving, add lemon juice, to taste.

Note: a richer sauce can be made by using sauce Béchamel (see page 59) as a foundation.

Celery Sauce

Ingredients

6 stalks celery, finely sliced
¾ pint (4½ dl) chicken stock
2 level tablespoons butter
2 level tablespoons flour
¼ pint (1½ dl) double cream
2 level tablespoons finely
    chopped parsley
Celery salt
Freshly ground black pepper
Lemon juice

1 Combine finely sliced celery and chicken stock in a saucepan and cook until celery is soft. Keep warm.

2 In the top of a double saucepan, melt butter. Add flour and cook gently over a low heat, stirring, until roux turns a pale golden colour.

3 Add hot celery stock (including celery) and cook over simmering water, stirring occasionally and skimming surface from time to time, until sauce has reduced to two-thirds of the original quantity.

4 Stir in double cream; add finely chopped parsley; correct seasoning, adding a little celery salt, freshly ground black pepper and lemon juice, to taste.

Opposite page *John Cleese learns a* tour de main *for Béarnaise Sauce (Recipe, page 62)*

Ingredients for a classic Béchamel Sauce. (Recipe, page 59)

Basic Sauce Espagnole

1 Heat butter in a thick-bottomed saucepan until it browns. Add thinly sliced onion and simmer, stirring constantly, until golden. Stir in flour and cook, stirring constantly, for a minute or two longer. The good colour of your sauce depends upon the thorough browning of these ingredients without allowing them to burn.

2 Remove saucepan from the heat and pour in the stock; return to heat and stir until it comes to the boil. Allow to boil for 5 minutes, skimming all scum from the top with a perforated spoon.

3 Wash and slice carrot, turnip, celery, mushrooms and tomatoes or tomato purée, and add them with the bouquet garni, cloves, peppercorns, and salt, to taste. Simmer the sauce gently for at least $\frac{1}{2}$ hour, stirring occasionally and skimming when necessary. Strain through a fine sieve; remove fat; reheat before serving.

Ingredients

2 level tablespoons butter
1 small onion, thinly sliced
2 level tablespoons flour
1¼ pints (7½ dl) well-flavoured
   brown stock
1 small carrot
1 small turnip
1 stalk celery or ¼ teaspoon
   celery seed
4 mushrooms
2-4 tomatoes or 1-2 level
   tablespoons tomato purée
1 bouquet garni (3 sprigs
   parsley, 1 sprig thyme and
   1 bay leaf)
2 cloves
12 black peppercorns
Salt

Madeira Sauce

1 Reduce sauce *espagnole* until it is half the original quantity.

2 Add Madeira. Heat the sauce well, but do not let it boil, or the flavour of the wine will be lost.

Ingredients

1 pint sauce espagnole (see
   above)
6 tablespoons Madeira

Glace de Viande

Ingredients

8 lb (3.6 kg) beef and veal
  bones
1 large Spanish onion, cut in
  half
1-2 chicken carcasses
½ lb (225g) carrots, cut in
  2-inch (5 cm) segments
½ lb (225g) celery stalks and
  leaves, cut in 2-inch (5 cm)
  segments
1 lb (450g) onions, cut in
  quarters
6-8 level tablespoons beef
  dripping
¾ pint (4½ dl) canned peeled
  tomatoes

Note: use half quantities of
the above if you do not
possess a very large stockpot

1 Ask your butcher to supply you with 8 lb (3.6 kg) beef and veal bones, with some meat on them, chopped into 4–6 inch (10–15 cm) segments. You'll have to give him warning.

2 Sear cut sides of onion in a griddle pan, or a large thick-bottomed frying pan, using no fat. Onion should be very dark on cut surfaces.

3 Brown the bones, together with 1 or 2 chicken carcasses, carrots, celery and onions, in beef dripping.

4 When bones and vegetables are well browned, transfer them to a very large stockpot or a large deep casserole. Fill the pot with unsalted water; add charred onion halves and peeled tomatoes and simmer bones and vegetables over the lowest of heats, or in the oven, for 18–24 hours.

5 Strain out the bones and vegetables; return stock to a clean stockpot and cook until it is reduced to half or less of the original quantity, skimming off fat and impurities as they rise to the surface of the stock.

6 Strain reduced stock into a clean saucepan through a muslin-lined sieve and cook again, stirring frequently, until it is very thick. Pour into jars, cool, and then store in the refrigerator until ready to use.

Glace de viande keeps for months in the refrigerator.

A Quick Meat Glaze

A good *glace de viande* or savoury meat glaze is not difficult to make, but it is expensive and takes more time to prepare than most home cooks, however enthusiastic, are prepared to give.

To make a quick meat glaze: take a 15-oz (425g) can of the best quality canned consommé that you can find; add 1 large onion and 2 tomatoes, finely chopped, and boil it fast until reduced to half its original quantity. Strain the sauce into a clean pan and reduce to just 3 to 6 tablespoons of dark glaze.

Basic Béarnaise Sauce

Ingredients

3 sprigs tarragon, coarsely
  chopped
3 sprigs chervil, coarsely
  chopped
1 level tablespoon chopped
  shallots
2 black peppercorns,
  crushed
2 tablespoons tarragon
  vinegar
¼ pint (1½ dl) dry white wine
3 egg yolks
½ lb (225g) softened butter,
  diced
Salt
Lemon juice
Cayenne pepper

Like its near cousin, Hollandaise sauce, the secret of successful Béarnaise is never to let the water in the bottom of the double saucepan boil, or the sauce will not 'take'. Béarnaise sauce is the perfect accompaniment to grilled steak; try it, too, with grilled, poached or fried fish.

1 Combine coarsely chopped herbs, chopped shallots, crushed black peppercorns, tarragon vinegar and dry white wine in the top of a double saucepan. Bring to the boil and cook over a high heat until liquid is reduced to about 2 tablespoons in the bottom of the pan. Remove from heat.

2 Beat egg yolks with a tablespoon of water and combine with reduced liquid in the top of the double saucepan. Stir briskly with a wire whisk over hot but not boiling water until light and fluffy.

3 Add pieces of butter to egg mixture one at a time, whisking briskly until completely incorporated. As sauce begins to thicken, increase the butter to several pieces at a time, whisking it in thoroughly as before until sauce is thick.

4 Season to taste with salt, lemon juice and cayenne pepper.

5 Strain sauce through a fine sieve and serve.

Sauce Hollandaise

1 Combine lemon juice, 1 tablespoon cold water and salt and white pepper in the top of a double saucepan or bain-marie.

2 Divide butter into four equal pieces.

3 Add the egg yolks and a quarter of the butter to the liquid in the saucepan, and stir the mixture rapidly and constantly with a wire whisk over hot, but not boiling, water until the butter is melted and the mixture begins to thicken. Add the second piece of butter and continue whisking. As the mixture thickens and the second piece of butter melts, add the third piece of butter, stirring from the bottom of the pan until it is melted. Be careful not to allow the water over which the sauce is cooking to boil at any time. Add rest of butter, beating until it melts and is incorporated in the sauce.

4 Remove top part of saucepan from heat and continue to beat for 2–3 minutes. Replace saucepan over hot, but not boiling, water for 2 minutes more, beating constantly. By this time the emulsion should have formed and your sauce will be rich and creamy. 'Finish' sauce with a few drops of lemon juice. Strain and serve.

Note: if at any time in the operation the mixture should curdle, beat in 1 or 2 tablespoons cold water to rebind the emulsion.

Ingredients
1 teaspoon lemon juice
Salt and white pepper
¼ lb (100g) softened butter
4 egg yolks
Lemon juice

Mayonnaise

1 Place egg yolks (make sure gelatinous thread of the egg is removed), salt and freshly ground black pepper and mustard in a bowl. Twist a cloth wrung out in very cold water round the bottom of the bowl to keep it steady and cool. Using a wire whisk, fork or wooden spoon, beat the yolks to a smooth paste.

2 Add a little lemon juice (the acid helps the emulsion), and beat in about a quarter of the olive oil, drop by drop. Add a little more lemon juice to the mixture and then, a little more quickly now, add more olive oil, beating all the while. Continue adding olive oil and beating until the sauce is of a good thick consistency. Correct seasoning (more salt, freshly ground black pepper and lemon juice) as desired. If you are making the mayonnaise a day before using it, stir in 1 tablespoon boiling water when it is of the desired consistency. This will keep it from turning or separating.

Notes: if the mayonnaise should curdle, break another egg yolk into a clean bowl and gradually beat the curdled mayonnaise into it. Your mayonnaise will begin to 'take' immediately.

If mayonnaise is to be used for a salad, thin it down considerably with dry white wine, vinegar or lemon juice. If it is to be used for coating meat, poultry or fish, add a little liquid aspic to stiffen it.

If sauce is to be kept for several hours before serving, cover the bowl with a cloth wrung out in very cold water to prevent a skin from forming.

Ingredients
2 egg yolks
Salt and freshly ground black pepper
½ level teaspoon Dijon mustard
Lemon juice
½ pint (3 dl) olive oil

Cucumber Cream

1 Flavour whipped cream with salt and lemon juice, to taste.

2 Peel, seed and dice cucumber, fold into the cream and chill until ready to use.

Ingredients
¼ pint (1½ dl) double cream, whipped
Salt
Lemon juice
½ cucumber

Egg Dishes, Omelettes and Soufflés

The greatest virtue of the egg to most of us today is that it is always there, handy in the refrigerator, ready to lend its sophisticated magic to delicate little ramekins of eggs and cream, light and insubstantial soufflés and moistly golden omelettes whenever there are unexpected guests.

We depend on the egg – one of the great basics of all cookery – to enrich and flavour chicken soups and sauces; to bind croquettes, meat loaves, and stuffings for meat, poultry and game; to coat meat, fish and vegetables for deep-frying; to add substance to batters and richness to cakes and pastry, and to act as the foundation for sauces made from butter and oil – mayonnaise, sauce Hollandaise and sauce Béarnaise (see pages 62 and 63).

I like to use raw eggs to dress a salad, and to add colour and quality to a spaghetti sauce. Even the shell can be used to clarify consommés and jellies.

Scrambled eggs
Most of us today think of scrambled eggs as a breakfast dish to be served with crisp slices of bacon or diminutive sausages sautéed until golden. But in France scrambled eggs can be a dish of creamy perfection, worthy of being served as a first course on its own at a luncheon party of distinction. I remember a remarkable luncheon at the elegant Plaza-Athenée in Paris, which started off with a delicious version of scrambled eggs (3 eggs per person cooked in butter until soft and moist) mixed with diced truffles and asparagus, and piled into a golden *croustade* of flaky pastry surrounded by individual moulds of ham mousse and asparagus tips. Elegant and different, and yet, except for the diced truffles and the ham mousses, not too extravagant or difficult to make.

Taking a leaf from the Plaza-Athenée's book, I have often served small, hot pastry cases filled just before serving with scrambled eggs lightly flavoured with a little grated Parmesan cheese, and tossed with diced ham and mushrooms simmered in butter. Try this, too, with thin slivers of sliced smoked salmon or flaked smoked trout and sliced radishes.

The omelette
Brillat-Savarin, giving a recipe for an omelette made with blanched carp's roe, tuna, shallot, parsley, chives and lemon juice, recommends: 'This dish should be reserved for breakfasts of refinement, for connoisseurs in gastronomic art – those who understand eating – and where all eat with judgment; but especially let it be washed down with some good old wine, and you will see wonders.'

Omelette Ratatouille. (Recipe, page 70)

Facing page *Eggs – a beautiful still-life by John Stewart.*

The most important thing to remember in omelette-making – indeed in all preparations based on eggs – is that only strictly fresh eggs should be used, and that the butter must be of the best quality.

The first essential of successful omelette-making is a good pan. I keep a pan exclusively for eggs. It is a pan expressly designed for omelettes – one of good weight, with rounded sides so that the omelette can slide easily on to the plate when cooked. The best omelette pans are made of copper, steel or aluminium.

The size of the pan is important. It must not be too small or too large for the number of eggs used in the omelette. Unless it is well proportioned to the number of eggs generally used, the omelette will either be unmanageably thick or too thin. I find a pan 7 or 8 inches (17½–20 cm) in diameter is just about right for a 4- to 5-egg omelette.

Never wash your omelette pan. Instead, just rub it clean after use with paper towels and a few drops of oil, then rub it dry with a clean cloth. If any egg adheres to the pan, it can be rubbed off with a little dry salt.

Once you have mastered the recipe for the basic omelette – *omelette nature,* the French call it – you are ready to try some of the many exciting variations on the omelette theme. Some of the most delicious are the easiest to make – but always remember to prepare the omelette filling before you make the omelette itself. In this way, your omelettes can come to the table crisply cased, with a wonderfully moist interior and filling. And always serve your omelette as soon as it is cooked, as the most successful omelette will spoil and toughen if kept waiting. It is far better to let your guests wait for the omelette than to let the omelette wait for the guests.

Soufflés

Soufflés, technically speaking, can be divided into three definite categories: the *soufflé de cuisine* – the famous savoury soufflé of France – makes the perfect beginning to a meal, whether it is a simple cheese affair (try a combination of Gruyère cheese and Parmesan cheese), a concoction of fish or shellfish, or one made with a well-seasoned base of puréed vegetables (endive, onion, or mushroom and cheese). Savoury soufflés can also make light-as-air entreés to dramatize a luncheon or supper party, for here you can let your imagination run riot. I remember one such superb duck soufflé, served to me in Rome, whose creamy interior was stuffed with olives stuffed in their turn with *pâté de foie gras.*

Why not experiment? What do you risk? The basic soufflé mixture of flour, butter, milk, eggs and grated cheese remains just the same whether you add a breakfast-cupful of diced kippers, chicken, lobster or sole.

Category number two in our soufflé line-up is the *soufflé d'entremets*; the choice is limitless. Chocolate, coffee, vanilla; *soufflé aux liqueurs*; or the whole gamut of sweet soufflés based on purées of fresh or cooked fruits (strawberries, raspberries, cherries, cranberries, or the sharp tang of lemon and orange, and the more muted note of mandarins).

Our third category, the *soufflé froid,* is not really a soufflé at all, but a moulded mousse made with a base of whipped cream and gelatine, and served in round moulds or soufflé dishes. Tie a strip of paper round the top of the dish to permit the mixture to be piled high above the edge, and *voilà,* when the paper is removed it gives the illusion of a real soufflé.

Soufflés are perfectly easy to make if you follow a few basic rules.

1 A rich, smooth sauce is the basis of all soufflés – a thick sauce Béchamel for a savoury soufflé (see page 59), a *crème pâtissière* for a sweet soufflé (see page 172).

2 The egg yolks must be beaten one by one into the hot sauce after the saucepan is removed from the heat, or they will curdle.

3 The egg whites must be beaten until stiff but not dry. In separating eggs, be sure there is no speck of yolk left in the whites, or you will not be able to beat your whites stiff.

4 A slow to moderate oven (325–350°F/170–180°C/Mark 3–4) is an essential for a perfect soufflé. If your oven is too hot, the soufflé will be well cooked on the top and undercooked inside.

5 Sweet soufflés should be softer than entrée or vegetable soufflés.

6 A soufflé must never be too liquid before it goes into the oven. The addition of the beaten egg whites should just about double the volume of your mixture. Cooking will double it again.

7 Finally, a soufflé must be eaten immediately.

Eggs Lucullus—for Special Occasions

1 Peel eggs, then cut each egg in half lengthwise and arrange, cut side down, on a porcelain serving dish. Garnish each egg with a small leaf of lettuce and 2 tomato wedges.

2 Blend mayonnaise with sour cream and mask each half-egg completely with a tablespoon of mayonnaise, tapping the bottom of the dish if the mayonnaise does not flow smoothly over the egg of its own accord.

3 Dot top of each egg with a few grains of caviar and chill lightly until ready to serve.

Serves 4

Ingredients
4 hard-boiled eggs
4 small lettuce leaves
8 tomato wedges
8 level tablespoons well-flavoured mayonnaise (see page 63)
4 tablespoons sour cream
2 teaspoons black caviar, or, for simpler occasions, red caviar

Eggs in Aspic *(Illustration, page 71)*

1 Coat the bottom of small individual moulds with Madeira aspic; allow to set.

2 Pour boiling water over tarragon leaves; dry and arrange on aspic. Place 2–4 thin strips of ham across leaves, and dribble a little aspic over them to hold them in place.

3 Trim poached eggs with scissors and place in moulds. Pour aspic over them to cover. Garnish, if desired, with cold cooked peas and diced cooked turnip and carrot. Cover with aspic. Chill. Unmould just before serving.

Serves 4

Ingredients
Madeira aspic
8 fresh tarragon leaves
1 slice cooked ham, cut en julienne
4 poached eggs
2 teaspoons each cold cooked peas, diced cooked turnip and diced cooked carrot (optional)

Fried Eggs

1 Melt butter in a small frying pan.

2 Break 1 egg at a time into a cup; season with salt and freshly ground black pepper; slide eggs quickly into the sizzling butter and cook for 1–2 minutes, or until done as you like them. Lift out with a spatula or a perforated spoon; drain and serve immediately.

Serves 1

Ingredients
2 eggs
1 level tablespoon butter
Salt and freshly ground black pepper

Oeufs sur le Plat

Ingredients

8 eggs
2 level tablespoons butter
Salt and fresh black pepper

1 Lightly butter 4 flat heatproof dishes and break the eggs into them without breaking the yolks. Season with salt and freshly ground black pepper, and place the remaining butter in small pieces on the top.

2 Bake in a preheated slow oven (325°F/170°C/Mark 3) for 4–5 minutes, or until the whites are set but not hard. Serve hot in the dishes in which the eggs were cooked.

Serves 4

Baked Eggs with Cream

Ingredients

¼ pint (1½ dl) double cream
2 level tablespoons grated Gruyère cheese
2 tablespoons lemon juice
2 tablespoons dry white wine
1-2 level teaspoons prepared mustard
Salt and fresh black pepper
8 eggs
Butter
Buttered breadcrumbs

1 Mix together double cream, grated cheese, lemon juice and dry white wine; add mustard and salt and freshly ground black pepper, to taste.

2 Break eggs into individual buttered ramekins or casseroles, 2 eggs in each.

3 Cover the eggs with the sauce and sprinkle buttered breadcrumbs over the top. Place ramekins in a pan of hot water and bake in a moderate oven (375°F/190°C/Mark 5) for about 15 minutes.

Serves 4

Spanish Tortilla, delicious served hot or cold. (Recipe, page 71)

Scrambled Eggs Provençal *(Illustration, page 70)*

1 Break the eggs into a mixing bowl; add salt and freshly ground black pepper, and cayenne pepper, to taste, and mix lightly with a fork.

2 Cut white bread into rounds about 4 inches (10 cm) in diameter and sauté lightly in a little butter and olive oil until just golden. Keep warm.

3 Scramble the eggs in butter and olive oil until they are just soft. Not too firm.

4 Spoon the scrambled eggs on to the fried toast rounds and garnish with a latticework of thin anchovy strips. Fill each lattice with a halved black olive and sprinkle with finely chopped parsley.

Serves 6

Ingredients

9 eggs
Salt and freshly ground black
    pepper
Cayenne pepper
6 slices white bread
Butter
Olive oil
12 anchovy fillets, sliced in
    half lengthwise
Black olives
3 level tablespoons finely
    chopped parsley

Scrambled Eggs with Asparagus Tips and Ham

1 Break eggs into a bowl. Add salt and freshly ground black pepper, to taste, and stir well with a fork (don't beat) until yolks and whites are thoroughly mixed. Stir in double cream.

2 Melt 1 level tablespoon butter in the pan in which you intend to scramble eggs. Add chopped asparagus tips and ham, and toss over a gentle heat for 1 or 2 minutes until thoroughly hot.

3 Pour in eggs all at once; set pan over a low heat and immediately start stirring with a large wooden spoon. Keep stirring, making sure the spoon reaches the corners of the pan and keeping the whole mass of liquid egg on the move, until eggs are creamy and almost ready.

4 Remove pan from the heat and stir for a few seconds longer until eggs are ready. Then fold in a few flakes of cold butter (almost $\frac{1}{2}$ level teaspoon). Correct seasoning with a little more salt and freshly ground black pepper if necessary, and serve at once on a hot plate, or container of your choice.

Serves 1 generously

Ingredients

3 eggs
Salt and freshly ground black
    pepper
1 tablespoon double cream
Butter
3 canned asparagus tips,
    chopped
2 level tablespoons finely
    chopped ham

Scrambled Eggs with Buttered Shrimps and Mushrooms

1 Wash or wipe mushrooms clean; trim stems and slice mushrooms. Sauté in 1 oz (25g) butter for 5 minutes until softened. Stir in buttered shrimps and keep warm.

2 Beat eggs lightly in a bowl with cream, milk or water – just enough to mix them. (Water will make extremely fluffy eggs; cream gives a richer, smoother texture.)

3 Slip prebaked pastry cases into a moderate oven (350°F/180°C/Mark 4) to heat through.

4 Melt remaining butter in a large, heavy saucepan (about 8 inches (20 cm) in diameter). When butter is hot but not brown, pour in eggs and cook over low heat, stirring constantly with a wooden spoon, until eggs are just on the point of setting. Add sautéed mushrooms, shrimps and salt and freshly ground black pepper, to taste, at the halfway stage.

5 As soon as eggs are on the point of setting, remove pan from heat. Divide mixture between pastry cases and serve immediately.

Serves 6

Ingredients

6 oz (175g) button
    mushrooms
$\frac{1}{4}$ lb (100g) butter
4-6 oz (100-175g) buttered
    shrimps
12 eggs
6 tablespoons cream, milk or
    water
6 3-inch (7$\frac{1}{2}$ cm) pastry cases,
    prebaked (see page 170)
Salt and freshly ground black
    pepper

Omelette Ratatouille *(Illustration, page 64)*

Ingredients

8 tablespoons olive oil
1 Spanish onion, sliced
1 green pepper, diced
1 aubergine, diced
2 small baby marrows, cut in
  thin slices
2-4 ripe tomatoes, peeled,
  seeded and chopped
Salt and freshly ground black
  pepper
1 level tablespoon chopped
  parsley
Pinch of marjoram or
  oregano
Pinch of basil
1 clove garlic, crushed
8 eggs
1-2 tablespoons melted
  butter

1 Heat half the olive oil in a heatproof casserole; add onion slices and sauté until they are transparent. Add diced green pepper and aubergine and, 5 minutes later, baby marrows and tomatoes. The vegetables should not be fried but simmered gently in a covered pan for about 30 minutes.

2 Add salt and freshly ground black pepper, to taste, chopped parsley, marjoram or oregano, basil and crushed garlic; then cook uncovered for about 10 – 15 minutes, or until ratatouille is well mixed.

3 Beat eggs lightly with a fork. Season to taste with salt and freshly ground black pepper.

4 Heat remaining oil in a large omelette pan; pour in eggs and stir over a moderate heat until they begin to thicken and have set underneath.

5 Spoon ratatouille mixture down centre, reserving 2 or 3 tablespoons for garnish.

6 Continue to cook omelette until firm and golden brown on the underside but still creamy on top; then slide it up one side of the pan and fold it over on itself.

7 Slip folded omelette out carefully on to a heated serving dish. Brush with melted butter and garnish with remaining ratatouille mixture. Serve immediately.

Serves 2 - 3 generously

Poached Eggs Florentine. (Recipe, page 73)

Scrambled Eggs Provençal. (Recipe, page 69)

Spanish Tortilla *(Illustration, page 68)*

1 Heat 2 tablespoons olive oil in a medium-sized frying pan; add diced potatoes, coarsely chopped onion and pepper and cook, stirring constantly, until the vegetables are soft. Season generously with salt and freshly ground black pepper. Keep warm.

2 Season well-beaten eggs to taste with salt and freshly ground black pepper. Heat 2 tablespoons olive oil in a large frying pan; pour beaten eggs into the pan, lifting up edges of the eggs with a spatula to allow uncooked egg to run under. Add sautéed vegetables, and continue to cook, lifting up tortilla with a spatula, until omelette has a golden crust on the bottom. Then place a large plate on the omelette pan and invert pan so that omelette is on plate, crust side up.

3 Scrape free any crusty bits from pan; add a little more olive oil; return omelette to pan, moist side down, and continue to cook until omelette has browned on both sides. Cut in wedges and serve.

Serves 4 - 6

Ingredients
Olive oil
2 potatoes, peeled and diced
½ large Spanish onion, coarsely chopped
½ green or red pepper, coarsely chopped
Salt and freshly ground black pepper
6-8 eggs, well beaten

Courgette Frittata

1 Sauté finely chopped onion in 4 tablespoons olive oil in a large thick-bottomed frying pan until onion is soft and transparent. Remove onion from pan with a slotted spoon.

2 Add thinly sliced courgettes to pan and sauté, stirring constantly, until courgettes are cooked through.

3 Combine onion and courgettes in a bowl with beaten eggs. Add salt and freshly ground black pepper, to taste.

4 Melt 2 level tablespoons butter in 2 tablespoons olive oil in a large frying pan. Pour in *frittata* mixture and cook *frittata*, proceeding as you would when making an omelette, slowly on one side until brown; add a little more butter before turning to cook other side.

5 Slip cooked *frittata* onto a heated serving dish and sprinkle with chopped fresh herbs.

Serves 4

Ingredients
1 Spanish onion, finely chopped
Olive oil
2 courgettes, thinly sliced
6–8 eggs
Salt and freshly ground black pepper
Butter
1–2 level tablespoons chopped fresh parsley or chives

Eggs in Aspic. (Recipe, page 67)

Souffléed Breakfast Egg. (Recipe, page 73)

Basic Cheese Soufflé

Ingredients
Butter
2 level tablespoons flour
½ pint (3 dl) hot milk
5 egg yolks
4-6 oz (100-175g) grated
  cheese
Salt and freshly ground black
  pepper
6 egg whites

1 Melt 2 level tablespoons butter in the top of a double saucepan; add flour gradually and mix to a smooth paste, stirring constantly. Add hot milk and cook until sauce is smooth and thick. Remove from heat and add egg yolks one by one, alternately with grated cheese. Mix well and return to heat. Cook until cheese melts. Add salt and freshly ground black pepper. Remove from heat and allow to cool slightly.

2 Beat egg whites until they are stiff but not dry, then gently fold into warm cheese mixture. Pile mixture in a buttered soufflé dish or casserole. Bake in a preheated moderate oven (350°F/180°C/Mark 4) for 35–40 minutes, or until soufflé is golden. Serve immediately.

Serves 4

Provençal Vegetable Soufflé

Ingredients
Butter
4 oz (100g) courgettes, diced
4 oz (100g) aubergines, diced
4 tablespoons olive oil
4 oz (100g) tomatoes, peeled,
  seeded and diced
½ pint (3 dl) milk
½ chicken stock cube
4 level tablespoons finely
  chopped onion
2 oz (50g) grated Gruyère
  cheese
1 oz (25g) grated Parmesan
  cheese
1 level tablespoon finely
  chopped parsley
¼ level teaspoon dried
  oregano
5 egg yolks
Salt and freshly ground black
  pepper
Cayenne pepper
10 egg whites

1 Preheat oven to moderate (350°F/180°C/Mark 4). Butter a 2-pint (1-litre) metal ring mould, paying particular attention to the rim.

2 Toss diced courgettes and aubergines in olive oil until tender. Add diced tomatoes and cook for 1 minute more.

3 Combine milk and stock cube in a pan. Bring to boiling point, making sure cube has dissolved, and remove from heat.

4 In a heavy, medium-sized pan, melt 3 level tablespoons butter. Add finely chopped onion and cook over a very low heat for 5 minutes.

5 Gradually add hot flavoured milk, beating vigorously to prevent lumps forming. Bring to the boil and simmer for 2 minutes, stirring. Add cooked vegetables, grated cheese, parsley and oregano and simmer for 1 minute longer. Remove from heat.

6 Beat egg yolks lightly. Pour them into the hot sauce, stirring vigorously. Return pan to a low heat and cook gently for 1 minute longer, or until sauce has thickened, taking great care not to let it boil, or egg yolks may curdle.

7 Remove pan from heat and allow to cool to lukewarm, stirring occasionally to prevent a skin forming on top. Season generously with salt and freshly ground black pepper and cayenne pepper.

8 Whisk egg whites until stiff but not dry. Using a large metal spoon or spatula, fold them gently but thoroughly into lukewarm sauce.

9 Spoon mixture carefully into prepared ring mould, and immediately transfer to the oven.

10 Bake for 25 to 30 minutes, or until soufflé has risen well above the top of the mould and is golden and firm to the touch.

11 To serve: cover ring mould with a heated serving dish and invert the two quickly so that soufflé is not squashed.

Serves 6

Souffléd Breakfast Egg *(Illustration, page 71)*

1 Separate eggs.

2 Beat whites very stiff, and season generously with salt and white pepper.

3 Butter 4 individual ramekins or *cocottes*, and spoon an egg white into each. Use rather large dishes to allow egg whites to rise. Make a depression with the back of your spoon for each egg yolk. Place yolks in hollows (1 to each ramekin); cover each yolk with 1 tablespoon cream, and sprinkle with grated cheese. Bake in a hot oven (450°F/230°C/Mark 8) for 8–10 minutes.

Serves 4

Ingredients
4 eggs
Salt and white pepper
Butter
4 tablespoons double cream
4 level tablespoons grated
  Parmesan cheese

Croustade of Poached Eggs Benedict

1 Bake 4 individual pastry cases; remove from tins.

2 Place 1 round cooked ham in each case; top with poached egg; season to taste with salt and freshly ground black pepper, and dot with butter; warm through for a few minutes in a moderate oven (375°F/190°C/Mark 5).

3 Top each egg with 2 tablespoons sauce Hollandaise; garnish with 2 tomato wedges and serve immediately.

Serves 4

Ingredients
4 individual pastry cases
  (see page 170)
4 slices cooked ham, cut to fit
  pastry cases
4 poached eggs
Salt and freshly ground black
  pepper
Butter
8 tablespoons sauce
  Hollandaise (see page 63)
8 tomato wedges

Poached Eggs Florentine *(Illustration, page 70)*

1 To prepare spinach mixture: combine frozen spinach with butter in a heavy pan and allow to defrost over a gentle heat, stirring and mashing occasionally with a wooden spoon. Then simmer spinach for 5–7 minutes longer, stirring to rid it of excess moisture. Beat in grated Parmesan cheese and cream, and season to taste with a few drops of lemon juice, salt and freshly ground black pepper, and a pinch of freshly grated nutmeg.

2 Fill pastry cases with hot spinach mixture and top each one with a poached egg. Spoon hot Mornay sauce over the top and sprinkle with grated Parmesan cheese.

3 Slip pastry cases under a hot grill for a few minutes until tops are bubbling and golden, and serve immediately.

Note: if you have no Mornay sauce or other rich cheese sauce available, simply sprinkle pastry cases more generously with grated Parmesan cheese and grill as above until cheese has melted.

Serves 6

Ingredients
6 prebaked individual
  fingertip pastry cases, 4
  inches, (10 cm) in diameter
  (see page 170)
6 eggs, poached and trimmed
6 level tablespoons Mornay
  sauce (see page 59)
2 level tablespoons freshly
  grated Parmesan cheese

SPINACH MIXTURE

$\frac{3}{4}$ lb (350g) frozen spinach
2 oz (50g) butter
4 level tablespoons freshly
  grated Parmesan cheese
3-4 tablespoons single cream
Lemon juice
Salt and freshly ground black
  pepper
Freshly grated nutmeg

Aioli, a great one-dish luncheon from the South of France. (Recipe, page 77)

Cooking in Water

You can cook anything in water – from the ubiquitous poached chicken to the unusual *gigot à l'irlandaise* of French classic cookery (a tender leg of mutton, boned and stuffed with herbs, then rolled in a suet pastry, wrapped carefully in a sheet of muslin and simmered gently in water until deliciously tender).

Cooking in water does not, however, mean that you should not flavour it. Salt is, of course, used even when boiling a potato. But many cooks in France would never think of preparing their bouillon (the liquid in which anything is boiled) without adding a few peppercorns, a sprig of thyme or other herbs, a bay leaf, some onions, a little vinegar or equal quantities of wine and stock. I like to cook new potatoes, for instance, in a covered saucepan with just ½ inch (1 cm) water and 2–3 tablespoons butter or olive oil. Try this, too, with peas, spinach, carrots or sliced courgettes.

You will find it makes all the difference, whether you are cooking a fish in a delicately prepared court-bouillon; a fat, herb-stuffed chicken in a rich stock spiked with dry white wine; or fresh egg noodles in a light white stock flavoured with a little olive oil and a touch of garlic.

Poaching

Other than when making tea or coffee, or when cooking the occasional new potato, green vegetable or hard-boiled egg, I prefer to think of boiling in terms of poaching (a boiling that does not quite boil), for the term 'poaching' extends to all slow processes of cooking which involve the use of a liquid, not necessarily water, no matter how small the quantity. Thus the term 'poach' applies equally to the cooking of a large fish – a turbot or a salmon – in an aromatic court-bouillon, as to fillets of sole simmered in a little fish *fumet*, or to eggs or vegetables cooked in stock or water.

Poached foods are usually served with a butter- or cream-based sauce or, more simply, with butter, olive oil or cream.

Cooking fish in water

Many cooks think that there is nothing in the world as difficult to cook really well as fish, for its delicate flavour is so easily lost, and its light, creamy flakiness so quickly destroyed. Yet if we follow the simple and elementary rules for its preparation, we can all cook fish to perfection.

To poach fish

Whole fish or thick pieces of fish such as salmon, halibut, cod, ling, hake or turbot are best for poaching. If small fish or thin slices, steaks, or fillets are to be cooked in liquid, they are better steamed, or 'poached' in the oven (see below).

Always put all fish – except salt fish – into water that is very hot but not bubbling too hard, to which you have added $\frac{1}{2}$ oz (15g) salt and 1 or 2 tablespoons vinegar or lemon juice per 4 pints (2–3 litres) water.

A simple court-bouillon (quickly made stock) can be made to lend extra savour by the addition of a bouquet garni (thyme, bay leaf and parsley), sliced carrots, onion and celery to the water, as well as salt and vinegar or lemon juice. For a more flavoursome court-bouillon, add $\frac{1}{2}$ bottle inexpensive dry white wine instead of vinegar, or half white wine and half water may be used. And if the fish tends to be dry, add 2 or more tablespoons olive oil.

A red court-bouillon can be made by substituting claret for the white wine to give the fish a bluish tinge.

A long, solid fish kettle, with a drainer to allow fish to be lifted out easily without being broken, is the best utensil to use for poaching fish. My kettle is 2 feet (60 cm) long, which is just large enough to hold a young salmon or a salmon trout comfortably. When poaching smaller fish or a centre cut of a larger fish I always fasten the fish loosely to the drainer with a piece of string to prevent it floating about during cooking.

A large saucepan or flameproof casserole can be used for poaching fish if a plate is placed on the bottom of the saucepan and the fish is tied in a piece of muslin or cheesecloth, with the end of the cloth hanging over the sides of the pan so that the fish can be lifted out of the water easily without being broken.

Do not use too much liquid to cook the fish or the skin will in all probability break. Just enough liquid to cover the fish by 1 or 2 inches ($2\frac{1}{2}$–5 cm) is a good rule. And if I use a proper fish poacher with a tight-fitting lid, I use only enough court-bouillon to come halfway up the fish; the steam does the rest.

Allow the liquid to come to the boil again after the fish is put in; then reduce heat to a bare simmer and cook for the required time. If the fish is cooked too quickly, the outside will crack and break before the inside is ready. Remove all scum that rises, for if allowed to remain it will spoil the appearance of the fish.

Test the fish by flaking it with a fork before it is lifted from the water; the flesh ought to have lost its clear appearance and to have become white and opaque. It should also come away from the bone easily; a wooden skewer may be pushed in gently to try this. Overcooked fish is flavourless.

As soon as the fish is ready, lift it out of the cooking liquid and drain well. If it cannot be served at once, keep it warm on the drainer placed across the fish kettle and covered over with a hot clean cloth. Garnish with fresh parsley and lemon wedges, and serve sauce separately. Boiled or steamed potatoes are usually served with boiled fish.

To pan-poach fish

One of the most delicate ways of cooking fish fillets and small fish steaks or cutlets is to pan-poach them in equal quantities of well-flavoured fish stock and dry white wine. Butter a shallow, heatproof *gratin* dish and place the fillets of fish in it; season with salt, freshly ground black pepper and a little lemon juice, and barely cover with fish stock and wine. Place a piece of well-buttered waxed paper over fish and cook in a hot oven (450°F/230°C/Mark 8) or on top of the stove until the fish is tender and opaque (about 8–12 minutes).

To serve: lift fish out carefully, draining it well, and place on a heated serving dish. Keep warm. Thicken pan liquids slightly with a *beurre manié* (equal quantities of flour and butter kneaded together) or with an egg yolk mixed with a little double cream and lemon juice, to taste. Serve with the fish. This manner of cooking is guaranteed to bring out the flavour of the most delicate fish.

To oven-poach fish

The most effective method of poaching fish fillets isn't really poaching at all. It is oven-poaching, or poaching without liquid. Just place your fillets, or fish steaks, in a well-buttered heatproof baking dish with a little finely chopped onion and mushroom, and salt and freshly ground black pepper, to taste; cover the dish with buttered waxed paper or foil, and cook in a moderate oven (375°F/190°C/ Mark 5) until fish flakes with a fork. The fish may be served with or without sauce.

Blanching

Blanching is not, properly speaking, a method of cooking at all, but a preliminary preparation. To blanch vegetables, meat or fish, put the ingredient into a generous saucepan of cold water; bring the water to boiling point; remove the pan from the fire and drain the ingredient, which is then 'blanched'.

Almonds and chestnuts are blanched to facilitate the removal of their skins. Certain vegetables – onions, cabbage and even Brussels sprouts – are blanched to remove bitterness before they are tossed in butter. Diced fat bacon is usually blanched to remove excess salt before it is sautéed in butter and olive oil and used as a flavouring agent in many stews and ragoûts. Veal and lamb are blanched to preserve their whiteness for certain 'white' stews such as *fricassées* and *blanquettes*.

Aioli *(Illustration, pages 74 and 75)*

1 Soak codfish overnight in cold water.

2 Boil fish and vegetables. Cook each vegetable separately – white and sweet potatoes in their jackets, whole baby marrows, carrots and French beans, making sure they are tender but still quite firm, and on no account over-cooked.

3 Serve hot vegetables, hard-boiled eggs in their shells and raw tomatoes on large serving dishes decorated with lettuce and sprigs of fresh herbs. Place fish in centre. For best effect, group well-drained vegetables by colour. Serve with *aioli* sauce, from which this famous dish gets its name.

Serves 4 - 6

Ingredients
1 lb (450g) salt codfish
6 white potatoes in their jackets
6 sweet potatoes in their jackets
6 baby marrows
1 lb (450g) small carrots
1 lb (450g) French beans
6 hard-boiled eggs
6 ripe tomatoes
Lettuce
Fresh herbs (parsley, basil and so on), to decorate

Aioli Sauce *(Illustration, pages 74 and 75)*

1 Crush the garlic to a smooth paste in a mortar with a little salt; blend in egg yolks until mixture is a smooth homogeneous mass. Now take the olive oil and proceed (drop by drop at first, a thin trickle later) to whisk the mixture as for a mayonnaise. The *aioli* will thicken gradually until it reaches the proper stiff, firm consistency. The exact quantity of olive oil is, of course, determined by the number of egg yolks used.

2 Season to taste with additional salt, a little freshly ground black pepper and lemon juice. This sauce is served chilled in a bowl. Guests help themselves.

Ingredients
4 fat cloves of garlic per person
Salt
1 egg yolk each for two persons
Olive oil (about ¼ pint (1½ dl) for each yolk)
Freshly ground black pepper
Lemon juice

Poached Salmon in Court-Bouillon

Ingredients

1 whole salmon (about 4 lb
  (1.8 kg))
Cucumber slices
Pimento strips
Aspic jelly

COURT-BOUILLON

4 pints (2.3 litres) water
1 bottle dry white wine
1 large Spanish onion, sliced
4 carrots, sliced
4 stalks celery, sliced
2 bay leaves
10 peppercorns
Salt
Bouquet garni

It is not that easy to poach a salmon *really* well. First of all, you need a fish poacher, with a removable rack, to allow you to lower the fish into the court-bouillon, and, what's more important, to remove the fish without breaking it. Then you need to measure your fish poacher, so that you can be certain the salmon will fit into it.

1 Combine elements of court-bouillon in a fish poacher large enough to hold salmon; bring to the boil; skim; lower heat and simmer for 20 minutes.

2 Let court-bouillon cool slightly; place the cleaned salmon on the metal rack of the poacher, and lower the rack gently into court-bouillon.

3 Bring court-bouillon to the boil again (about 3 minutes); reduce heat to a simmer; cover poacher and simmer salmon gently for 35–45 minutes, or until fish flakes easily with a fork.

4 Remove fish carefully from court-bouillon; transfer it to a board and remove the skin with a sharp knife, leaving head and tail intact.

5 To serve cold: arrange the salmon on a serving platter and garnish fish with overlapping 'scales' of paper-thin halved cucumber slices and 'fins' made of strips of cooked pimento. *Note*: I always use tiny toothpicks to hold cucumber 'scales' to fish until aspic glaze holds them in place.

6 Brush fish with liquid aspic jelly; allow jelly to set; remove toothpicks. Serve with a well-flavoured mayonnaise (see page 63).

Catch of the day: a fine fresh salmon.

Graves

One doesn't expect a world famous vineyard to be located in the centre of a big city like Bordeaux. But Château Haut-Brion – one of the greatest names in Bordeaux wines – is located in the centre of a mass of small buildings, right on a main road.

In the past it was always thought that the best land would produce the best grapes and the best wines, but nothing is further from the truth. The very word Graves is derived from 'gravelly' and it is just this gravelly soil which produces the quality of the wines in Bordeaux. The more gravel you have in the soil the deeper the roots are forced to go to find their necessary nutrients. This makes for a strong vine. The gravel airs the soil, it forces the roots of the vines to go deep into the earth, and it also acts as a sort of solar 'radiator' accumulating the heat of the sun's rays during the day and then, when the sun is set, the warm gravel gives warmth to the vine.

When people talk about a Graves in England or America, they usually mean a sweet white wine. But, in fact, Graves is famous for the delicate, yet full-flavoured red wines of the Graves region. They do, of course, produce some white wines which are of superlative value, but these represent a much smaller percentage of the total crop, even though a great quantity of white wine is exported.

There is not that much demand for red Graves outside France, consequently the prices are still quite low. So, look out for a red Graves when you visit the supermarket or local wine shop. Ask for a Graves and make sure they know that you know what you want: a red Graves.

2

1

3

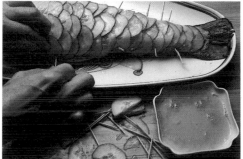

4

Poached Salmon in Court-Bouillon.
One of the most attractive ways of
decorating a cold fresh salmon is to
coat it with a thin layer of
overlapping cucumber slices.
1 Place 4 lb (2 kg) salmon on rack
in fish poacher and cook in
prepared court-bouillon for
35–45 minutes.

2 Remove fish on rack from
court-bouillon; let it cool slightly
and then carefully remove skin.

3 To make cucumber 'scales': slice
cucumber in half lengthwise and
then cut each half cucumber into
paper-thin half-rounds.

4 To cover fish with 'scales': dip
each 'scale' in aspic jelly which is
just beginning to set. Then, starting
at the tail end, place cucumber
slices in overlapping rows until fish
is entirely covered. Half toothpicks
are invaluable for holding
'difficult' slices to sides of fish.

Smoked Haddock in Court-Bouillon

Ingredients

2 lb (900g) smoked haddock
    fillets
Water and milk
Thin lemon slices
Sprigs of fresh parsley
Boiled new potatoes
¼ lb (100g) butter
Juice of ½ lemon
Salt and freshly ground black
    pepper

1 Soak haddock in water for 2 hours.

2 Drain fish and put in a saucepan; cover with equal amounts of water and milk, and bring to a fast boil. Remove from the heat and allow to stand for 15 minutes. Drain haddock, reserving stock for some other use.

3 Serve haddock on a heated serving dish, garnished with thin lemon slices, sprigs of fresh parsley and boiled new potatoes. Serve with butter melted with lemon juice and seasoned with salt and freshly ground black pepper, to taste.

Serves 4 - 6

Filets de Sole du Pays Normand

Ingredients

2 Dover sole (1-1¼ lb (450-
    550g) each)
2 shallots, finely chopped
½ pint (3 dl) reduced fish
    fumet (see below)
½ pint (3 dl) dry white wine

FISH FUMET

Butter
Bones and trimmings from
    sole
1 small piece turbot with
    bone
4 sprigs parsley
2 sprigs thyme
2 bay leaves
1 shallot, finely chopped
¼ pint (1½ dl) dry white wine
2 mushrooms, sliced
⅛ level teaspoon fennel seed
6 peppercorns
Salt and freshly ground black
    pepper

GARNISH

12 poached mussels
24 small cooked prawns
4 mushroom caps simmered
    in butter and lemon juice
Crescents of flaky pastry
    (optional)

Ingredients

¼ pint (1½ dl) double cream
4 mushroom stalks, finely
    chopped
1-2 egg yolks
Salt and freshly ground black
    pepper
Cayenne pepper or freshly
    grated nutmeg

1 Ask your fishmonger to fillet Dover sole. Reserve bones and trimmings.

2 To make fish *fumet*: butter the saucepan; combine bones and trimmings from sole with small piece of turbot, parsley, thyme, bay leaves, finely chopped shallot, dry white wine, ¼ pint (1½ dl) water, sliced mushrooms, fennel seed and peppercorns, and salt and freshly ground black pepper, to taste. Bring to the boil; skim and simmer for 10–15 minutes. Strain fish *fumet* and reduce to half the original quantity (there should be about ½ pint (3 dl)).

3 To prepare fish: poach fillets of sole with finely chopped shallots in equal quantities of fish *fumet* and dry white wine until fish flakes easily with a fork (about 7 or 8 minutes). Remove fillets and keep warm in a low oven.

4 To serve: place sole fillets on a heated serving dish and keep warm. Prepare Normandy Cream Sauce (see below). Strain sauce over sole. Garnish with poached mussels, prawns, and mushroom caps which you have poached in a little butter and lemon juice. Add crescents of flaky pastry, if desired.

Serves 4

Normandy Cream Sauce

1 Reduce poaching liquids from fish until they are syrupy.

2 Bring cream to the boil with finely chopped mushroom stalks and add reduced poaching liquid little by little, stirring briskly with a wooden spatula or whisk until sauce is well blended.

3 Remove saucepan from heat and stir in egg yolks, which you have first mixed with a little of the hot sauce. Whisk well, return to heat and simmer, stirring continuously, until sauce is smooth and thick. Do not allow the sauce to boil after the eggs have been added.

4 Correct seasoning.

Sole in Court-Bouillon with Herb or Caviar Tartlets

1 To make court-bouillon: butter an enamelled saucepan or baking dish; lay half the fish bones and trimmings on bottom of pan; add lemon juice, parsley, bay leaf, onion, mushrooms, and salt and freshly ground black pepper, and enough water and dry white wine in equal quantities to cover fish. Bring to the boil; add fish fillets; cover with remaining bones and simmer gently, covered with a piece of buttered paper, for 10–15 minutes, or until fish flakes easily with a fork. Remove fish fillets from court-bouillon and keep warm.

Cook court-bouillon over a high heat until reduced to about ½ pint (3 dl). Strain.

2 To serve: place fish fillets on a heated serving dish; pour over the Fish Velouté Sauce (see below); garnish with thin slices of lemon and sprigs of fresh watercress. Surround with tiny tartlets filled with sour cream and topped with finely chopped fresh fennel and chives, or, for a more extravagant occasion, black caviar.

Serves 6

Ingredients

2 lb (900g) fillets of sole

COURT-BOUILLON

Butter
Bones and trimmings of sole
Juice of 1 lemon
4 sprigs parsley
1 bay leaf
¼ Spanish onion, finely chopped
4 mushrooms, finely chopped
Salt and freshly ground black pepper
Water and dry white wine

GARNISH

6 baked 1-inch (2½ cm) tart shells (see page 170)
Thinly sliced lemon
Sprigs of watercress
Sour cream
Finely chopped fresh fennel and chives, or black caviar

Fish Velouté Sauce

1 Melt butter in the top of a double saucepan; stir in flour and cook over water, stirring continuously, until smooth.

2 Add strained court-bouillon and cook, stirring from time to time, until thick

and smooth. Add double cream and continue cooking until sauce is reduced to the desired consistency.

3 Correct seasoning, adding a little salt and pepper if necessary.

Ingredients

2 level tablespoons butter
2 level tablespoons flour
¼ pint (3 dl) double cream
Salt and fresh ground pepper (optional)

Stuffed Fillets of Sole in Hollandaise Sauce

1 Lay fillets of sole out flat on a clean surface; brush with softened butter; season with salt and freshly ground black pepper; place 1 level tablespoon prawns on each fillet and roll fillets up, starting from head; fasten with toothpicks.

2 Place rolled fillets in a well-buttered gratin dish. Sprinkle with chopped shallots and mushroom stalks, add salt and freshly ground black pepper to taste, and cover with fish bones and

trimmings. Cover with buttered paper and 'poach' in a hot oven (450°F/230°C/Mark 8) for 10 minutes, or until fish flakes easily with a fork. Keep warm.

3 To serve fillets: place pastry cases on a baking tray; place 1 cooked fillet in each case and spoon over sauce Hollandaise. Heat in a hot oven for a few minutes until sauce bubbles.

Serves 4

Ingredients

2 sole, filleted
Butter
Salt and freshly ground black pepper
4 level tablespoons peeled prawns
2 shallots, finely chopped
Mushroom trimmings
Fish bones and trimmings
4 baked pastry cases (see page 170)
1 recipe sauce Hollandaise (see page 63)

Steaming

Steaming is one of the principal forms of Oriental cooking and one not to be by-passed in Western kitchens. It is rapid and also one of the most effective methods of cooking I know for preserving the maximum degree of original taste.

Flavour the water with salt, a clove of garlic or a few spring onion tops to give a subtle flavour to the steamed food. Or follow an ancient Arabian recipe and flavour your steaming bouillon with salt, powdered cumin, ginger, cinnamon, paprika and cayenne pepper.

Your cooking utensil should be large enough to hold comfortably, with a stand, the dish containing the food to be cooked.

Heat the dish; place the food in it and put the dish on the stand in the pan only when the water is actually boiling and steam is rising. To cook: cover the pan immediately and turn up the heat so that the steam is at its height.

Steamed food cooks quickly. It should be neither overdone nor underdone. All meat – except pork, which must be well done – should be a little pink when removed from the steamer.

Serve steamed food the moment it is considered cooked. Otherwise it will be overdone, for because of the intense heat it has absorbed the cooking process will continue away from the heat until the food cools. Steam-cooked food should be eaten hot, or it will lose its flavour and texture.

Sea Bass Steamed in Watercress is a nouvelle cuisine *version of an age-old cooking process. The fish is at once tender and moist, impregnated with the flavours of watercress, lemon and prawns. (Recipe, page 84)*

Steamed fish

Fish steaks or fillets – salmon, cod, sole, turbot – or whole small fish can be cooked to perfection by steaming.

To steam fish: place fish in a well-buttered oval baking dish; sprinkle with 1 or 2 tablespoons each finely chopped onion and mushrooms; moisten with 4–6 tablespoons dry white wine, canned clam juice or well-flavoured fish stock; season to taste with salt and freshly ground black pepper, and place over boiling water to which you have added a clove or two of garlic. Cover tightly and steam until fish flakes easily with a fork.

Steamed poultry

A whole chicken or duck (or even a lean leg of baby lamb) may be steamed in this way if your steamer is large enough. The legendary Alexandre Dumaine, often called the world's greatest chef when he was alive, used to serve a whole steamed chicken at his famous restaurant, *La Côte d'Or*, in Saulieu, Upper Burgundy. The chicken was marinated overnight in a few tablespoons of port or Madeira before being steamed in its own juices and a little butter in a heatproof dish. The secret here? The chicken was steamed for an hour over a superbly flavoured beef bouillon complete with onions, carrots, turnips and fresh herbs, which lent their flavours and juices to the finished dish.

Steamed vegetables

Most vegetables – cauliflower, peas, Brussels sprouts, green beans – steam to perfection in 15–20 minutes. Try steamed peas dressed with sautéed onion, diced ham, sugar and mint leaves; or dressed steamed cauliflower with lemon juice and fresh breadcrumbs or slivered almonds sautéed in butter. Serve steamed Brussels sprouts with a sprinkling of fresh breadcrumbs sautéed in butter until golden. Dress steamed green beans with butter, finely chopped parsley and crumbled bits of crisp-fried bacon.

Steaming equipment

There are special steamers on the market for whole chickens, whole fish or asparagus. These consist of a double saucepan with a perforated bottom to allow the steam to rise. Or you can improvise with one of the folding round steamer attachments designed to fit almost any size saucepan or casserole. These handy little steamers fit easily into a round saucepan or casserole, with the water simmering below.

Whichever pan you use, cover it tightly so that the food is completely surrounded by steam and continues to cook in it until tender. Wet towels wrapped around the join between the lid and pan help to prevent the steam from escaping.

Vegetable Couscous

For Virginia McKenna I served *couscous* steamed on its own as a vegetable accompaniment for meats and poultry, the grains subtly flavoured with my own version of a Moroccan spice blend.

Couscous should be light and fluffy and marvellously flavoured. Flavour the broth with 1 Spanish onion, 4 or 5 carrots, 4 stalks celery, 1 fat clove garlic, mashed with the point of a knife, some ground ginger, a little cayenne pepper and a little ground cumin seed. Put on the steamer top and then line it with a wet cloth so the steam can come right up through it, and the fine grains of *couscous* can't fall through. Dampen the *couscous* before putting it in the cloth-lined steamer top so that the steam can go through it more quickly.

Sea Bass Steamed in Watercress *(Illustration, page 82)*

Ingredients

1 sea bass (about 2 lb (900g))
2 bunches watercress,
    trimmed and washed
Lemon juice
Salt and freshly ground black
    pepper
2 cloves garlic
2 sprigs thyme
¼ pint (1½ dl) chicken stock
4 Dublin Bay prawns
Butter
Fennel seeds
Finely chopped parsley

1 Ask your fishmonger to scale and clean the fish and cut away its fins.

2 To steam sea bass: put a layer of half the watercress sprigs in an enamelled oval casserole large enough to contain the fish comfortably. Season the fish, inside and out, with lemon juice and salt and freshly ground black pepper, to taste. Lay fish on top of layer of watercress. Add garlic cloves and thyme and top with remaining watercress (leaving a few sprigs for garnish). Add stock. Top with Dublin Bay prawns; cover casserole and cook over a fast heat for 20 minutes, or until fish flakes easily with a fork.

3 To serve sea bass: bring the fish to the table in the casserole, lifting lid so the full flavour of the dish escapes as you serve it. Then transfer fish to a serving platter and lift fillets away from bone. Season fillets with salt and freshly ground black pepper and arrange on hot plates. Garnish each plate with a few sprigs of fresh watercress and 2 Dublin Bay prawns. Serve with a hot butter sauce to which you have added fennel seeds, finely chopped parsley and salt, freshly ground black pepper and lemon juice, to taste.

Serves 2

Steamed Mussels in the Crock

Ingredients

48 mussels
3 shallots, finely chopped
1 level tablespoon butter
¼ pint (1½ dl) white wine
¼ pint (1½ dl) chicken stock
4 slices of leek
1 small carrot, cut in quarters
1 small bay leaf
4 sprigs parsley
¼ pint (1½ dl) double cream
    (optional)
Salt and freshly ground black
    pepper
Lemon juice

1 Scrape and beard mussels; place in a fireproof crock with shallots, butter, white wine and chicken stock. Add leek, carrot, bay leaf and parsley. Cover and steam for 5 minutes, or until mussels are all open.

2 Add cream, if desired, and salt and freshly ground black pepper, and lemon juice, to taste. Bring to the boil again and serve.

Serves 4

Steaming in the Chinese manner

Steaming in the Chinese manner is extremely simple: all you have to do is to slice the food concerned (a whole fish, fish fillets or steaks, a fillet of beef, a loin of pork, or breast of chicken or turkey) diagonally across the grain into thin strips. Flavour in the Chinese manner with 3 tablespoons dry white wine and 1 tablespoon soy sauce, with a little cornflour added to thicken the sauce. Then add 6–8 thinly sliced button mushrooms for every pound of food used.

Place the meat, fish or poultry, and mushroom slices, in a heatproof *gratin* dish or shallow casserole with 1 or 2 thinly sliced shallots or green onions and season to taste with salt and freshly ground black pepper. When ready to cook, set dish on a stand in a large pan containing about 2 inches (5 cm) rapidly boiling water. Cover pan and steam for 10–12 minutes. The sauce will be translucent, light and delicious.

Chinese Steamed Fish with Ginger and Green Onions

1 Place cleaned fish in a flat dish large enough to hold them.

2 Slice mushrooms thinly. Add sliced ginger and sliced green beans.

3 Combine finely chopped garlic and chopped spring onion with grated lemon peel, olive oil, soy sauce, cornflour, dry white wine and salt and freshly ground black pepper, to taste. Mix well and pour over fish.

4 Place dish in a large steamer, or on a rack in a large saucepan wide enough to hold it, with about 2 inches (5 cm) of rapidly boiling water. Cover and steam for 15 minutes.

5 Remove to a hot platter and serve immediately, decorated with some of the mushrooms, ginger and green beans and lemon knots. Boiled rice (see page 154) or steamed sliced carrots (see page 149), new potatoes and green beans should accompany this dish.

Serves 2

Ingredients
2 whiting or sole (about ¾ lb (350g) each)
¼ lb (100g) button mushrooms
2-3 slices fresh ginger
12 green beans, sliced
1 clove garlic, finely chopped
2 chopped spring onions
Peel of ½ lemon, grated
4 tablespoons olive oil
2 tablespoons soy sauce
1 level tablespoon cornflour
2 tablespoons dry white wine
Salt and fresh black pepper
2 strips lemon peel

Chinese Steamed Lobster *(Illustration, pages 86 and 87)*

1 Fill a large saucepan three-quarters full of salted water (1 tablespoon to 2 pints (1 litre)), or well-flavoured court-bouillon, and bring to the boil. Plunge in the lobsters head first and boil quickly for 2 minutes. Remove lobsters from saucepan and slice over a shallow bowl into 1-inch (2½ cm) slices, shell and all. Reserve juices.

2 Transfer enough of the salted water that you cooked the lobster in to cover the bottom of a large *wok* and bring to the boil. Reserve the rest of the liquid for stock.

3 Place spinach leaves in the bottom of a Chinese bamboo steamer. Arrange sliced lobster on this green 'bed' and sprinkle with sliced fresh ginger and spring onion segments.

4 Place bamboo steamer over water; cover steamer with bamboo lid and steam lobster over gently boiling water for 10–15 minutes, or until tender.

5 Transfer sliced lobster and spinach to a heated serving platter. Heat ginger and spring onion segments in ¼ pint (1½ dl) stock with reserved lobster juices; add soy sauce and Tabasco, to taste, and spoon over.

Serves 4

Ingredients
2 live lobsters (about 2 lb (900g) each)
Salted water or well-flavoured court-bouillon (see page 78)
8-12 fresh spinach leaves
8-12 thin slices fresh ginger
8-12 spring onions, sliced in 1-inch (2½ cm) segments
Soy sauce
Tabasco

Chinese Steamed Prawns

1 Defrost prawns; roll in cornflour and place on a platter in steamer* with finely chopped shallots, finely sliced mushrooms and cucumber, soy sauce and white wine. Season with freshly ground black pepper, and cook over 2 inches (5 cm) fast-boiling water, covered, so platter is entirely confined in steam, until tender.

* If you do not have a steamer, place a trivet in the bottom of a casserole large enough to contain platter and cook, covered, over fast-boiling water.

2 Serve hot from the steamer on a bed of rice, garnished with fresh tomatoes.

Serves 4

Ingredients
1½ lb (675g) frozen prawns
Cornflour
4 shallots, finely chopped
¼ lb (100g) mushrooms, finely sliced
2 oz (50g) cucumber, finely sliced
4 tablespoons soy sauce
4 tablespoons dry white wine
Freshly ground black pepper
Rice
Tomatoes

Arabian Steamed Couscous

Ingredients

1 3-3½ lb (1.3-1.6kg) roasting
  chicken, or 2½ lb (1.1kg)
  shoulder of lamb
Salt and freshly ground black
  pepper
3 tablespoons olive oil
2 Spanish onions, quartered
8 small turnips, quartered
8 small carrots, quartered
2 medium-sized green
  peppers, seeded, cored
  and quartered
2 level teaspoons paprika
1 level teaspoon ground ginger
½ level teaspoon ground
  cinnamon
¼ level teaspoon saffron
  strands
8 small courgettes
2 chicken stock cubes
2 level tablespoons tomato
  purée
¼ lb (100g) chick peas, soaked
  overnight
1 lb (450g) couscous
½ lb (225g) packet frozen
  broad beans (optional)
4 level tablespoons chopped
  parsley
2 level tablespoons butter
Ground ginger, cayenne
  pepper and tomato purée
  to finish sauce

BOUQUET GARNI

1 celery stalk, cut into 1-inch
  (2½ cm) lengths
6 black peppercorns
3 cloves
1 bay leaf
1 clove garlic, peeled
½-1 level teaspoon cumin seed

Preceding pages *Chinese
Steamed Lobster. The recipe
is simplicity itself: take 1
Chinese wok, 1 Chinese steamer
basket; add 2 sliced lobsters,
8-12 slices fresh ginger, 8-12 leaves
spinach or escarole, 8-12 spring
onion segments, and steam over
bubbling water seasoned with
ginger, spring onion and soy.
Delicious. (Recipe, page 85)*

1 Cut chicken into serving pieces (or cut the lamb into chunks) and season with salt and freshly ground black pepper.

2 Collect ingredients for bouquet garni and tie them up in a square of muslin.

3 Place the bottom section of a *couscoussière* over a medium heat; or steamer which will fit it tightly. Heat 2 tablespoons olive oil in the *couscoussière* or saucepan, and sauté chicken or lamb steadily until golden brown all over, for 10-15 minutes. Transfer meat to a plate.

4 In the same oil, sauté quartered onion, turnips, carrots and green peppers for 15 minutes, or until golden. Sprinkle with paprika, ginger, cinnamon and saffron and mix well. Add meat.

5 Pour over 2 pints (1.1 litre) boiling water; add courgettes, stock cubes, tomato purée, the bouquet garni and soaked chick peas. Bring to the boil; reduce heat to a gentle simmer; cover and cook gently for 15 minutes.

6 Meanwhile prepare couscous: place the grain in a bowl and moisten with 6 tablespoons cold water, 1 at a time, working it in evenly with your fingertips, rather as though you were rubbing fat into flour to make pastry. The grain will absorb the water without any trouble, and look and feel almost as it did when it came out of the packet.

7 Line steamer top with a clean tea cloth (wrung out in boiling water just in case any trace of detergent remains). Place couscous in this.

8 Remove lid from pan in which meat and vegetables are simmering. Fit steamer over the top and continue to simmer gently, uncovered. Steam couscous in this way for 30 minutes, occasionally drawing a fork through the grains to aerate them and ensure that they do not stick together in lumps.

9 After 30 minutes, remove couscous from steamer. Spoon grain into a heat-proof bowl that will fit snugly over the pan. Sprinkle with remaining tablespoon of olive oil and gradually add a further 6 tablespoons cold water, working it in evenly as before. Season to taste with salt.

10 Add frozen broad beans to stew, if desired. Stir in chopped parsley. Fit bowl over the pan; cover bowl with lid and continue to simmer for a further 30 minutes or until meat is tender.

11 Add butter to couscous and leave it to melt while you finish making sauce.

12 Strain off ½ pint (3 dl) liquid from stew. Pour into a small pan. Flavour with a further ¼ level teaspoon ground ginger, a pinch of cayenne pepper and a level teaspoon of tomato purée. Taste and adjust the flavourings/seasonings – sauce should be quite strong. Reheat to boiling point.

13 Toss couscous with a fork to mix in melted butter. Heap it around the sides of a large heated serving platter.

14 Arrange cooked chicken or lamb pieces in the centre. Spoon over as much of the vegetables and juices as your dish will take and serve immediately, handing hot sauce around separately. Any remaining vegetables and juices can be kept hot, in reserve.

Serves 6

Note: sometimes, this wonderful combination is further garnished with hot little sausages called *merguez*, spicy little balls of minced lamb called *kefta* and chick peas and onions simmered in honey.

Basic Steamed Chicken

1 Rub cleaned and trussed chicken with cut side of ½ lemon; sprinkle with salt and freshly ground black pepper, to taste; place in a *gratin* dish just large enough to hold it.

2 Add butter, chicken stock and finely chopped onion to *gratin* dish; place dish in a large double steamer over 3 inches (7½ cm) rapidly boiling water, and steam for 1–2 hours, according to size of chicken.

3 Serve chicken with pan juices and parsley sauce or celery sauce.

Serves 4

Ingredients
1 roasting chicken
½ lemon
Salt and freshly ground black pepper
4 level tablespoons butter
4 tablespoons chicken stock
2 level tablespoons finely chopped onion
Parsley sauce or celery sauce (see page 60)

The White Wines of Burgundy

In Burgundy, wines are not château-bottled; even at a prestigious château like the Château de Meursault. They are bottled 'at the *domaine*' or 'on the estate', '*mise en bouteille au domaine*' is the phrase seen on bottles here. This is because most of the parcels of land that make up the vineyards of Burgundy are really very small. Most are owned by one proprietor, but some have as many as 60 or 70 owners.

Puligny
From Puligny everywhere you look there are vineyards, tiny parcels of land owned by different growers. Some of the greatest names in white wines are produced in this small area – Puligny-Montrachet, Meursault, Corton-Charlemagne.

Château de Meursault
The *domaine* of the Château de Meursault, a few miles south of Beaune, produces both red and white Burgundy. Meursault is a strong, firm wine, which has a lovely scent, and when it's at its best, on a chalky slope in the sun, gets an almost luscious, velvety taste, with a wonderful after-taste.

Corton-Charlemagne
Corton-Charlemagne is one of the greatest white wines. Warm, fruity, golden, it is a superb first course wine to enjoy with pâté, mousseline of salmon, or a delicate *salade folle* of the *nouvelle cuisine*.

Chablis
Just above Dijon, where we take the Great Wine Road to Mâcon, we find Chablis. The vines of Chablis, like those in much of Burgundy, are centuries old, dating back to Roman times, in fact. Chablis *Grand Cru* is grown on the right-hand bank of the River Serein, facing the town of Chablis. Chablis *Premier Cru* is produced by scattered vineyards on both sides of the river. The third A.O.C. qualification is Chablis, used by the various vineyards of the region, growing their vines on less favoured slopes of these same hills. The fourth category is Petit Chablis, a name given to white wines grown in a more spread-out area.

Chablis, at its best, is a spirited wine, with body and a delicate fragrance. Some say it has a faint after-taste of fresh mushrooms in the rain.

Roasting

Prime cuts of beef, veal, lamb or pork make successful roasts, but only the prime cuts. If you are ever in any doubt about the quality of a piece of meat, casserole it or pot-roast it instead.

A small joint – anything 2 lb (900g) or under – doesn't make a successful roast either, however good its quality. By the time the inevitable shrinkage has occurred, there will be little of it left. Again, settle for more gentle pot-roasting or casseroling instead.

The cuts of beef suitable for roasting are the ribs, the sirloin, the fillet and, in best-quality beef, the rump. Suitable cuts of lamb are the leg, the saddle, the loin and the shoulder. Pork roasts include the leg, the loin and the spare rib. The loin, the saddle, the leg, the shoulder, the rump and often the breast of veal can all be roasted.

The true secret of successful roasting is the even circulation of heat on all sides of the meat. It is best to roast your joint on a rack set in a shallow roasting pan in the oven. Never use just a roasting pan without a rack, as the meat tends to stew in the fat and juices in the bottom of the pan as the top over-browns.

To test roasts for doneness

Take a sharp, *thin*, metal skewer or a long fork with no more than *two* sharp prongs to it. Push the skewer or fork into the thickest part of the meat – right through to the bone, if there is one – and pull it out again. You will be able to tell the state of the meat from the colour of the juices that spurt out. The test spot in poultry is right through the thickest part of the inside leg (i.e. where the leg lies close to the body).

With roast beef, blood-red juice means that the meat is very rare, pink that it is medium done, and a clear liquid that it is well cooked. For pork or veal, the juices that run out should be perfectly clear. For lamb, the liquid should be clear or lightly touched with pink. With poultry, the juices should be perfectly clear.

One or two tests should be enough. Resist the temptation (understandable in a nervous novice) to jab your roast full of holes like a pin cushion.

Joanna Lumley, glamorous blonde star of the Avengers, is a girl who loves food as much as filming. I enjoyed enormously having her on the series.

Opposite page *Roast Guinea Fowl with Aromatic Butter, photographed in the Long Hall at Hintlesham, is one of the house specialities. The guinea-fowl, farm-reared locally, are brushed inside and out with a* pommade *of softened butter flavoured with crushed juniper berries, thyme and rosemary, finely chopped onion, garlic and parsley and lemon and orange juice, before being roasted in the oven. (Recipe, page 93)*

To serve a roast

To be at its best, roast meat should be served either really hot or really cold. Nothing is less appetizing than lukewarm meat or congealing gravy. (The exception is delicate meat like veal or poultry, which loses flavour if served too cold.)

Choose a large, flat serving platter that will give you plenty of room to carve without having to retrieve morsels from the table.

Make sure your platter, sauceboat and dinner plates are as hot as safety allows.

When the roast is ready, transfer it to the serving dish; *then leave it for 15–20 minutes in the turned off oven with the door ajar* to allow the cooking to subside and the juices, which were still flowing freely when you last pierced the joint, to be reabsorbed by the meat. You will find this 'rest' makes the meat far easier to carve into slices, and it also gives you time to make the gravy and do any other last-minute preparation.

Finally, to avoid that awkward pause during carving, which usually results in a polite guest of honour being forced to watch his meat grow cold before him as he waits for the others to be served, it is a good idea to carve enough for the first round before serving. Second helpings can then be sliced to order as needed.

Beef

I like to roast beef at a low temperature for an even texture. Roast beef in a fairly hot oven (400–425°F/200–220°C/Mark 6–7) for 15–30 minutes to seal it. Then reduce oven heat to 325°F/170°C/Mark 3 and continue to cook until done.

Veal

It is very important to roast veal slowly, too, so that it is still juicy with just a hint of firmness. Most cooks make the mistake of letting it go on to the stage of being stringy and dry. You'll be amazed at the difference if you try low-temperature roasting the next time you roast veal.

Always lard veal – or cover it with a protective layer of fat or bacon – before you roast it. Do not sear veal at a high temperature as you do beef. Cook it in a slow oven (325°F/170°C/Mark 3) for 20–35 minutes per pound (450g). Veal is at its succulent best when well cooked but with a delicate hint of pink still in evidence.

Lamb and mutton

Lamb should never be overcooked. It is at its succulent best – moist and richly flavoured – when it is a little pink on the inside. So do not roast it until it is a dull greyish-brown in colour, with the meat falling off the bones, the flesh dry and tough. Instead, treat lamb gently in the French fashion, roasting it until the juices run pink. For maximum juiciness and minimum shrinkage, I like to cook it for 20–25 minutes per pound at a relatively low temperature (300–325°F/150–170°C/Mark 2–3) for roasting, and a bare simmer for cooking in liquid. Cook mutton at the same temperature for 40 minutes per pound (450g).

Pork

Pork is best if roasted at about 300–325°F/150–170°C/Mark 2–3 – with plenty of cooking time and basting to give the skin or crackling a nice flavour and texture. All cuts of pork, provided they are tender and fairly fat, can be roasted. Cook pork slowly in an uncovered shallow pan or casserole. Maximum flavour is reached only when the pork is slowly and well cooked. Cook it until the meat has lost its pinkish tinge and is pale beige in colour. I like to roast pork in a slow to moderate oven (300–325°F/150–170°C/Mark 2–3) for about 35 minutes per pound (450 g).

To glaze pork roasts after cooking: increase the oven temperature to 425°F/220°C/Mark 7; sprinkle fat with 2–3 level tablespoons brown sugar; return meat to oven to glaze.

Duck

There are two schools of thought on the cooking of duck. One widely held theory is that for maximum flavour and succulence duck should be roasted for 15–20 minutes per pound (450g) at a high temperature (450°F/230°C/Mark 8).

I find that cooking a duckling in a slow oven gives the best results, with a straight 350°F/180°C/Mark 4 temperature right through the cooking time.

To roast duck

Place duck, breast side up. on a rack in a roasting pan. Cover breast of the bird with buttered foil and roast in a moderate oven (350°F/180°C/Mark 4) for 1½–1¾ hours. Baste frequently with butter or dripping. Remove foil 20 minutes before removing duck from the oven; dredge breast with flour and leave in oven until well browned. Transfer to a hot serving dish; remove trussing threads and strings, and keep duck warm while preparing gravy.

Goose

A plump, well-fattened goose is one of the most delectable birds there is. Like duckling, it needs slow roasting to bring it to the peak of succulent perfection. I like to place diced apple and onion, flavoured with a little finely chopped garlic and dried thyme or sage, in the cavity of the goose; rub it outside with coarse salt, dried thyme and freshly ground black pepper, and roast it in a moderately hot oven (400°F/200°C/Mark 6) for 15 to 20 minutes or until fat starts to run, then reduce temperature to 300°F/150°C/Mark 2, and continue cooking for 10–15 minutes per pound (450g), basting occasionally with a little white wine, butter and dried thyme. The skin should be pricked from time to time during cooking to release melted fat.

To roast goose

Place goose, breast side down, on a rack in a shallow roasting pan. Prick fatty parts of goose with a fork to help draw out remaining fat during cooking. Roast goose at 400°F/200°C/Mark 6 for 15 minutes, and then in a very slow oven (300°F/150°C/Mark 2) for 2 hours, pouring off fat during roasting as it accumulates. Then turn goose and cook for 1½–2 hours more, or until goose is nicely browned and the meat is very tender. You will find that long, slow cooking at this temperature will cook out excess fat and leave meat juicy and tender.

Turkey

To prepare a turkey for roasting, rub with softened butter and place the bird, breast side up, in a roasting pan. Cover breast with thin strips of unsmoked bacon and then cover bacon with a piece of muslin brushed with melted butter to prevent bird drying out during roasting.

To roast turkey

Roast stuffed turkey in a slow oven (325°F/170°C/Mark 3) for 3½–4 hours for a 10-12-pound (4.5-5.4kg) oven-ready bird, allowing about 15 minutes per extra pound (450g) of weight for larger birds. To let turkey brown and crisp, remove bacon and muslin 20–30 minutes before turkey is done.

Roast Guinea Fowl with
Aromatic Butter *(Illustration, page 90)*

1 Combine crushed thyme, rosemary, garlic and juniper berries in a mortar and pound until well blended. Add diced butter and lemon and orange juice, alternately, pounding again until well blended.

2 Stir in chopped onion and finely chopped parsley, a pinch of grated nutmeg or mace, and generous amounts of salt and freshly ground black pepper. Mixture should be highly flavoured. Brush birds – inside and out – with this aromatic butter and allow meat to absorb flavours overnight.

3 To roast birds: place in a heatproof roasting pan and cook in a fairly hot oven (425°F/220°C/Mark 7) for 25–35 minutes, basting frequently with melted aromatic butter. Birds are cooked when juices run quite clear when you insert a skewer through the thickest part of the leg.

Serves 6

Ingredients

3 guinea fowl, poussins or partridges
1 level teaspoon crushed thyme
½ level teaspoon rosemary leaves
1 clove garlic
6 juniper berries
¼ lb (100 g) butter, diced
Juice of ½ lemon
Juice of 1 orange
1 Spanish onion, chopped
3 level tablespoons finely chopped parsley
Pinch of grated nutmeg or mace
Salt and freshly ground black pepper

Roast Rib of Beef

Ingredients

1 3-rib roast of beef
2 cloves garlic, cut in slivers
6-8 sprigs of rosemary
4-6 level tablespoons beef
    dripping
1 level tablespoon dry
    mustard
Freshly ground black pepper
2 level tablespoons lightly
    browned flour
1 flattened piece beef suet
Red wine
Salt
Butter
Worcestershire sauce

1 To prepare beef for roasting: make 6–8 insertions in beef with the point of a sharp knife and insert slivers of garlic and sprigs of rosemary. Spread beef with dripping and sprinkle with a mixture of dry mustard, freshly ground black pepper and flour (which you have browned lightly in a frying pan or in the oven). Tie a flattened piece of beef suet over the top.

2 When ready to roast beef: place meat on a rack over a roasting pan and brown in a preheated fairly hot oven (425°F/220°C/Mark 7) for 15 minutes. Reduce oven to 325°F/170°C/Mark 3; add a little warmed red wine to the pan and continue to roast, basting frequently, allowing 15–18 minutes per pound (450g) if you like your beef rare, 20–24 minutes per pound (450g) for medium, and 25–30 minutes per pound (450g) if you prefer it well done. *Note:* if desired, add a little more red wine or

water to pan from time to time.

3 When meat is cooked to your liking, season to taste with salt and additional freshly ground black pepper. Remove beef to a warm serving platter and let it stand for 15–20 minutes at the edge of the open oven before carving. During this time the beef sets and the cooking subsides; the roast is then ready for carving.

4 In the meantime, pour off the fat in the roasting pan and use the pink juices that pour from the roast as it sets; stir all the crusty bits into it to make a clear sauce. Add a little more red wine, a knob of butter and a dash of Worcestershire sauce. Bring to the boil, reduce heat and simmer for 1 or 2 minutes. Strain and serve in a sauceboat with roast.

Serves 8 – 10

Roast ribs of beef with 'attendant' vegetables. What could be better than a huge roast of beef, charred on the outside, meltingly rare on the inside, served with its traditional vegetables? **Main picture** *Roast potatoes and Brussels sprouts.* **Top right** *Buttered new potatoes and peas.* **Centre right** *Carrot and turnip strips.* **Bottom right** *Creamed button onions with buttered breadcrumbs.*

Roast Loin of Veal

Ingredients

1 loin of veal (4-6 chops)
Salt and freshly ground black pepper
Crushed rosemary
2-4 level tablespoons softened butter
¼ pint (1½ dl) dry white wine

1 Have your butcher bone and trim a loin of veal. Season to taste with salt and freshly ground black pepper and crushed rosemary. Spread with softened butter and roast the meat in a slow oven (325°F/170°C/Mark 3) for about 20–30 minutes per pound (420g), or until it is well done, basting frequently. Add a little hot water if fat tends to scorch during cooking.

2 Remove veal from oven; add dry white wine and make sauce with the pan juices in the usual manner.

Serves 4-6

Rack of Lamb in Pastry with Walnuts

Ingredients

1 rack of lamb (8 chops)
Salt and freshly ground black pepper
Butter
1 Spanish onion, finely chopped
3 tablespoons olive oil
½ lb (225g) mushrooms, finely chopped
2 slices cooked ham, finely chopped
¼ lb (100g) coarsely chopped walnuts
½ lb (225g) frozen puff pastry
1 egg yolk, beaten

1 Ask your butcher to trim off fat from rack of lamb, separate meat from bone, and chine bone.

2 Season lamb generously with salt and freshly ground black pepper; brush with softened butter and roast in a moderate oven (375°F/190°C/Mark 5) for 10 minutes, or until lamb is half cooked. Allow meat to cool.

3 Sauté finely chopped onion in 3 level tablespoons each butter and olive oil until onion is transparent; add finely chopped mushrooms and continue to cook, stirring constantly, until mixture is almost dry. Add finely chopped ham and coarsely chopped walnuts; season with salt and freshly ground black pepper, to taste, and cook for 1 minute more. Allow mixture to cool.

4 Spread lamb generously with chopped onion, mushroom, ham and walnut mixture; brush with softened butter.

5 Roll out puff pastry into a thin sheet and wrap the lamb in it, allowing bones to protrude from pastry. Decorate pastry with 'leaves' and 'tassels' cut from pastry, fixing them on to pastry with a little beaten egg yolk. Brush pastry with water; cover 'leaves' and 'tassels' loosely with a little aluminium foil.

6 Place lamb in pastry on a baking sheet and bake in a hot oven (450°F/230°C/Mark 8) for 15 minutes. Remove foil, brush pastry slightly with beaten egg yolk and continue baking until the crust is browned (about 10–15 minutes more).

Serves 3-4

Roast Loin of Pork

Ingredients

1 loin of pork (4-6 chops), chined
6 level tablespoons softened butter
1½ level tablespoons French mustard
2 bay leaves, crumbled
¼ level teaspoon dried rosemary or thyme
Salt and freshly ground black pepper
3-4 sage leaves, quartered
12-16 slivers of garlic

GARNISH

4-6 tomato halves
Sliced mushrooms

1 Preheat oven to hot (450°F/230°C/Mark 8).

2 With the point of a sharp knife, make 12–16 incisions all over the joint about 1 inch (2½ cm) deep.

3 Blend butter with French mustard, crumbled bay leaves and rosemary or thyme.

4 Season pork with salt and freshly ground black pepper and spread with mustard butter, making sure it goes deep into the incisions.

5 Stick a quartered sage leaf and a sliver of garlic in each incision with the point of a sharp knife.

6 Roast in the usual way, lowering heat to 300°F/150°C/Mark 2 after the first 15 minutes. Serve with tomato halves scooped out and filled with sliced mushrooms, which have been sautéed in butter.

Serves 4-6

Basic Roast Chicken

1 Loosen the skin at the neck end of a cleaned and trussed roasting chicken as much as possible from the breast; insert stuffing over the flesh of the breast and fill the loose skin of the neck with as much as it will hold. Fold the skin over and fasten with 1 or 2 stitches. Stuff body cavity as well.

2 Tie 1 or 2 slices of fat bacon over the breast, making 1 or 2 slits in the bacon to prevent it from curling. Cover the bird with waxed paper and roast in a slow oven (325°F/170°C/Mark 3), basting frequently with butter, for 1–1½ hours, according to the size and age of the bird. Test it by feeling the flesh of the leg; if it gives way to pressure it is ready. A few minutes before the end of cooking time, remove the paper and bacon; sprinkle the breast lightly with flour; baste well, turn up the oven temperature to 400°F/200°C/Mark 6 and brown quickly.

3 When ready to serve: put bird on a hot serving dish; remove the trussing string, and garnish with watercress seasoned with lemon juice and salt.

4 Pour away the fat from the roasting pan in which the bird was roasted; add chicken stock and stir over a high heat until boiling, scraping in any brown bits from sides of pan. Season to taste with salt and freshly ground black pepper, and serve in a sauceboat.

Serves 4

Ingredients

1 roasting chicken (3½-4 lb (1.6-1.8 kg))
Parsley stuffing
2 slices fat bacon
Butter
1 level tablespoon sifted flour
Watercress
Lemon juice
Salt
½ pint (3 dl) chicken stock
Freshly ground black pepper

Roast Chicken à la Provençale

1 Ask your butcher to clean and truss chicken.

2 Peel garlic and cut into 12 slivers.

3 Make 12 deep slits into chicken with the point of a sharp knife, and push a strip of garlic and a sprig of rosemary well down into each slit. Season meat generously with salt and freshly ground black pepper. Place it on a dish, cover with foil and leave at room temperature for 1 hour to absorb flavours.

4 Preheat oven to hot (450°F/230°C/Mark 8).

5 Transfer chicken to a roasting tin; add finely chopped onion, olive oil, butter and dry white wine and roast for 15 minutes; then reduce heat to 300°F/150°C/Mark 2 and continue to roast until chicken is cooked through but still moist (37–38 minutes per pound (450g)), basting occasionally with pan juices plus a tablespoon or two of boiling water if juices are scarce.

6 To serve: transfer chicken to an oval heated serving dish and moisten with pan juices. Sprinkle with finely chopped herbs and serve immediately.

Serves 4

Ingredients

1 2-lb (900g) chicken
2 large cloves garlic
12 small sprigs rosemary
Salt and freshly ground black pepper
½ Spanish onion, finely chopped
2 tablespoons olive oil
4 level tablespoons butter
6 tablespoons dry white wine
2 level tablespoons finely chopped parsley
¼ level teaspoon each finely chopped fresh tarragon and chives

Roast Goose with Baked Apples

1 Place the goose on a rack in a roasting pan and spread with 4 tablespoons butter which you have mixed with crumbled sage leaves and crushed juniper berries. Season generously with salt and freshly ground black pepper.

2 Place bird in a preheated hot oven (450°F/230°C/Mark 8), and roast for 30 minutes. Spoon off excess fat and baste goose with pan juices. Return to oven and roast for 18 minutes per pound (450g), removing excess fat from pan juices and basting every 15 minutes.

3 Forty-five minutes before goose is done, place peeled and cored cooking apples around bird; dot apples with remaining butter and continue to cook.

4 To serve: place goose on a large heated serving dish and surround with baked apples. Remove all fat from sauce; whisk in currant preserve and add Calvados or Cognac; correct seasoning and spoon a little sauce over goose and each baked apple. Serve remaining sauce separately.

Serves 8

Ingredients

1 oven-ready goose (8-10 lb (3.6-4.5 kg))
6 level tablespoons softened butter
Crumbled dried sage leaves
Crushed juniper berries
Salt and fresh black pepper
8 cooking apples, peeled and cored
Red currant preserve
4 tablespoons Calvados or Cognac

Grilling

Grilling–the roasting of meat, poultry, game or fish on an open fire – was probably the starting point of all cooking.

Grilling is really only a matter of applying direct, intense heat to whatever you are going to cook. In other words, if you are going to cook a steak, a chop or a piece of game, all you want to do is get that piece of meat as hot and as charred on the outside and as moist and tender on the inside as you possibly can.

It is best to remember when grilling, whether over charcoal or under gas or electricity, that the metal grid of the grill should always be very hot when the objects to be grilled are placed upon it; otherwise they tend to stick to the bars of the grid. I like to heat the grid thoroughly, wipe it clean with a damp cloth and then rub a bit of suet over the bars to prevent the meat from sticking.

Open-fire grilling

One of the hazards of open-fire grilling is that fat dripping from the meat causes the fire to flare up and smoke. So keep coals under the meat for a short time until the meat becomes brown, then spread the coals in a circle with none directly under the meat. If flames still flare up, put a dripping pan under the meat. You will find that the meat will cook sufficiently even though there is no fire under it. If after the meat is done you still want a little more charring, push coals back under the meat and cook until it is as brown as you wish.

If you want a fire that sears quickly – perfect for grilling small fish, minute steaks or skewered meats – the charcoal should be piled about two or three inches high. If you need a lazy, more controlled heat for a whole leg of lamb or a large duck, the charcoal should be spread out in a single layer, with the coals separated a little from each other.

Keep a circle of fresh charcoal at the outer edge of your fire and push it into the centre as needed. Do not put fresh coals on top of the lighted charcoal, or you will find that you have set up a dense smoke screen. A bulb syringe filled with water should be kept handy to tame flames when necessary.

It is important not to start cooking too soon with charcoal. For perfect grilling, charcoal should look ash-grey by day and have a warm, red glow after dark. If your charcoal is still flaming, it is too early to start cooking.

Grilling meat over an open fire

Always give meat on the spit or grill a chance to warm up and relax over the coals before you start basting. The meat will absorb the flavours of your basting sauce better this way. A word to the wise: if your sauce has a tomato base, do not begin to use it until the last 15 minutes of cooking time. This gives a rosy brown glaze to barbecued meats and avoids unnecessary scorching.

When grilling steak or lamb, cut a garlic clove in half and toss it on the coals for a wonderful flavour. For pork or ham on the spit, wait until meat is almost done and then drop a spiral of orange or lemon peel in the fire. I like to use herbs in this way too: a sprig of rosemary, a bay leaf or two, or a sprig of sage or thyme, make all the difference.

Charcoal-grilled Sole, Coulis de Tomates à la Provençale *(Illustration, pages 98 and 99)*

Ingredients

2 large sole, 1¼-1½ lb (550-675g) each, trimmed and cleaned
Olive oil
Salt and freshly ground black pepper

COULIS DE TOMATES À LA PROVENÇALE
6 ripe tomatoes, skinned, seeded and diced
6 tablespoons olive oil
4 level tablespoons freshly chopped parsley
2 level tablespoons freshly chopped tarragon
½ clove garlic, finely chopped
6 coriander seeds, crushed
4 fennel seeds, crushed
Salt and freshly ground black pepper

1 To prepare sole: wash fish and score the skins in a criss-cross pattern with the point of a sharp knife. Brush fish with olive oil and season with salt and freshly ground black pepper.

2 To prepare *coulis de tomates*: combine diced tomatoes with olive oil, chopped parsley and tarragon and finely chopped garlic in a frying pan. Add crushed coriander and fennel seeds and heat through. Season with salt and freshly ground black pepper, to taste, Keep warm.

3 To grill sole: brush the charcoal grill rack with olive oil. Place fish on it, white skin down, lying diagonally across the ridges and grill for 2 minutes. Place fish diagonally across the grill in the opposite direction, to mark it. Then grill for a further 2 minutes. Turn the fish over and grill for 4–6 minutes on the other side, in the same manner.

4 To serve sole: lift the fillets from the fish in 4 unbroken pieces, cutting along the length of backbone with a sharp knife, and sliding the blade between flesh and bones to loosen the fillets. Serve with *coulis de tomates*.

Serves 4

Seafoods Kebabs *(Illustration, page 102)*

Ingredients

6 scallops
9 small bacon rashers, cut in half
¼ lb (100g) large peeled prawns
Finely chopped parsley

MARINADE
6 tablespoons olive oil
4 tablespoons dry white wine
2 shallots, finely chopped

1 Separate orange coral 'tongues' from scallops and cut white sections in half. Trim.

2 Roll a small strip of bacon around each coral tongue and piece of scallop. Thread scallop and bacon rolls on to kebab skewers alternately with peeled prawns.

3 Place marinade mixture in a shallow bowl; brush kebabs with mixture and allow them to stand in the mixture for at least 2 hours.

4 When ready to cook: brush kebabs again lightly with marinade mixture and cook gently over charcoal, turning frequently, for 8–10 minutes. Sprinkle with finely chopped parsley.

Serves 3

Charcoal-grilled Chuletas *(Illustration, page 102)*

1 Pierce steaks with a thick barbecue skewer.

2 Combine remaining ingredients and brush steaks with this mixture, forcing mixture well down into holes in meat. Allow meat to marinate for at least 2 hours before cooking.

These may be spread on hot steak before serving.

DEVIL SPREAD
Cream 1 tablespoon Worcestershire sauce and 4 drops Tabasco with $\frac{1}{4}$ lb (100g) butter

3 To grill: rub hot grid with a piece of suet; place steaks on grid, brush with marinade and grill over charcoal for 5 minutes on each side for a rare steak; grill a few minutes longer if you prefer steak to be medium rare.

Serves 4-6

ROQUEFORT SPREAD
Cream 2 oz (50g) Roquefort cheese with $\frac{1}{4}$ lb (100g) butter

MUSTARD SPREAD
Cream 4 tablespoons Dijon mustard with $\frac{1}{4}$ lb (100g) butter

Ingredients

4-6 sirloin steaks, 1-inch ($2\frac{1}{2}$ cm) thick
8 tablespoons olive oil
4 tablespoons dry white wine
1 tablespoon lemon juice
2 level tablespoons coarsely chopped Spanish onion
2 cloves garlic, chopped
$\frac{1}{4}$ level teaspoon rubbed oregano
$\frac{1}{4}$ level teaspoon crumbled bay leaves
1 level tablespoon chopped parsley
Salt and freshly ground black pepper

Old English Grilled 'Skuets'

1 Cut beef and lamb into 2-inch (5 cm) cubes; cut kidney into thinner pieces.

2 Marinate meats in olive oil and lemon juice with finely chopped garlic and herbs for at least 1 hour.

3 When ready to grill: thread meats on skewers with mushroom caps and small parboiled onions.

4 Rub hot grid with a piece of suet; place 'skuets' on grid; brush with marinade sauce and grill over charcoal for 5 minutes on each side for rare, a few minutes longer for medium rare.

Serves 4

Ingredients

$\frac{1}{2}$ lb (225g) boned sirloin
$\frac{1}{2}$ lb (225g) boned shoulder of lamb
$\frac{1}{2}$ lb (225g) lamb's kidney
4 tablespoons olive oil
4 tablespoons lemon juice
1 clove garlic, finely chopped
$\frac{1}{2}$ level teaspoon each dried thyme and sage
Mushroom caps
Small white onions, parboiled

Grilled Lamb with Oriental Spices

1 Cut lamb into 1-inch ($2\frac{1}{2}$ cm) cubes and combine in a porcelain bowl with remaining ingredients. Mix well and allow lamb cubes to marinate in this mixture for at least 4 hours, turning lamb from time to time so that it becomes impregnated with all the flavours.

2 When ready to grill: drain and reserve marinade. Thread meat on to skewers, 4-6 cubes on each; brush with marinade and grill for 5 minutes about 3 inches ($7\frac{1}{2}$ cm) from the coals. Turn lamb and baste with marinade every 5 minutes until done – 20-25 minutes in all.

Serves 6

Ingredients

$2\frac{1}{2}$ lb (1.1 kg) lamb, cut from leg
Salt and freshly ground black pepper
2 level teaspoons coriander
2 level teaspoons cumin seed
1 Spanish onion, finely chopped
2 level teaspoons brown sugar
4 tablespoons soy sauce
4 tablespoons lemon juice
$\frac{1}{4}$ level teaspoon powdered ginger

John Schlesinger (on the other side of the camera for once) joins me for a glass of champagne after filming a sequence for 'Food, Wine & Friends'.

Grilling under gas or electricity

Grilling is a wonderfully quick way to cook, but because it is so quick, it is difficult to grill perfectly. A minute too long under the grill, or the wrong temperature – too hot for a thin slice of ham or gammon or a joint of chicken; not hot enough for a thick slice of beef – will ruin the end result.

Practice, of course, will teach you how to deal most successfully with your grill. One easy rule to remember: thick cuts of meat and fish should be cooked at a greater distance from the heat, thinner cuts, near the heat.

To grill steaks or chops successfully: season meat with freshly ground black pepper and place on preheated grid. The thicker cuts of meat should be 'seized' on both sides with a very high heat to preserve their juices, before cooking at a more moderate heat to allow its gradual penetration into the juicy centre of the meat. The smaller cuts – tournedos, chops, cutlets – can be cooked without lowering the heat once the juices have been sealed in. For best results, season meats to taste with salt after cooking.

Ingredients

1 large rump steak (about
  1½ inches (4 cm) thick) or
  4 small sirloin steaks (½ lb
  (225g) each)
Freshly ground black pepper
Butter
Olive oil (optional)
Cracked peppercorns
  (optional)
Salt

Open-fire grilling is one of the oldest and most delicious ways of dealing with top-quality beef, lamb, poultry and game. We use open-fired real charcoal grills in both my restaurants to give a superb flavour to cuts of beef, lamb, veal, poultry, game and seafood.

Grilled Rump or Sirloin

1 Remove meat from refrigerator at least 30 minutes before cooking; trim off excess fat and score remaining fat in several places around side to prevent meat from curling up during cooking.

2 Preheat grill for 15 to 20 minutes.

3 Either sprinkle both sides of steak, or steaks, with freshly ground black pepper and spread with 4 level tablespoons softened butter; or brush steak, or steaks, on both sides with olive oil seasoned with cracked peppercorns.

4 Rub hot grill with a piece of excess fat; place steak, or steaks, on grid, and grill for 8 minutes on each side for a rare steak; brushing with melted butter or olive oil from time to time; grill a few minutes longer if you prefer steak to be medium rare. Sprinkle with salt, to taste.

Serves 4

Right *Seafood Kebabs.*
Far right *Charcoal-grilled Chuletas.*
Facing page *Charcoal-grilled Sirloin Steak. (Recipes, pages 100, 101 and 102).*

Brochettes of Halibut or Turbot

Ingredients

1½ lb (675g) halibut or turbot (thick end of fillet)
4 firm medium-sized tomatoes
3 small onions
Rice or shredded lettuce

BASTING SAUCE

8 tablespoons olive oil
4 tablespoons dry white wine
½ Spanish onion, finely chopped
2 bay leaves, crumbled
Salt and freshly ground black pepper

1 To make basting sauce: combine olive oil, dry white wine, finely chopped onion, crumbled bay leaves and salt and freshly ground black pepper, to taste, in a large shallow bowl.

2 Cut halibut or turbot into chunks (1–1½ inches (2½–3½ cm) square). You should have about 30 in all – any thin pieces should be rolled up into pieces the same size as chunks.

3 Slice tomatoes and onions ¼ inch (½ cm) thick.

4 Place fish pieces in bowl with basting sauce. Toss fish carefully in sauce; cover half the bowl with slices of tomato and the other half with slices of onion. Place bowl in refrigerator for at least 2 hours.

5 When ready to cook, thread six 8- or 9-inch (20 or 22½ cm) metal skewers with alternate pieces of fish and tomato and onion slices, starting and ending with a chunk of fish, and dividing ingredients equally between skewers.

6 Line rack of grill pan with foil. Arrange skewers on it; brush with half the basting sauce and place under a preheated hot grill. Reduce heat to moderate and grill for 4–5 minutes.

7 Turn skewers; baste with remaining sauce and continue to grill for 4–5 minutes longer, or until fish flakes easily with a fork.

8 Serve immediately on a bed of rice or shredded lettuce, spooning some of the cooking juices over skewers.

Serves 6

Grilled Turbot Steaks with Garlic Butter

Ingredients

6 turbot steaks, about 1-inch (2½ cm) thick
2-3 tablespoons olive oil
Salt and freshly ground black pepper
Lemon juice

GARLIC BUTTER

3 oz (75g) butter
2 large cloves garlic, crushed
1 level tablespoon very finely chopped shallot
½ level teaspoon very finely chopped parsley
Lemon juice
Salt and freshly ground black pepper

1 Prepare garlic butter in advance. Work butter in a bowl with a wooden spoon until slightly softened. Add crushed garlic and chopped shallot and continue to beat until thoroughly blended; then beat in finely chopped parsley and lemon juice, to taste. Season to taste with salt and freshly ground black pepper. Roll butter into a long thin sausage shape; roll in foil and chill until firm again.

2 Turn on the grill set at maximum heat about 20 minutes before cooking turbot. Line grill pan with a large sheet of aluminium foil.

3 Brush both sides of each turbot steak with olive oil and sprinkle with salt and freshly ground black pepper; arrange steaks side by side on the foil in grill pan; squeeze a little lemon juice over steaks.

4 When ready to cook steaks, turn grill down to moderate and grill steaks for about 15–20 minutes, depending on their thickness, turning them once and squeezing a little more lemon juice over. They are ready when the fish can easily be prised away from the bone with a fork.

5 Transfer turbot steaks to a heated dish and top each one with a thin slice of chilled garlic butter. Serve immediately.

Note: this same recipe is also good for salmon steaks, tuna steaks or tournedos of beef.

Serves 6

Basic Grilled Chicken

1 Only very young and tender chickens can be cooked in this way. Split cleaned chickens open through the back, flatten and trim birds, cutting off feet and wing tips; wipe with a damp cloth, and season generously with salt and freshly ground black pepper, paprika and a little lemon juice.

2 Skewer birds open; brush both sides with melted butter and sprinkle with fine browned breadcrumbs. Grill over charcoal or under grill for 25–30 minutes, turning the birds occasionally and basting frequently with melted butter. Serve very hot, garnished with watercress and lemon wedges.

Serves 4

Ingredients

2 tender poussins (young chickens)
Salt and freshly ground black pepper
Paprika
Lemon juice
Melted butter
4 level tablespoons fine browned breadcrumbs
Sprigs of watercress
Lemon wedges

Grilled Chicken with Lemon and Garlic

1 Cut chicken into serving pieces. Place chicken pieces in a generously buttered shallow heatproof baking dish. Sprinkle with grated lemon rind, finely chopped garlic and dried oregano and pour over strained lemon juice and olive oil. Flavour to taste with salt and freshly ground black pepper; dot with remaining butter and refrigerate for at least 2 hours.

2 Preheat grill and cook chicken under it for about 15 minutes, basting frequently with marinade juices, until chicken pieces are brown on one side. Turn pieces over and grill on other side until well browned.

3 Baste chicken pieces with pan juices; cover baking dish (or cover chicken pieces with aluminium foil) and continue to cook in a preheated slow oven (325°F/170°C/Mark 3) for 30–40 minutes, or until chicken is tender, basting from time to time. Sprinkle with finely chopped parsley and serve immediately.

Serves 4 - 6

Ingredients

1 roasting chicken
$\frac{1}{4}$ lb (100g) butter
Grated rind and juice of 1 lemon
2 cloves garlic, finely chopped
$\frac{1}{2}$ level teaspoon dried oregano
2 tablespoons olive oil
Salt and freshly ground black pepper
2 level tablespoons finely chopped parsley

Magret de Canard au Poivre Vert

1 To prepare *glace de canard*: chop duck carcass and trimmings coarsely with a chopper. Combine $\frac{1}{4}$ chicken stock cube and tomato purée with finely chopped carrot and onion and sauté in butter until ingredients are well browned. Add 1 pint (6dl) water and dry white wine and cook, skimming from time to time, until sauce is reduced to half its original quantity. Strain sauce into a small saucepan, pressing vegetables and bones to extract all juice. Continue to cook sauce over a low heat until it is reduced to about $\frac{1}{4}$ pint ($1\frac{1}{2}$ dl). Season with freshly ground black pepper, to taste.

2 Brush duck breasts with melted butter and season generously with salt and freshly ground black pepper, to taste. Grill for 10 minutes on each side.

3 Then, using a kitchen towel to protect your hands from the heat of the cooked duck, remove skin. Keep warm.

4 Place duck breasts on a heatproof serving dish or shallow casserole (an oval enamelled iron *gratin* dish is very good for this as it can go directly on to the heat). Keep warm in oven. Make a new 'skin' for each breast of duck by covering with overlapping thin slices of apple which you have sautéed in butter until golden brown.

5 Place *gratin* dish on a medium heat and heat duckling; brush apple slices with a little *glace de canard*; add green peppercorns to remainder and pour around duck breasts in pan. Garnish with watercress and serve at once.

Serves 4

Ingredients

4 breasts of duck
Butter
Salt and freshly ground black pepper
2 tart eating apples
Green peppercorns
Sprigs of watercress

GLACE DE CANARD

Carcass and trimmings of duck
$\frac{1}{4}$ chicken stock cube
1 level tablespoon tomato purée
1 carrot, finely chopped
$\frac{1}{2}$ Spanish onion, finely chopped
6 level tablespoons butter
$\frac{1}{4}$ pint ($1\frac{1}{2}$ dl) dry white wine
Freshly ground black pepper

Beaujolais

Henri de Rambuteau, a towering giant of a man, was one of the stars on our television series. We spent the day with him at the twelfth-century Château des Granges in the heart of the Beaujolais vineyards where they produce light and fresh wines, sweet to the taste.

Beaujolais consists of 6000 acres of vines, extending 30 to 40 miles from north to south, and less than 15 miles from east to west, producing about 110 million bottles of Beaujolais per year. The 30 to 40 *villages* are located in the centre of the region, as are the 9 *Grands Crus* (Great Growths).

Ordinary Beaujolais is a red wine, but it is very near to white wine in its taste, lightness and the way it is made. The main difference between red and white wines is in the fermentation. The reds are fermented with grape skins, and the whites with the juice of the grape only. In Beaujolais, the wine is fermented with skins only as long as they are needed to set a typical Beaujolais colour. The fermentation is then completed without skins in the barrel, like white wine. The result is a light, fruity, almost flowery wine.

Beaujolais is divided into four grades of wine: Beaujolais, Beaujolais Supérieur, Beaujolais Villages and the 9 *Grands Crus*. According to Henri de Rambuteau, 'You should be able to taste the *crus*, drink the *villages* and quaff the Beaujolais.' That serves wonderfully well to delineate the different categories produced in this fascinating region.

Beaujolais *nouveau* comes from last year's harvest, and goes on being '*nouveau*' for that year, right up to the next harvest. However, according to French regulations, wine of this type is not allowed to leave the cellar

before 15 December, so from that day to the next crop a wine can be called *nouveau*. This wine is fermented in the cellar intentionally to make a light, fresh wine, to be drunk before March and served slightly chilled. According to Henri de Rambuteau, 'the lighter the wine, the more chilled it should be'.

The Grands Crus de Beaujolais

Moulin-à-Vent–the King of Beaujolais, is considered with Beaujolais Fleurie to be first among noble growths. It is a big, fat wine, almost a Burgundy.

Brouilly has a marvellous, almost purplish colour and a dry, fruity taste with a hint of raspberry.

Côte de Brouilly is situated in the very centre of Brouilly, on the slopes of Mont de Brouilly.

Fleurie is a round wine with a wonderful fruitiness. Not as heavy as Moulin-à-Vent.

Morgon, the hardiest of Beaujolais, improves with a little ageing. A true Morgon is not bottled until 8 or 9 months after harvest, and is still better a year after bottling.

Chénas mostly lies within the Moulin-à-Vent district. An excellent wine, but not of the same quality as a good Moulin-à-Vent.

Juliénas ages well, keeping its pleasant fruitiness for years.

Chiroubles is as elegant as Fleurie, but more violet-coloured like a Morgon, though less hard in quality. It should be drunk very young.

St-Amour is the lightest of the *Grands Crus*, with the white wines approaching Pouilly-Fuissé in quality and flavour.

Pan grilling

An excellent method of grilling steaks at home is to grill them in an iron frying pan or in one of the special corrugated iron grill pans made for this purpose. For best results, you need a heavy iron pan with a raised grid. The ridges mark meat in an appetizing way. You can use an ordinary old-fashioned iron frying pan, however, if you cover the entire bottom surface with a little coarse sea salt, just enough to keep the meat away from the actual pan so that it will not stick.

If the pan or grill is hot enough, it should not be necessary to add fat. If desired, rub the pan with a piece of suet. Season meat to taste with freshly ground black pepper, sear quickly on one side, reduce the heat and cook for a minute or two longer. Turn the steaks; sear on the other side and continue cooking and turning until the steak is done to your taste.

Baste all meats with butter or olive oil before placing them on the hot grid and repeat this operation several times during the cooking process to keep the meat from drying out during cooking. Little beads of blood on the outside surfaces indicate that the meat is done.

To grill meat

Meat is often marinated in olive oil and wine to tenderize and flavour it before cooking. Add salt and freshly ground black pepper, to taste, and one or more of the following: sliced onion, shallot, garlic, soy sauce, bay leaf, thyme or parsley. Marinate meat for at least 2 hours in this mixture, turning it occasionally to ensure maximum penetration. Pat dry with a clean tea towel before grilling.

Beef

Beef is the most popular meat for grilling. The best cuts to use for grilling are the fillet, the rump and the upper cut of sirloin. I like a good thick rib steak, cut from the sirloin, complete with bone. The most expensive cuts of beef for grilling are those cut from the fillet. Slices of fillet are usually named according to their thickness: a tournedos is a small piece of fillet about $1\frac{1}{2}$ inches ($3\frac{1}{2}$ cm) thick; the famous filet mignon of American restaurant parlance is a piece $1\frac{3}{4}$–2 inches (4–5 cm) thick; while a piece 2–3 inches (5–$7\frac{1}{2}$ cm) thick is known as a Châteaubriant.

White meats

When grilling white meats – veal, lamb or chicken – a moderate heat will ensure that you cook and colour the meat simultaneously. Baste white-meat grills fairly often with butter, or butter and olive oil. They are done when the juices coming from them are colourless.

To grill fish

Wash and clean fish; dry lightly and score the skin across diagonally on both sides to prevent it cracking during cooking. Season with salt and freshly ground black pepper, and brush with olive oil or melted butter. Or marinate fish for 2 hours before cooking in equal quantities of olive oil and dry white wine with a little finely chopped garlic and a crumbled bay leaf or two. Or split open the fish, remove the bones, then lightly coat the fish with flour, egg and breadcrumbs, or fine oatmeal.

For best results, always heat the grid thoroughly and grease it well before you place the fish on it. Keep the fish rather close to the fire if cooking over an open fire or it will become flabby. Cook fish for 8–12 minutes according to thickness, and turn at least once during the cooking time. I like to serve grilled fish with lemon quarters and *fines herbes* butter, where butter is beaten with finely chopped parsley, chives, tarragon and a hint of marjoram and lemon juice.

Pan-grilled Tournedos with Corncakes

(Illustration, pages 110 and 111)

1 Heat a large, heavy-bottomed grill pan over a moderately high heat until drops of water shaken on to the surface bounce and sizzle on contact.

2 Grease pan thoroughly with a piece of beef fat impaled on a fork, or with a wad of absorbent paper soaked in olive oil.

3 When pan is practically smoking, add fillet steaks and sear for just 2 minutes on each side or until steaks are well marked, turning once. Season generously with salt and freshly ground black pepper.

4 Reduce heat to very moderate and time carefully according to chosen degree of 'doneness': 5–6 oz (150–175g) /2 inches (5 cm) thick; $3\frac{1}{2}$–4 minutes/ blue; $5\frac{1}{2}$–6 minutes/rare; 7 minutes/ medium; $8\frac{1}{2}$ minutes/well done.

5 Half a minute before steaks are due to come out of pan, add a good lump of butter. Let it froth and turn golden.

6 Transfer steaks to a heated serving dish.

7 Pour buttery pan juices over steaks. Place prepared corncakes in pan and heat through. Transfer corncakes to serving dish with steaks. Top each steak with a piece of 'Snail' butter and serve immediately.

Serves 4 - 6

Ingredients
4 small fillet steaks
Beef fat or olive oil to grease grill pan
Salt and freshly ground black pepper
4 level tablespoons butter
Prepared corncakes (see page 116)
'Snail' butter (see page 111)

Pan-grilled Steaks with Spring Onions

1 Flatten steaks with the side of a cleaver and season both sides with salt and freshly ground black pepper.

2 Heat grill pan over a high heat; brush with olive oil and sear steaks 2 at a time, on both sides over a high heat, 30–45 seconds per side. Return all steaks to pan. Remove from heat.

3 Add sherry and brandy to the pan; stand back and set alight with a match.

When flames die down, transfer steaks to a heated serving platter and keep warm.

4 Add butter to grill pan; return to heat and bring cooking juices to the boil again.

5 Sprinkle steaks with chopped spring onions and pour sauce over. Serve immediately.

Serves 4

Ingredients
4 thin slices sirloin steak, about 6 oz (175g) each
Salt and freshly ground black pepper
Olive oil
4 tablespoons dry sherry
2 tablespoons brandy
4 level tablespoons butter
2 level tablespoons chopped spring onions

Southern American Beefsteak

1 Brush steaks with olive oil and season with freshly ground black pepper, to taste.

2 Make a paste of the remaining ingredients, with freshly ground black pepper, to taste. Set aside.

3 Heat a large, heavy-bottomed grill pan over a moderately high heat until drops of water shaken on to the surface bounce and sizzle on contact.

4 Brush ridges of grill pan with olive oil and grill steaks on both sides for 3–4 minutes per side for rare, 5–6 minutes per side for medium, and a few minutes more for well done.

5 When steaks are done, spread with paste and serve immediately.

Serves 4

Ingredients
4 small sirloin steaks
Olive oil
Freshly ground black pepper
1 level teaspoon dry mustard
1 level teaspoon salt
2 level teaspoons brown sugar
2 level teaspoons grated onion
4 level tablespoons butter

Pan-grilled Steak Satés

Ingredients

1½ lb (675g) rump steak,
 1-inch (2½ cm) thick
2 tablespoons soy sauce
6 tablespoons olive oil
2 tablespoons lemon juice
¼ Spanish onion, finely
 chopped
1 clove garlic, finely chopped
1 level tablespoon powdered
 cumin
Freshly ground black pepper

1 Cut steak into thin strips 3 inches (7½ cm) long and marinate for at least 4 hours in a mixture of soy sauce, olive oil, lemon juice, finely chopped onion and garlic, and powdered cumin.

2 When ready to cook, thread the beef on skewers and brush with marinade.

Heat a large, heavy-bottomed grill pan over a moderately high heat until drops of water shaken on to the surface bounce and sizzle on contact. Grill kebabs, turning from time to time, until cooked through. Season to taste with freshly ground black pepper.

Serves 4

Pan-grilled Marinated Lamb Steaks

Ingredients

2 lamb steaks, cut from leg
 of lamb
4 tablespoons olive oil
4 tablespoons lemon juice
2 level teaspoons ground
 cumin
1 level teaspoon ground
 coriander
Freshly ground black pepper
Coarse salt

1 Place lamb steaks in a shallow *gratin* dish or baking pan.

2 Mix olive oil and lemon juice and pour over steaks. Sprinkle both sides of steaks with ground cumin and coriander and freshly ground black pepper, to taste. Rub spices in well. Cover dish with aluminium foil and refrigerate for 12-24 hours, turning steaks once or twice during this time so that they absorb all the flavours.

3 When ready to cook: heat iron grill pan over a medium heat until it is very hot. Place steaks on grill pan and grill for 3-5 minutes on one side. Season with coarse salt, to taste; turn steaks, brush with marinade and grill on other side for 3-5 minutes. Test meat for 'done-ness' by cutting into edge of steak to check colour. Serve immediately.

Serves 2

Pan-grilled Tournedos with Corncakes and 'Snail' Butter. Pan-grilling is an age-old manner of cooking tender cuts of beef, lamb and poultry. Use a ridged iron pan to mark meat. The corncakes—a cross between fritters and pancakes—are first pan-fried and then grilled for a moment or two in the ridged pan to give them the added flavour of the meat juices. To make 'Snail' Butter, combine 4 oz softened butter with 4 level table-spoons finely chopped parsley and chives and flavour with finely chopped garlic and lemon juice, to taste. (Recipes, pages 109 and 116).

Pan-grilled Lamb's Kidneys en Brochette

1 Split kidneys in half from rounded edge; remove thin outer skin; open and run skewer through them to keep them open. Brush kidneys with melted butter; season with salt and freshly ground black pepper and sprinkle generously with breadcrumbs.

2 Heat a large, heavy-bottomed grill pan over a moderately high heat until drops of water shaken on to the surface bounce and sizzle on contact.

3 Brush ridges of grill pan with olive oil and grill kidneys until cooked through. Do not overcook kidneys, however, or they will be tough.

4 Just before serving, place a knob of garlic butter on each kidney half. Garnish with grilled bacon and sprigs of watercress. Serve with boiled new potatoes.

Serves 4

Ingredients
8-12 lamb's kidneys
4-6 tablespoons melted butter
Salt and freshly ground black pepper
Fresh breadcrumbs
Olive oil
Garlic butter
4 slices grilled bacon
Sprigs of watercress
Boiled new potatoes (see page 148)

Pan-grilled Liver and Bacon

Ingredients

4 thin slices bacon
4 slices calf's liver, 6-8 oz
(175-225g) each
Melted butter
Salt and freshly ground black
pepper
Béarnaise sauce (see page 62)

1 Heat a large, heavy-bottomed grill pan over a moderately high heat until drops of water shaken on to the surface bounce and sizzle on contact.

2 Grill bacon slices until crisp on each side. Remove from pan.

3 Brush liver slices with melted butter and arrange slices in grill pan, buttered side down. Cook until lightly browned; turn liver slices over; brush with melted butter and cook until lightly browned on the other side. Do not overcook. Liver should be pink on the inside.

4 Remove liver slices to a heated serving platter; sprinkle with salt and freshly ground black pepper. Garnish each liver slice with crisp bacon and serve with Béarnaise sauce. **Serves 4**

Pan-grilled Veal Steak 'Mode d'Ici'

Ingredients

4 veal steaks, ⅓-inch (1 cm)
thick
Freshly ground black pepper
4 shallots, finely chopped
4–6 tarragon leaves, finely
chopped
¼ pint (1½ dl) dry white
Chablis
¼ pint (1½ dl) rich beef stock
4 level tablespoons tomato
purée
¼ pint (1½ dl) double cream
Salt
Butter
Oil
Fresh watercress

1 Remove veal steaks from refrigerator and season with freshly ground black pepper.

2 To make sauce: combine finely chopped shallots and tarragon leaves with dry white Chablis in a small saucepan and cook over a high heat until there are only 1 to 2 tablespoons liquid left in the bottom of the saucepan. Add rich beef stock and tomato purée; stir well; cover saucepan and simmer gently for 30 minutes over a very low flame.

3 Add cream and simmer for 10 more minutes; add salt and freshly ground black pepper, to taste; stir in 1 level tablespoon butter and keep warm.

4 To cook veal: heat a heavy frying pan over a moderately high heat until drops of water shaken on to the surface bounce and sizzle away on contact.

5 Grease pan thoroughly with a thick wad of absorbent paper soaked in oil.

6 When pan is practically smoking, slap on the veal steaks and sear for just 2 minutes on each side, turning once.

7 Reduce heat to moderate and fry for a few more minutes on each side, until veal is cooked through and tender.

8 Just before steaks are due to come out of pan, add a good lump of butter. Let it froth and turn golden.

9 Transfer steaks to a heated serving dish.

10 Strain sauce through a fine sieve over steaks. Garnish with a few sprigs of watercress and serve immediately.

Serves 4

Pan-grilled Turkey

Ingredients

2 cooked turkey legs
(drumsticks and thighs)
Butter (6 oz (175g))
1 level teaspoon dry mustard
1 level teaspoon Dijon
mustard
½ level teaspoon curry
powder
Cayenne pepper
Salt
Toasted breadcrumbs
Olive oil (optional)

1 Cut meat from turkey legs and thighs into cubes about ¾-inch (2cm) in diameter.

2 Mix softened butter with mustards, curry powder, cayenne pepper and salt, to taste, and roll turkey cubes in this mixture. Let turkey marinate in this mixture at room temperature at least ½ hour before cooking.

3 When ready to cook, heat a large, heavy-bottomed grill pan over a moderately high heat until drops of water shaken on to the surface bounce and sizzle on contact. Toss turkey with toasted breadcrumbs and pan-grill turkey for 7–8 minutes, or until nicely browned on all sides, basting from time to time with a little melted butter or olive oil. Serve very hot.

Serves 4

Pan-grilled Chicken

1 Sprinkle chicken pieces with salt and freshly ground black pepper and marinate in Lemon Sauce (see below) for at least 4 hours.

2 To grill chickens: drain chicken pieces, reserving marinade juices. Heat a large heavy-bottomed grill pan over a moderately high heat until drops of water shaken on to the surface bounce and sizzle on contact. Pan-grill chicken pieces slowly until tender, turning and basting with marinade juices from time to time.

Serves 4

Ingredients
2 young frying chickens, quartered
Salt and freshly ground black pepper

Lemon Sauce

1 Combine olive oil, lemon juice, finely chopped mushrooms, onion, garlic and parsley and dried tarragon in a flat dish large enough to hold chicken pieces.

2 Season sauce to taste with salt and freshly ground black pepper. Add a dash of Tabasco for extra flavour.

Ingredients
4 tablespoons olive oil
4 tablespoons lemon juice
6 button mushrooms, finely chopped
3-6 level tablespoons finely chopped onion
1 clove garlic, finely chopped
1 level tablespoon finely chopped parsley
½ level teaspoon dried tarragon
Salt and freshly ground black pepper
Tabasco

Pan-grilled Chicken with Paprika Sauce

1 Melt butter and chicken fat in a small saucepan; add garlic clove and simmer for 1 minute. Season generously with salt and freshly ground black pepper. Remove garlic clove and pour garlic-flavoured fat into a shallow *gratin* dish.

2 Dip chicken pieces in garlic-flavoured fat and sprinkle with freshly grated lemon peel and freshly ground black pepper.

3 Preheat oven to moderate (375°F/190°C/Mark 5).

4 Heat iron grill pan to very hot; place chicken pieces on pan and grill for 7 minutes on each side, turning pieces 2 or 3 times during cooking, basting each time with garlic-flavoured fat. Finish cooking chicken pieces in preheated oven until tender, about 10 minutes.

5 In the meantime, make paprika sauce: sauté finely chopped onion and paprika in butter until onions are transparent. Add chicken stock and salt and freshly ground black pepper, to taste, and cook over a high heat, stirring constantly until stock is reduced to a glaze. Stir in sour cream and lemon juice, to taste. Keep warm.

6 To serve: arrange chicken pieces on a heated serving platter and strain paprika sauce over them.

Serves 4

Ingredients
2 level tablespoons butter
2 level tablespoons rendered chicken fat
1 clove garlic
Salt and freshly ground black pepper
1 3½-lb (1.6 kg) chicken, cut up for frying
Freshly grated peel of 1 lemon

PAPRIKA SAUCE
¼ Spanish onion, finely chopped
1½ level tablespoons paprika
3 level tablespoons butter
9 tablespoons chicken stock
Salt and freshly ground black pepper
½ pint (3 dl) sour cream
Lemon juice

Frying

Frying, strictly speaking, is simply the immersing of food in very hot fat or oil. The term is also extended, in this country, to pan-frying, which has come to mean the same as sautéeing, and in America many foods are oven-fried, a new combination of sautéeing and baking which has much to recommend it for simple dishes.

Pan-frying

This popular method of cooking uses butter to sauté meat, fish or fresh vegetables in a frying pan. Finely chopped fresh parsley, lemon juice or slivered almonds are sometimes added to the sauce obtained. It is a good idea to add a little olive oil (but only a very little) to the butter at first; then, when what you are cooking begins to take on colour, add more butter. This will prevent butter from browning during the cooking process.

For pan-frying, you need a good heavy frying pan or sauté pan and a little fat: lard, vegetable oil or a combination of vegetable oil and butter, or clarified butter. Professional cooks always clarify butter to get all the impurities and salt particles out of the butter, leaving a clear liquid which does not burn (see page 59).

Only very tender foods are suitable for pan-frying: fish, young chicken, chops, liver, beef fillets and vegetables. Thick slices of meat – other than fillet steak and chops – cannot be pan-fried successfully.

Do not crowd food in the pan and do not cover the pan when frying, because the steam thus held in will moisten the food and destroy its surface crispness.

Oven-frying

Beloved of American cooks, this process is a very useful method of cooking fish or chicken. Heat the oven to moderately hot (400°F/200°C/Mark 6). Use enough olive oil, or olive oil and butter, to cover the bottom of a shallow baking dish. Heat the dish in the oven for a minute or two and then put in the food, which you have first basted with melted butter and rolled in breadcrumbs mixed with chopped fresh herbs (parsley, chervil, chives, etc.) and a little grated lemon rind. Turn once during cooking time. Cook in the oven until tender.

Pan-frying is quick cooking at its gourmet best. Here we have—left to right—Pan-fried Scallops, Calf's Liver with Sage and Avocado, and Pan-fried Veal with Lemon. (Recipes, pages 119 and 120).

Pan-fried Tournedos

Ingredients

4 small fillet steaks

Beef fat or olive oil to grease frying pan

Salt and freshly ground black pepper

4 level tablespoons butter

Prepared corncakes (see below)

1 Heat a large, heavy-bottomed frying pan over a moderately high heat until drops of water shaken on to the surface bounce and sizzle on contact.

2 Grease pan thoroughly with a piece of beef fat impaled on a fork (do not forget sides of pan), or with a wad of absorbent paper soaked in olive oil.

3 When pan is practically smoking, add 4 small steaks and sear for just 2 minutes on each side, turning once. Season generously with salt and freshly ground black pepper.

4 Reduce heat to very moderate and time carefully according to chosen degree of 'doneness': 4–6 oz (100–175 g)/2 inches (5 cm) thick; 3½–4 minutes/blue; 5½–6 minutes/rare; 7 minutes/medium; 8½ minutes/well done.

5 Half a minute before steaks are due to come out of pan, add a good lump of butter. Let it froth and turn golden.

6 Transfer steaks to a heated serving dish. Pour buttery pan juices over steaks. Place prepared corncakes in pan and heat through. Transfer corncakes to serving dish with steaks. Serve immediately.   Serves 4–6

Variations on the tournedos theme:

TOURNEDOS IMAM BAYELDI

Sauté tournedos in butter and serve with half a small stuffed aubergine, a pilaff of rice (see page 154), and sauce *diable*.

TOURNEDOS POMMES ANNA

Sauté tournedos in butter and serve on top of a small round of *pommes Anna* (see page 148) made in an individual tart tin. Serve with a small cooked artichoke heart mounded with puréed *foie gras* and a slice of truffle. Serve with sauce Perigourdine.

TOURNEDOS OPERA

Sauté tournedos in butter and accompany with individual tart shells filled with diced sautéed chicken livers mixed with Madeira sauce (see page 61).

Corncakes

Ingredients

¼ Spanish onion, finely chopped

4 level tablespoons butter

1 small can sweet corn

1 egg, beaten

¼ pint (1½ dl) cold Béchamel sauce (see page 59)

Salt and fresh black pepper

Milk

Oil or fat, for frying

1 Sauté finely chopped onion in butter until onion begins to take on colour. Stir in drained sweet corn, and continue to cook, stirring constantly, for 2 minutes. Stir in beaten egg and cold Béchamel sauce and season to taste.

2 Add just enough milk to make a loose batter which should be just enough to produce thin corn pancakes when fried in hot oil or clarified butter as detailed in Step 3 following.

3 To make corncakes: pour 2–3 tablespoons of mixture into hot oil or clarified butter and fry until golden on both sides. Drain well and keep warm until ready to serve.

This quantity will serve 4–6

Fillet 'Hare and Hounds'

Ingredients

4 fillet steaks

Salt and fresh black pepper

4 level tablespoons butter

2 tablespoons olive oil

1 tablespoon Dijon mustard

2 level tablespoons brown sugar

1 Season steaks generously with salt and freshly ground black pepper.

2 Heat butter and olive oil in a thick-bottomed frying pan. Sauté steaks on each side until tender. Spread mustard over top of steaks; sprinkle with brown sugar; transfer steaks to a *gratin* dish and glaze under preheated grill for a few minutes until golden brown.

3 Pour off fat from pan juices; heat remaining juices and pour over steak. Serve immediately.

Serves 4

Pan-glazed Sliced Sirloin

1 Trim fat from sirloin and slice into thin strips across the grain.

2 Heat 2 level tablespoons butter and olive oil in a large, thick-bottomed frying pan. When hot, add a quarter of the sirloin strips, and sauté, stirring constantly, until beef browns and crusts slightly on the outside but remains rare and tender on the inside.

3 Remove strips from the pan and keep warm.

4 Continue to cook remainder of beef, in batches, as above. Keep warm.

5 Add chopped shallots to the pan and cook, stirring constantly, until they are just coloured. Add lemon juice, dry sherry and red wine vinegar and continue to cook for a second or two more.

6 Add beef stock. Stir thoroughly and cook over a low heat until stock is reduced to a quarter of the original quantity.

7 Work in 5 level tablespoons butter, tablespoon by tablespoon. Season to taste with salt and freshly ground black pepper; add finely chopped parsley and tarragon. Return beef strips to pan and reheat them in the sauce. Serve immediately.

Serves 4

Ingredients
2-2½ lb (about 1 kg) sirloin steak, about 1½ inches (3½ cm) thick
Butter
1 tablespoon olive oil
2 level tablespoons chopped shallots
2 tablespoons lemon juice
2 tablespoons dry sherry
2 tablespoons red wine vinegar
½ pint (3 dl) beef stock
Salt and freshly ground black pepper
4 level tablespoons finely chopped parsley
4 level tablespoons finely chopped tarragon

Ham-and-Beefburgers

1 Form beef into 8 thin, oval-shaped patties.

2 Spread 4 patties with French mustard, and season generously with salt and freshly ground black pepper. Place a slice of cooked ham on each patty, trimming ham to size of each patty with a pair of kitchen scissors. Place ham scraps on top of ham slice and top with remaining patties, pressing meat firmly together.

3 Sauté patties in equal quantities of butter and olive oil for 2 or 3 minutes on each side. Serve patties with knobs of anchovy butter, made by combining butter with anchovy paste, to taste.

Serves 4

Ingredients
1 lb (450g) freshly minced beef
French mustard
Salt and freshly ground black pepper
4 thin slices ham
Butter
Olive oil

ANCHOVY BUTTER
2 level tablespoons softened butter
Anchovy paste

Ham Hash

1 Boil potatoes in salted water. Drain thoroughly and toss in the dry pan over a moderate heat to evaporate excess moisture.

2 Put potatoes, cooked ham, quartered onion and green pepper through the coarse blade of a mincer. (Or chop them up together very finely indeed.) Season to taste with salt and freshly ground black pepper; add thyme and mix well.

3 Heat butter and olive oil together in a heavy, 8-inch (20 cm) frying pan. Add hash mixture; shape into an even cake with a spatula or the back of a spoon, and cook over a moderate heat for 5 minutes, or until cake is crisp and golden underneath.

4 Brown top under a hot grill for 3-4 minutes.

5 Garnish with onion rings and a sprig of parsley. Serve immediately, cut into thick wedges.

Serves 2-4

Ingredients
4 medium-sized potatoes (about 1¼ lb (550g))
Salt
½ lb (225g) cooked ham
1 small onion, quartered
½ green sweet pepper, seeded and cored
Freshly ground black pepper
¼ level teaspoon thyme
2 level tablespoons butter
1 tablespoon olive oil
Onion rings and a sprig of parsley, to garnish

Swedish-born model and actress Maud Adams takes a final sip (you have to taste, taste!) as she learns another cooking hint on the show.

Pan-fried Veal with Lemon *(Illustration, page 115)*

1 Slice veal into 8–16 pieces according to the size. Pound slices flat. Season veal on both sides with salt and freshly ground black pepper.

2 Heat olive oil and 2 level tablespoons butter in a frying pan. When fat froths, add pieces of veal, lemon slices (they must be paper-thin), onions and herbs and cook veal for 1 minute on each side, or until cooked through but still juicy.

3 Transfer veal and lemon slices to a heated dish with a slotted spoon. Keep warm. Add remaining butter to the pan, together with a little dry white wine (or water) and heat gently, scraping surface of the pan clean with a wooden spoon. Pour pan juices over hot veal and lemon and serve immediately.

Serves 4

Ingredients

1 lb (450g) boneless veal, loin or fillet
Salt and freshly ground black pepper
1 tablespoon olive oil
4 level tablespoons butter
8 thin slices lemon
4 green onions, sliced thinly
1 sprig fresh tarragon or rosemary
2 level tablespoons finely chopped parsley
4 tablespoons dry white wine (optional)

Calf's Liver with Sage and Avocado *(Illustration, page 115)*

1 Peel avocados and remove stones; slice thinly. Brush each slice with a little lemon juice to preserve colour.

2 Dip liver slices in flour well seasoned with salt and freshly ground black pepper.

3 Melt butter and olive oil in a frying pan; add sage leaves and sauté calf's liver very quickly on both sides. Add veal or beef stock and a squeeze of lemon juice to pan; top liver slices with sliced avocado; warm through and serve immediately.

Serves 4

Ingredients

2 avocado pears
Lemon juice
8 thin slices calf's liver
Flour
Salt and freshly ground black pepper
4 level tablespoons butter
1 tablespoon olive oil
6 sage leaves
6 tablespoons veal or beef stock

Opposite page *Sauté of Duckling with Wine Vinegar. Tender duckling sautéed in clarified butter until golden on all sides, splashed with sherry vinegar and then gently pan-simmered in a sauce enriched with wine and finely chopped shallots. (Recipe, page 120).*

Sauté of Duckling *(Illustration, page 118)*

Ingredients
1 tender duck (5–6 lb (2–3 kg)),
  or 2 smaller ones
Salt and fresh black pepper
2 stalks celery, chopped
2 carrots, sliced
2 large onions, sliced
4 tablespoons Cognac
¾ pint (4 dl) dry red wine
¼ lb (100g) green bacon, diced
4 tablespoons olive oil
2 tablespoons dry sherry
1 tablespoon wine vingear
2 level tablespoons butter
1 level tablespoon flour
Bouquet garni
2 cloves garlic

1 Cut duck into serving pieces and place in a porcelain or earthenware bowl. Add salt and freshly ground black pepper, chopped celery, sliced carrots and onions, Cognac and red wine, and marinate the duck in this mixture overnight.

2 Remove duck pieces from the marinade; drain and pat dry.

3 Pan-fry diced green bacon in olive oil in a large frying pan until golden. Remove bacon bits and reserve. Pan-fry duck pieces over a low heat in remaining fat until brown on all sides. Return bacon bits to pan; cover frying pan and simmer gently for 20 minutes.

4 Skim excess fat from pan juices. Add sherry and wine vinegar and stir over high heat for 2–3 minutes. Remove from heat.

5 To prepare sauce: while duck is cooking, make a roux. Strain marinade juices into roux mixture and stir over a low heat, until smooth.

6 Add marinade vegetables, bouquet garni and garlic to the thickened sauce and simmer over a very low heat for 20 minutes.

7 When ready to serve: remove bouquet; skim off excess fat; strain sauce through a fine sieve over duck and bacon pieces in pan, pressing vegetables well, to extract full flavour. Simmer duck pieces in sauce until tender. Serve with boiled noodles.

Serves 4 – 6

Basic Sautéed Chicken with Aromatics

Ingredients
1 tender chicken (2½-3 lb
  (1.1-1.3 kg))
Salt and freshly ground black
  pepper
2 level tablespoons butter
2 tablespoons olive oil
Bouquet garni
¼ Spanish onion, finely
  chopped
1 small clove garlic, finely
  chopped
¼ pint (1½ dl) dry white wine
¼ pint (1½ dl) double cream
4 ripe tomatoes, peeled,
  seeded and chopped
4 button mushrooms,
  simmered in butter and
  lemon juice

1 Cut chicken into serving pieces, reserving backbone. Season well with salt and freshly ground black pepper, and put chicken pieces, flesh side down, in a sauté pan or thick-bottomed frying pan just large enough to hold them comfortably. Add butter and olive oil and sauté chicken pieces until they are browned on all sides – about 10 minutes.

2 Add backbone and bouquet garni; cover pan and simmer gently for 20 minutes. Remove wings and breasts after 15 minutes. They are the most delicate, and cook most quickly. Keep warm.

3 Remove remaining chicken pieces and sauté finely chopped onion in pan juices until transparent. Add garlic and dry white wine, and continue cooking until wine is reduced to half the original quantity. Add double cream and chopped tomatoes and simmer gently for 5–10 minutes more. Do not allow sauce to boil.

4 Return sautéed chicken to the pan and allow it to steep gently, covered, over the lowest of heats for 5 minutes Do not allow liquid to boil or your sauce will separate and the chicken will be tough. Garnish chicken with button mushrooms.

Pan-fried Scallops *(Illustration, pages 114 and 115)*

Ingredients
8 scallops
2 eggs, beaten
4 tablespoons double cream
Salt and fresh black pepper
Cornmeal, or breadcrumbs
¼ lb (100g) butter
¼ pint (1½ dl) oil, for frying
Lemon wedges

1 Wash and trim scallops; slice in half.

2 Combine beaten eggs and cream in a bowl. Add salt and freshly ground black pepper, to taste. Dip scallops in egg mixture, then in cornmeal or crumbs, and allow to set on aluminium foil for about 5 minutes before cooking.

3 Melt butter in a thick-bottomed frying pan. Add oil; bring to frying temperature and cook scallops in fat until they are golden brown. Serve. immediately with wedges of lemon.

Serves 4

Deep-frying

The way you fry is more important than the fat or oil you use. If anyone asked me to define the quality of a fried food, I would say that its quality was in inverse proportion to the oil or fat absorbed by the food. Deep-fried food should never be greasy. *Thus, the temperature of the fat is of prime importance*: it must be hot enough to 'carbonize' the exterior of what is being fried at the very moment of immersion. This prevents grease from penetrating the food, conserves the juices, and allows the food to retain all its taste. Deep-frying is simple and quick when you know how.

Vegetable fats and vegetable oils are good for all deep-frying. Rendered beef fat is a good choice for meats, fish croquettes and less delicate foods. Chicken fat and butter are not suitable for deep-frying because they scorch at low temperatures. *The quality and freshness of the oil or fat used is of great importance.*

A frying medium uses itself up quickly, especially when it is heated to excess. I have found that I can double the life of my frying oil if I never allow it to smoke or boil. Use the bread test instead: drop an inch (2½ cm) cube of day-old bread in the hot oil. If your temperature is right for deep-frying (375°F/190°C) the bread should brown in about 60 seconds.

1 Do not allow fat to smoke or boil.

2 The temperature of the fat should vary as little as possible during cooking.

3 If you plunge food into the fat a second time, the temperature of the second cooking must be higher than that of the first.

To deep-fry fish

When properly fried, fish should be a light golden brown and dry and crisp in texture, as free from fat as if it had never touched it. I like to deep-fry fish in a combination of lard and oil to give added flavour; for pan-frying I use butter or olive oil, or a combination of the two.

Small fish are better fried whole, large ones should be filleted or cut into steaks or cutlets.

To fry well, fish should be perfectly dry. Always pat fish dry with a clean cloth or paper towel before coating with seasoned flour, fine oatmeal or cornmeal, beaten egg and dry breadcrumbs, or a frying batter. This serves two purposes: (1) to keep fat from entering the fish while it is immersed in the hot cooking fat or oil; and (2) to add a flavoursome, crunchy coating to the fried fish, which adds enormously to the delicately flavoured flesh within.

If seasoned flour or flour and milk are used as a coating, apply just before the fish is to be cooked, or the flour will become moist and the fish will not fry well. Batter, too, should be applied only at the last moment.

Délices au Gruyère. Make a thick white sauce; flavour it with freshly grated Gruyère cheese and nutmeg; spread it out in a baking-tin to cool; cut into rectangles. Dip each délice in flour, in beaten egg and then in breadcrumbs. Then deep-fry them for a minute or two in deep fat.

Délices au Gruyère

1 Melt butter in the top of a double saucepan; stir in 4 level tablespoons flour and cook over water, stirring continuously with a wooden spoon, until smooth. Pour in boiling milk and mix with a whisk to make a thick sauce.

2 Simmer sauce for a few minutes longer; add freshly grated Gruyère cheese and a little freshly grated nutmeg, and continue cooking, stirring continuously, until cheese is completely blended into sauce.

3 Remove sauce from heat; stir in egg yolks; season to taste with salt and freshly ground black pepper, and more nutmeg if desired. Continue to cook over water, stirring continuously, for 2 or 3 minutes, being careful not to let mixture boil. Spread in a rectangular baking tin and allow to cool. Cover with paper or foil and chill in refrigerator for 3 hours, or until needed.

4 Just before serving, cut into rectangles; flour lightly and dip in egg beaten with milk and olive oil; drain, roll in fresh breadcrumbs and fry in hot oil (temperature 375°F/190°C) until golden. Serve immediately.

Serves 4 – 6

Ingredients
4 level tablespoons butter
Flour
¾ pint (4½ dl) boiling milk
8 level tablespoons freshly grated|Gruyère cheese
Freshly grated nutmeg
2 egg yolks
Salt and freshly ground black pepper
1 egg beaten with 2 tablespoons milk and 1 tablespoon olive oil
Fresh breadcrumbs
Oil, for frying

Délices aux Fruits de Mer

Deliciously different little deep-fried *délices* of crab, salmon or prawns can be made in much the same way as Délices au Gruyère.

Simply drain the canned fish of your choice – crab, Alaska King crab, salmon or Norwegian prawns; chop finely; flavour to taste with salt, fresh black pepper, cayenne pepper and lemon juice. Add to sauce in Step 3 of above recipe at the same time as you add the egg yolks; proceed as above.

Batter-dipped Prawns

Ingredients

1½ lb (675g) frozen prawns
½ chicken stock cube
Lemon juice
Cayenne pepper.
Salt and fresh black pepper
Oil for frying
Mayonnaise (see page 63)
Lemon wedges

BEER BATTER

5 oz (150g) plain flour
Pinch of salt
2 tablespoons olive oil
¼ pint (1½ dl) beer, preferably
   lager
1 egg white

1 Dissolve chicken stock cube in 2 tablespoons boiling water. Add juice of 1 lemon and a dash of cayenne pepper.

2 Defrost prawns; season with salt and freshly ground black pepper and marinate in flavoured lemon juice.

3 To make beer batter: sift flour and salt into a bowl, and make a well in the centre. Pour in olive oil and gradually add beer, stirring with a wooden spoon to incorporate flour from sides of well. Batter should be completely smooth and slightly thicker than a crêpe batter. Leave to rest for 2 hours. When ready to use batter: whisk egg white until stiff but not dry, and fold in gently but thoroughly.

4 Preheat oven to very slow (275°F/140°C/Mark 1).

5 To cook prawns: half-fill deep-fryer with oil and heat it to 375°F/190°C using bread cube test (see page 121). Dip prawns, one at a time, in batter so that they become completely coated and lower them – 4–6 at a time – into hot fat. Cook in hot fat for 3–4 minutes, or until batter is puffed and golden brown.

6 To keep prawns hot: as prawns are fried, lift them from frying basket, let them drain for a minute or two on a baking sheet lined with paper kitchen towels and then keep warm in preheated oven.

7 Serve with mayonnaise and lemon wedges.

Deep-fried Fillets of Plaice or Sole

Ingredients

8–12 fresh fillets of plaice
   or sole
½ chicken stock cube
Juice of 1 lemon
Cayenne pepper
Salt and freshly ground black
   pepper
Flour
1 egg, well beaten
Fresh breadcrumbs
Hot lard or oil, for frying
Lemon wedges

1 Dissolve chicken stock cube in 2 tablespoons boiling water in a large flat soup bowl or serving dish. Add lemon juice and a dash of cayenne pepper.

2 Season fillets of plaice or sole with salt and freshly ground black pepper and marinate in flavoured lemon juice for at least 2 hours.

3 When ready to cook, remove fillets from marinade; pat dry with a paper towel; dip in flour, then in beaten egg, and then in breadcrumbs, pressing breadcrumbs into fillets with a spatula to make them adhere well.

4 Shake off loose crumbs and fry in hot lard or oil (temperature 375°F/190°C) until golden brown. Serve with lemon wedges.

Serves 4

Deep-fried Aubergines and Courgettes

Ingredients

2 aubergines
4 courgettes
Oil, for deep-frying
Flour
2–3 eggs, lightly beaten
Fine breadcrumbs
Salt and freshly ground black
   pepper

1 Do not peel aubergines or courgettes. Cut aubergines crosswise into ¼-inch (½ cm) slices; then cut each slice into strips ¼-inch (½ cm) thick. Trim ends from courgettes and cut each across into 2 equal-sized pieces. Cut each piece in 2 lengthwise and remove seeds. Then cut into ¼-inch (½ cm) thick strips.

2 Preheat oven to very slow (275°F/140°C/Mark 1).

3 Half-fill the deep-fryer with oil and heat it to 375°F/190°C using the bread cube test (see page 121).

4 Dip aubergine and courgette strips, a few at a time, into flour, then into lightly beaten eggs and then into breadcrumbs. Fry strips, 12–20 at a time, in hot oil until golden brown.

5 To keep vegetable strips hot: as vegetable strips are fried, lift them from frying basket; let them drain for a minute or two on a baking sheet lined with paper kitchen towels and then keep warm in preheated oven.

6 Season generously and serve at once.

Serves 4–6

Chinese stir-frying

Chinese cooking has much to recommend it when it comes to quick, easy dishes with a truly fabulous flavour. I often serve my friends a quickly prepared dish of strips of lean beef and green peppers, tossed for minutes only in a *wok* – a Chinese round-bottomed frying pan – before being steamed for a moment or two in a pungent sauce made of equal quantities of Chinese soy sauce, oyster sauce, dry white wine and peanut oil, softened in flavour with a little honey.

So, if you are like so many friends of mine – who admit that they love Chinese food but are afraid to cook it themselves because it is too different, too exotic, to try – change your mind, I beg of you. Chinese food *is* different, of course. But the stir-fry recipes I have chosen for you are simple, quick and easy.

The Canton school of cooking, one of the best known in the Western world, is famous for quick-stir-frying of meats and vegetables together. The secret here is the cutting of the ingredients to the same size so that they not only look well together in the finished dish, but they cook more quickly in the hot oil.

Quick-stir-frying is as easy as it sounds. All that is needed is a round-bottomed shallow frying pan or *wok*. (The Chinese supermarkets in Soho's Gerrard Street sell *woks* from £1.80.)

The foods to be stir-fried are cut into small, uniform pieces before they are cooked so that more surface is exposed to the heat. As a result the foods cook quicker and do not lose their character, flavour or vitamin content. Vegetables cooked in the *ch'ao* manner are cooked for minutes only (spinach, 3–5 minutes; green beans, 9 minutes). Thinly sliced pieces of meat are cooked through almost as soon as they touch the pan. Even pork can be cooked in a matter of minutes in this particular way.

To quick-stir-fry beef: cut fillet or rump steak into pieces 2 inches (5 cm) square and then slice each square against the grain into thin strips $\frac{1}{16}$-inch ($\frac{1}{8}$ cm) thick. Marinate the slices for at least 30 minutes in a mixture of cornflour mixed with water, soy sauce and sake, or sherry, to keep in juices and add flavour during cooking time.

Tender vegetables such as spring onions and young leeks are cut across the grain. Carrots, celery and asparagus are usually cut diagonally so that a large area of the cut vegetable will be exposed to the heat during cooking.

All ingredients should be prepared before you start cooking. Cut vegetables and meats to size and place them near the stove on individual plates. You won't have time, once you start cooking, to chop or cut an extra ingredient. And remember, a high heat is essential for quick-stir-frying. The *wok* has rounded sides which allow every part of it to become very hot.

In the Chinese meal, rice bowls are always individual. I like to use mine as a 'dripping bowl', carrying each morsel of prawn in oyster sauce, or pork ball in sweet and sour, or crisp stir-fried vegetables by the chopstickful (if there is such a word) from the central dish over my bowl to allow some of the juices to drip into the fluffy rice, adding their own subtle flavour to the rice in passing.

I find that food eaten in this manner actually tastes better than when it is served Western style, all on one plate and eaten with a fork. Enjoyed the Chinese way, in little morsels from the bubbling hot central dish, each single nugget is a small mystery, its flavour a nagging reminder of some subtle ingredient just beyond your palate's memory.

Stir-fried Duck with Mixed Vegetables

Ingredients

2 breasts of lightly roasted
duck
2 tablespoons Chinese
oyster sauce
1 tablespoon Chinese chili
sauce
2 tablespoons soy sauce
2 tablespoons peanut oil
2 tablespoons honey
2 tablespoons dry white wine
¼ lb (100g) haricots verts
cooked in boiling salted
water until just tender
4 canned water chestnuts,
thinly sliced
¼ lb (100g) button
mushrooms, thinly sliced
8 spring onions, cut into
2-inch (5cm) segments

1 Cut duck into even-sized cubes. Place in a large flat bowl and add Chinese oyster sauce, chili sauce and soy sauce (obtainable in some supermarkets and all Chinese provision stores), peanut oil, honey and dry white wine. Toss and marinate duck in sauce for at least 2 hours.

2 When ready to cook, heat a Chinese *wok,* or a large thick-bottomed frying pan, over a high heat; add duck pieces and stir-fry until duck is crisp and heated through. Add marinade juices, *haricots verts,* thinly sliced water chestnuts and mushrooms, and spring onion segments. Continue to cook, stirring constantly, for 1 minute more. Serve immediately.

Serves 4 as part of a Chinese meal, or 2 as a separate dish on its own.

Below *Chinese Stir-fried Rice. Toss cooked rice over a high heat with sausage or diced ham, chicken and pork and sliced mushrooms, and chopped onions. Top with thin strips of Chinese omelette. (Recipe, page 128)*

Right *Stir-fried Duck with sliced mushrooms, water chestnuts, haricots verts and spring onions is first marinated in a mixture of soy, oyster and chilli with dry white wine, honey and peanut oil.*

Stir-fried Chicken with Courgettes and Walnuts

Ingredients

2 raw chicken breasts
1 level tablespoon cornflour
Dry white wine
1 egg white, unbeaten
16 walnut halves
2 courgettes, thinly sliced
4 tablespoons peanut oil
2 thin slices fresh ginger, cut into thin strips
1 small clove garlic, finely chopped
2 tablespoons soy sauce
1 level tablespoon sugar

1 Slice raw chicken breasts lengthwise into $\frac{1}{4}$-inch ($\frac{1}{2}$ cm) slices. Cut each slice across into 3 sections and cut each section into strips $\frac{1}{4}$-inch ($\frac{1}{2}$ cm) thick.

2 Dissolve cornflour in $1\frac{1}{2}$ tablespoons dry white wine and combine with unbeaten egg white.

3 Place chicken strips in a large flat bowl; pour over egg white mixture and toss well.

4 Place walnut halves in a small frying pan; add cold water to just cover them and bring to the boil. As soon as water boils, drain and pat dry, removing any skins to take away bitter flavour.

5 Heat peanut oil in a Chinese wok, or large frying pan; add blanched walnut halves and stir-fry until they are lightly browned. Add courgettes and stir-fry for 1 minute more. Transfer walnuts and courgettes to a plate.

6 Add chicken, ginger strips and finely chopped garlic to wok or frying pan, and stir-fry until chicken pieces change colour. When chicken pieces change colour, add fried walnuts and courgettes, soy sauce, sugar and 2 tablespoons dry white wine and continue to cook for 1 minute more. Serve immediately.

Serves 4 as part of a Chinese meal, or 2 as a separate dish on its own.

Chinese Beef with Oyster Sauce

Ingredients

2 raw fillet steaks
2 green peppers
4 level tablespoons Chinese fermented beans

CHINESE MARINADE

3 tablespoons Chinese oyster sauce
1 tablespoon Chinese chili sauce
3 tablespoons soy sauce
3 tablespoons peanut oil
3 tablespoons dry white wine

1 Trim beef fillets of fat and cut diagonally into thin strips.

2 Cut peppers in half and remove stems and seeds. Cut peppers into 1-inch ($2\frac{1}{2}$ cm) squares.

3 Place meat in a shallow bowl and peppers in another. Combine Chinese marinade ingredients and pour half over peppers and half over meat. Toss each well and leave for 2 hours.

4 When ready to cook, heat a Chinese wok, or a large thick-bottomed frying pan, over a high heat; add pepper pieces and stir-fry until peppers are tender. Return cooked pepper pieces to bowl in which they were marinated.

5 Wipe wok, or frying pan, clean with a paper kitchen towel; add marinated beef pieces and stir-fry until tender; add green pepper pieces; pour over marinade juices and fermented beans and heat through. Serve immediately.

Serves 4 as part of a Chinese meal, or 2 as a separate dish on its own.

Chinese Stir-fried Rice *(Illustration, page 126)*

Ingredients

2 eggs
2 tablespoons water
Soy sauce
5 tablespoons vegetable oil
$\frac{1}{2}$ Spanish onion, chopped
$\frac{1}{2}$ lb (225g) cooked rice
6 level tablespoons diced cooked pork
6 level tablespoons diced cooked chicken
6 level tablespoons diced Italian sausage
6 mushrooms, diced
Salt and freshly ground black pepper

1 Make a thin omelette with eggs, water and $\frac{1}{2}$ teaspoon soy sauce cooked in 1 tablespoon vegetable oil; cut in strips and set aside.

2 Heat remaining oil in wok or large frying pan; when it is very hot add finely chopped onion and sauté until golden. Add cooked rice that has been left to become cold, and diced pork, chicken, sausage and mushrooms and sauté gently for 3–5 minutes.

3 Just before serving, add egg strips, 2 teaspoons soy sauce and salt and freshly ground black pepper, to taste. Serve immediately.

Serves 4

Stir-fried Eggs with Soy Pork Sticks

1 Place a Chinese *wok*, or an omelette pan, over a medium heat; heat 1 tablespoon peanut oil; pour in beaten egg mixture and stir-fry until eggs begin to cook. Remove from heat and transfer half-cooked eggs to a dish.

2 Cut leeks into 1-inch (2½ cm) segments and then finely slice each segment lengthwise.

3 Cut pork into matchstick-sized segments.

4 Cut spring onions into 1-inch (2½ cm) segments.

5 Heat 6 tablespoons peanut oil in *wok*, or omelette pan; add shredded leeks and cook for 2 minutes; add pork sticks and cook until pork changes colour. When pork changes colour, add spring onion segments, soy sauce, sugar and dry white wine. Toss once; add stir-fried eggs and continue to cook, stirring constantly, until heated through. Serve immediately.

Serves 4 as part of a Chinese meal, or 2 as a separate dish on its own.

Ingredients
6 eggs, well beaten with 1 teaspoon each water and soy sauce
Peanut oil
2 leeks
½ lb (225g) lean pork
4 spring onions
3 tablespoons light soy sauce
½ level teaspoon sugar
2 tablespoons dry white wine

Stir-fried Prawns and Asparagus Tips

1 Combine 1 tablespoon peanut oil, dry sherry and 1 tablespoon soy sauce in a shallow porcelain or earthenware bowl. Add shelled prawns and toss well. Sprinkle with cornflour and toss again.

2 Beat egg white in a small bowl until it begins to froth. Add to prawns and toss. Refrigerate for 30 minutes.

3 When ready to cook prawns, heat a wok or a large frying pan over a high heat until hot. Pour in just enough peanut oil to fry prawns. Spoon in prawns – 5 or 6 at a time – and cook, stirring. Remove prawns when they are pinky white. Drain fried prawns on a paper towel until ready to finish dish.

4 To prepare asparagus: break off tough ends of asparagus and trim ends with a sharp knife. Rinse asparagus carefully to remove any sand and cut diagonally into 1½-inch (3½ cm) segments.

5 To stir-fry asparagus: heat a *wok* or large frying pan over a high heat. Add 2 tablespoons peanut oil, ginger strips and finely chopped garlic and stir-fry asparagus segments, tossing them in oil over a high heat for 1 minute. Add 4 tablespoons water and stir for a few seconds more. Cover *wok* and steam asparagus over a high heat for 1 minute.

6 Add prawns and stir; add 1 tablespoon soy sauce and sesame oil and stir-fry for 1 minute more. Serve at once.

Serves 4 as part of a Chinese meal, or 2 as a separate dish on its own.

Ingredients
1 lb (450g) shelled prawns, 1–1½ inches (2½–3½ cm) long
Peanut oil
1 tablespoon dry sherry
1 tablespoon soy sauce
1 level tablespoon cornflour
1 egg white
8–10 asparagus stalks
2 thin slices fresh ginger, cut in thin strips
1 clove garlic, finely chopped
1 tablespoon sesame oil

Stir-fried Prawns with Snow Peas

1 Defrost prawns.

2 Dissolve cornflour in 1½ tablespoons dry white wine and combine with unbeaten egg white.

3 Pat prawns dry and place in a large flat bowl. Pour over egg white mixture and toss well.

4 Heat peanut oil in a Chinese *wok* or large frying pan, and stir-fry prawns until they change colour. Add 2 tablespoons dry white wine, soy sauce, sugar and blanched snow peas. Toss over a high flame until heated through. Serve immediately.

Serves 4 as part of a Chinese meal, or 2 as a separate dish on its own.

Ingredients
½ lb (225g) frozen prawns
1 level tablespoon cornflour
Dry white wine
1 egg white, unbeaten
6 tablespoons peanut oil
2 tablespoons soy sauce
1 level tablespoon sugar
¼ lb (100g) snow peas (mange touts), cooked in boiling salted water until just tender

Cooking in a Casserole

Braising is simply a combination of roasting, stewing and steaming. The meat to be braised is sometimes (Step 1) larded; often (Step 2) marinated; always (Step 3) browned in fat and then (Step 4) cooked gently, covered, in a little liquid to preserve juices and flavour. In the classic French method, the casserole is lined with a layer of diced or sliced vegetables before slow simmering begins.

For the most part meat, poultry or fish to be braised is not cut up, but is braised in the piece, but the braising techniques listed below can also be used with great facility for cut-up pieces of meat, poultry or fish in the stews, ragoûts, daubes and casseroles of many countries.

1 Larding
Top-quality beef – rib or fillet – does not have to be larded, but it is usually wise to lard a rump or round of beef, a roast of veal or a leg of mutton with strips of bacon fat as long as the piece of meat to be cooked and about ½ inch (1 cm) wide. Season these first with freshly ground black pepper and spices, sprinkle with chopped parsley and marinate for about 2 hours in a little brandy; then insert the strips into the meat with a special larding needle. Most butchers will lard meat for you.

2 Marinating
The flavour of meat intended for braising is greatly improved by marinating it for a few hours in the wine which is to be the moistening agent in cooking. Roll the meat in a mixture of salt, freshly ground black pepper and finely chopped herbs, and place it in an earthenware casserole just large enough to hold it, on a bed of thickly sliced and fried carrots and onions, a generous bouquet garni, a clove or two of garlic, and some blanched, fried fat bacon. Cover the meat with wine and marinate for at least 2 hours in this mixture, taking care to turn it several times during this period.

3 Sautéeing
After marinating the meat, drain it well and wipe dry with a clean cloth. Sauté in a little olive oil, bacon fat, butter or lard, or a combination of these, to colour it and seal in its juices. Then place the vegetables and herbs from the marinade in the bottom of a heavy casserole or braising pan just large enough to hold the meat; place the meat on this bed of aromatics and pour in enough of the juices from the marinade to cover the vegetables amply.

Opposite page *Ragoût of Lamb à la Provençale. Strips of orange peel and black olives add both colour and flavour to this rustic casserole. Other aromatics are onions and carrots. (Recipe, page 137)*

4 Casseroling

Add well-flavoured beef stock; bring it to the boil; cover the casserole and cook gently on top of the stove or in a moderate oven (250°F/120°C/Mark ½) until the meat can be pricked deeply with a fork without giving blood. Remove the meat to another casserole just large enough to hold it; strain the sauce over meat through a piece of muslin and place casserole, covered, in the oven. Cook until meat is tender, basting from time to time to keep the top moist. Before serving, correct seasoning and thicken the sauce, if necessary, with a *beurre manié* (equal quantities of flour and butter kneaded together).

Cook very slowly so that the meat will be tender and the fat will rise gradually to the surface of the liquid.

Vegetables – as well as meats, poultry and fish – can be braised in this way with excellent results.

Osso Bucco

Ingredients

4 thick slices shin of veal
Flour
Salt and freshly ground black
   pepper
2 tablespoons olive oil
2 level tablespoons butter
2 cloves garlic, finely
   chopped
½ Spanish onion, finely
   chopped
¼ pint (1½ dl) boiling water or
   light stock
¼ pint (1½ dl) dry white wine
4 level tablespoons tomato
   purée
4 anchovy fillets, finely
   chopped
4 level tablespoons chopped
   parsley
Grated rind of ½ lemon
   or orange

1 Choose shin of veal with plenty of meat and have it sawn into pieces 2 inches (5 cm) thick.

2 Dredge veal pieces with flour; season with salt and freshly ground black pepper and brown them in olive oil and butter. Add half the finely chopped garlic and the onion; pour over boiling water or light stock, dry white wine and tomato purée; cover the pan and sim-mer gently over a very low heat for 1½ hours.

3 Add finely chopped anchovy fillets and remaining finely chopped garlic. Blend thoroughly, heat through and serve sprinkled with chopped parsley and grated lemon or orange rind, and accompanied by saffron rice (see page 154).

Serves 4

Italian Braised Beef

Ingredients

1 level tablespoon lard
1 tablespoon olive oil
½ lb (225g) fat salt pork, diced
1 onion, sliced
2 cloves garlic, chopped
2½ lb (1.1 kg) lean beef, cut
   into bite-sized pieces
Salt and freshly ground black
   pepper
1 generous pinch marjoram
¼ pint (1½ dl) dry red wine
4 level tabelspoons tomato
   purée, diluted in water

1 Combine lard and olive oil in a thick pan or flameproof casserole; when fat begins to bubble, add diced salt pork, sliced onion and chopped garlic and sauté until golden.

2 Add pieces of meat seasoned with salt and freshly ground black pepper and marjoram, and cook, stirring frequently, until meat is well browned on all sides. Now add dry red wine (one of the rougher Italian ones) and continue cooking until the wine has been reduced to half the original quantity.

3 Add diluted tomato purée and enough boiling water to cover the meat. Cover the pan and simmer gently over a very low heat for about 2 hours, or until the meat is tender and the savoury sauce is thick and richly coloured. A tablespoon or two of red wine just before serving will add extra bouquet to this dish, which should be served directly from the casserole.

Serves 4-6

Chicken in White Wine *(Illustration, page 135)*

1 Heat 2 level tablespoons butter and olive oil in an iron *cocotte* or a heavy flameproof casserole just large enough to hold chicken.

2 Sauté bacon pieces in fat until golden. Remove bacon; add coarsely chopped shallots and carrots and cook, stirring constantly, until vegetables 'soften'; then add chicken and brown on all sides.

3 Return bacon bits to the pan; pour over Cognac and flame. Then add bouquet garni, salt and freshly ground black pepper, to taste, dry white wine and chicken stock. Cover the bird with a piece of buttered paper cut to fit the casserole, with a small hole in the centre to allow steam to escape. Cover casserole and simmer gently over a very low heat until tender (1–1¼ hours). Add more wine or a little chicken stock if the sauce reduces too quickly during the cooking.

Serves 4

Ingredients
1 tender chicken (about 4 lb (1.8 kg))
Butter
2 tablespoons olive oil
¼ lb (100g) fat bacon, diced
4 shallots, coarsely chopped
2 carrots, coarsely chopped
2 tablespoons Cognac
1 bouquet garni
Salt and freshly ground black pepper
½ pint (3 dl) dry white wine
¼ pint (1½ dl) chicken stock

Braised Chicken Mediterranean

1 Sauté chicken and diced green bacon in butter and olive oil in a flameproof casserole until chicken is golden on all sides.

2 Add pitted green olives, which you have previously soaked in hot water for 15 minutes to remove excess salt, and button mushrooms. Season to taste with a little salt and freshly ground black pepper. Moisten with Cognac. Cover casserole and cook in a slow oven (325°F/170°C/Mark 3) for 45 minutes.

3 Add sautéed potatoes and tomatoes and simmer gently for another 15 minutes, or until chicken is tender. Serve in the casserole or on a serving dish.

Serves 4

Ingredients
1 3½-lb (1.6 kg) chicken
½ lb (225g) fat green bacon, diced
2 level tablespoons butter
2 tablespoons olive oil
½ lb (225g) green olives, pitted
½ lb (225g) button mushrooms
Salt and freshly ground black pepper
6 tablespoons Cognac
1 lb (450g) diced sautéed potatoes
4 tomatoes

Casserole of Duck with Red Wine

1 Cut duck into serving pieces and place in a porcelain or earthenware bowl. Add salt and freshly ground black pepper, to taste, chopped celery and carrots, sliced onion, Cognac, lemon peel and red Burgundy, and marinate the duck in this mixture overnight.

2 Remove duck pieces from the marinade; drain and dry with a clean cloth. Reserve marinade juices.

3 Dice bacon and sauté in olive oil until golden. Remove bacon bits and brown duck pieces in fat.

4 Place bacon bits and duck pieces with pan juices in a large flameproof casserole and cook, covered, over a moderate flame for 20 minutes. Add the marinade juices and vegetables to the casserole; add rich duck stock, bouquet garni and garlic. Cook over a low flame for 1½ hours or until duck is tender. Remove bouquet; skim fat; correct seasoning; remove duck pieces and bacon to a serving platter; strain over sauce and garnish with boiled potatoes and sliced mushrooms which you have simmered in butter and lemon juice. Serve immediately.

Serves 4

Ingredients
1 tender duck
Salt and freshly ground black pepper
1 stalk celery, chopped
2 carrots, chopped
1 Spanish onion, sliced
6 tablespoons Cognac
1 strip of lemon peel
½ pint (3 dl) red Burgundy
¼ lb (100g) bacon (1 piece)
2 tablespoons olive oil
¼ pint (1½ dl) rich duck stock, made with trimmings and giblets
1 bouquet garni (parsley, bay leaf and thyme)
2 cloves garlic
12 small new potatoes
½ lb (225g) mushrooms

Top left *Indian Lamb Curry.*

Bottom left *Lamb in Burgundy.*

Bottom right *Chicken in White Wine.*
(Recipes, pages 133, 135 and 136)

Indian Lamb Curry

1 Dust lamb with seasoned flour and sauté in butter and olive oil, stirring continuously, until meat is golden on all sides. Remove meat from pan with a slotted spoon; add sliced onion, garlic, green pepper and celery and sauté vegetables, stirring from time to time, until they are soft.

2 Mix *kari* blend thoroughly in a bowl and stir half the mixture into vegetables.

3 Make coconut milk by simmering a handful of dried coconut in ¼ pint (1½ dl) milk with 1 level tablespoon butter. Press this mixture through a fine sieve; combine with stock and add to vegetables and spices. Now check flavour of sauce and add more *kari* until the sauce is of desired pungency. Cover and simmer for 15 minutes.

4 Add meat and raisins and continue cooking over a low heat or in a very slow oven (275°F/140°C/Mark 1) until meat is tender, stirring occasionally.

5 Remove from heat, stir in yoghurt; correct seasoning and serve with boiled rice, *pappadoms,* and traditional curry condiments: mango chutney, apple chutney, preserved *kumquats,* chopped cooked bacon, etc.

Serves 4–6

Ingredients

2½ lb (1.1 kg) boned lamb, cut into 1¼-inch (3 cm) cubes
Salt and freshly ground black pepper
4 level tablespoons flour
4 level tablespoons butter
2 tablespoons olive oil
1 large Spanish onion, sliced
1 clove garlic, sliced
1 green pepper, sliced
2 stalks celery, sliced
¼ pint (1½ dl) coconut milk (made with dried coconut, milk and butter)
½ pint (3 dl) well-flavoured stock
2 oz (50g) seedless raisins
6 level tablespoons yoghurt
Boiled rice (see page 154)
Curry condiments

KARI BLEND

3 level tablespoons curry powder
1 level teaspoon each cumin and coriander
1 level teaspoon each ginger and turmeric
¼ level teaspoon each paprika and cayenne pepper
2 level tablespoons flour
Coarse salt
Freshly ground black pepper

Lamb in Burgundy *(Illustration, page 134)*

Ingredients

2 level tablespoons butter
2 tablespoons olive oil
1¼ lb (550g) small white
onions
2½ lb (1.1 kg) lamb, trimmed
and cut into 2-inch (5 cm)
cubes
2 level tablespoons flour
2 level tablespoons tomato
purée
½ pint (3 dl) Burgundy
Salt and freshly ground black
pepper
1 bay leaf
¼ level teaspoon dried thyme
leaves
¼ level teaspoon dried
marjoram leaves
4 parsley sprigs
½ lb (225g) mushrooms
Chopped parsley

1 Preheat oven to slow (325°F/170°C/ Mark 3).

2 Heat butter and olive oil in a large, thick-bottomed casserole. Add onions and sauté in combined fats for 5 minutes; remove.

3 Add lamb, a third at a time, and brown well on all sides. Remove lamb with a slotted spoon and reserve.

4 Remove casserole from heat; discard all but 2 tablespoons fat. Stir in flour and tomato purée; return casserole to a

low heat and stir until smooth. Gradually add Burgundy, stirring until smooth. Then add lamb, salt and freshly ground black pepper, herbs and mushrooms, stirring until well mixed. Cover casserole and cook in a preheated oven for 1½ hours.

5 Add onions; bake 1 hour longer, or until meat is tender. Sprinkle with chopped parsley. Serve with mashed potatoes or boiled rice (see page 154).

Serves 4

Braised Shoulder of Lamb with Herb Stuffing

Ingredients

1 shoulder of lamb
Olive oil
Salt and freshly ground black
pepper
Lemon juice
Flour
2 level tablespoons butter
6 tablespoons dry white wine
6 tablespoons chicken stock

Ingredients

½ lb (225g) boneless lean pork
¼ lb (100g) bacon, trimmed of
rind
1 Spanish onion,
finely chopped
4 level tablespoons butter
½ lb (225g) spinach, chopped
2 level tablespoons finely
chopped parsley
2 level tablespoons finely
chopped tarragon
¼ level teaspoon dried
oregano
2 eggs, beaten
Salt and freshly ground black
pepper
Freshly grated nutmeg

1 Have your butcher bone and trim a shoulder of lamb ready for rolling. Do not have him roll this.

2 Brush lamb with olive oil and sprinkle with salt and freshly ground black pepper, to taste. Sprinkle with lemon juice.

3 Preheat oven to slow (325°F/170°C/ Mark 3).

4 Spoon Herb Stuffing (see below) on meat; roll up and sew up with fine string. Dust the lamb roll with flour.

5 Melt butter and 2 tablespoons olive oil in an oval heatproof casserole; brown stuffed shoulder of lamb on all sides over a medium heat; add dry white wine and chicken stock; cover casserole; transfer to preheated oven and cook for 1½–2 hours, basting from time to time with pan juices.

Herb Stuffing

1 Put lean pork and trimmed bacon through the mincer or process in a food processor.

2 Sauté onion until soft in butter. Add spinach and continue to sauté until spinach is well flavoured.

3 Add finely chopped parsley, tarragon, dried oregano, beaten eggs and salt and freshly ground black pepper and freshly grated nutmeg, to taste. Mix well.

Ragoût of Lamb à la Provençale *(Illustration, page 130)*

1 Cut lamb into 1½-inch (3½ cm) cubes and season generously with salt and freshly ground black pepper, rubbing seasoning well into meat with your fingers. Reserve bones and trimmings for stock.

2 Combine meat in a porcelain bowl with marinade ingredients and marinate in this mixture, turning from time to time, for at least 8 hours.

3 Drain meat (reserving marinade juices and vegetables) and season again with salt and freshly ground black pepper.

4 To make stock: place bones and trimmings in a baking tin; moisten with olive oil and brown in a hot oven, turning bones from time to time. Place bones and pan juices in a large heatproof casserole with marinade vegetables and cook over a high heat, stirring constantly, until vegetables are browned. Dust with flour and continue to cook for 5 more minutes. Add tomato purée, mashed garlic, well-flavoured stock, leeks, celery, parsley, bay leaf, thyme, rosemary and sage. Simmer gently for 1½ hours, adding a little more liquid if necessary. Strain stock through a fine sieve; allow to cool, remove fat; dot with butter and reserve.

5 To cook lamb: heat 3 level tablespoons butter in a heatproof thick-bottomed casserole until it sizzles; place all lamb pieces in casserole and sauté over a reasonably high heat until lamb is golden on all sides; place casserole in a preheated moderate oven (350°F/180°C/Mark 4) and simmer gently for 1 hour, or until lamb is almost tender. Transfer lamb to a clean casserole and keep warm in a low oven.

6 Add strained stock to casserole in which you have cooked lamb cubes and cook over a high heat, stirring in all the crusty bits from the sides of the pan, until sauce is reduced to half the original quantity. Add remaining 2 tablespoons butter, diced, and whisk until sauce is smooth. Correct seasoning and pour over lamb pieces. Bring to the boil; reduce heat and simmer gently for 30–40 minutes, or until tender. Serve immediately garnished with black olives, sliced cooked carrots, glazed button onions and button mushrooms, and sprinkled with finely chopped tarragon and parsley.

Serves 4 – 6

Ingredients

3 lb (1.3 kg) young lamb taken from shoulder and leg

Salt and freshly ground black pepper

5 level tablespoons butter

MARINADE

2 Spanish onions, finely chopped

6 carrots, finely chopped

3 tablespoons olive oil

¾ pint (4½ dl) dry white wine

STOCK

Bones and trimmings from lamb

3 tablespoons olive oil

Marinade vegetables

1 level tablespoon flour

2–3 level tablespoons tomato purée

2 cloves garlic, mashed

½ pint (3 dl) well-flavoured stock

2 leeks, white parts only

2 stalks celery

4 sprigs parsley

1 bay leaf

1 sprig thyme

1 sprig rosemary

4 sage leaves

Butter

GARNISH

24 black olives

4 carrots, peeled, sliced and simmered in butter with 2 strips of orange peel

12 button onions, simmered in butter and lemon until tender

12 button mushrooms simmered in butter and stock until tender

1 level tablespoon finely chopped tarragon

1 level tablespoon finely chopped parsley

Red Wines of the Loire

One of my favourite summer excursions is a leisurely trip through the Loire, stopping off in each of the little villages to visit the local *châteaux* and taste the local wines. The red wines are my particular favourites here because they are soft and gentle, not harsh on the tongue, and definitely not 'drunk-making'. For example, Bourgueil, a light delicate red wine, which is softer than a Beaujolais, and yet with a certain firmness to it. It has a roundness and what the French call a 'purple robe', because it is almost purple in colour.

White Wines of the Loire

The white wines of the Loire – better known than the reds – are delightfully crisp and light. Try pale, golden Muscadet with its faint, fruity sharpness of flavour, as the perfect accompaniment for fresh oysters and seafood. Serve pale, green-tinted Sancerre on its own as an aperitif or as a first course wine for party lunches. But the most famous white wine of the area is undoubtedly Pouilly-Fumé, full-bodied and slightly drier, with almost a smoky taste. Serve it with salmon, salmon trout and light chicken and veal dishes.

Cooking au Gratin

The term *au gratin* (from the French verb *gratiner*: to brown) applies to oven-cooked dishes – macaroni, noodles, *gnocchi*, meats, fish and vegetables – which are baked in shallow, heatproof *gratin* dishes, usually covered with a sauce, sprinkled liberally with breadcrumbs, dotted with butter and browned in the oven or under the grill until a crisp *gratin* coating forms. Cooking *au gratin* is associated in most people's minds with cheese, but although dishes *au gratin* often contain cheese, this is not an essential ingredient.

In order that there may be plenty of the characteristic crisp, golden brown top, a shallow heatproof dish is used, hence the familiar term, '*gratin* dish'.

When browning in the oven, it is wise to set the dish in a pan half full of water. This prevents the sauce from spoiling or separating.

Left-overs – poached fish, chicken or turkey and sliced hard-boiled eggs – make an excellent luncheon or supper dish when cooked *au gratin*.

Left *Most vegetables can be gratinéed. Perhaps the most famous of these is Gratin Dauphinois: thinly sliced new potatoes and grated cheese, browned in the oven until smooth and flavourful, with a crisp golden crust.*
Near left *Gratin of Baby Turnips is a modern version.*
(Recipes, pages 140 and 141)

Fish and shellfish

Gratins can be made with either raw fish or leftovers. The most common raw *gratins* are made of whole fish, fish fillets or fish steaks. These can be sautéed in butter or poached in a little concentrated fish stock for a few minutes. They are then covered with a sauce *duxelles* (finely chopped mushrooms, onion and parsley, sautéed until smooth in butter) or a well-flavoured cream or cheese sauce, then sprinkled with freshly grated breadcrumbs and Parmesan cheese. Or, a little sauce Béchamel (see page 59) or velouté sauce (see page 30) may be poured around the fish before it is dotted with butter and sprinkled with chopped parsley, mushrooms, shallots and cheese.

Vegetables

Most vegetables can be *gratinéed*. Perhaps the most famous of these is *gratin dauphinois* (thinly sliced new potatoes, cream and grated cheese, browned in the oven until smooth and flavourful, with a crisp golden crust), a wonderful accompaniment to steaks and roasts (see opposite). *Gratin savoyard* exchanges beef stock for cream in an equally delicious variation of this great dish. Try adding diced celery, finely chopped onions or shallots, or a hint of garlic to this basic recipe. You will be delighted with the result.

Larousse Gastronomique (published in the United Kingdom by Paul Hamlyn) talks of a delicious *gratin languedocien* of peeled and sliced aubergines and tomato halves sautéed in olive oil and then placed in alternate layers in a buttered baking dish. The vegetables are covered with a mixture of fresh breadcrumbs and finely chopped garlic and parsley, sprinkled with olive oil (or dotted with butter), brought to the boil on the top of the stove and then baked slowly in the oven till the top is crisp and well browned.

Other vegetables – French beans, broccoli, endive, celery, leeks, onion and marrows – can be *gratinéed* in a similar fashion.

Gratin of Baby Turnips or Carrots *(Illustration, page 139)*

Ingredients

1½ lb (675g) small French turnips, or baby carrots
Butter
1 egg
¼ pint (1½ dl) double cream
8 level tablespoons freshly grated Gruyère cheese
4 level tablespoons freshly grated Parmesan cheese
Salt and freshly ground black pepper

1 Peel or scrape turnips (or carrots) and slice them very thinly (about 1/16th-inch (⅛ cm) thick). Rinse thoroughly and leave to soak in a bowl of cold water for 15 minutes.

2 Select a shallow ovenproof dish about 9 x 5 inches (22½ x 12½cm). Grease with 1 level tablespoon butter.

3 Preheat oven to very slow (300°F/150°C/Mark 2).

4 Drain turnip (or carrot) slices and dry them thoroughly with a cloth or absorbent paper.

5 Whisk egg and cream together until well blended.

6 Arrange a quarter of the turnip (or carrot) slices in the dish in overlapping rows; pour over 2 level tablespoons egg and cream mixture; sprinkle with 2 level tablespoons Gruyère cheese and 1 level tablespoon Parmesan cheese; dot with 1 level teaspoon butter; and, finally, season to taste with salt and freshly ground black pepper.

7 Repeat layers exactly as above, making four in all, and ending with grated cheese and butter.

8 Bake *gratin* for 1 hour 20 minutes, or until vegetables feel tender when pierced with a sharp skewer and are golden and bubbling on top. Allow to 'settle' for a few minutes before serving.

Note: if top browns too quickly, cover with a sheet of foil.

Serves 4

Gratin Dauphinois *(Illustration, pages 138 and 139)*

1 Peel and slice potatoes thinly and soak in cold water for a few minutes. Drain and dry thoroughly with a clean tea towel.

2 Butter a shallow fireproof casserole or deep *gratin* dish.

3 Place a layer of sliced potatoes on bottom of dish in overlapping rows; pour over a quarter of the cream, sprinkle with 2 level tablespoons grated cheese (mixed Gruyère and Parmesan),

dot with butter and season to taste with salt and freshly ground black pepper. Continue this process until dish is full, finishing with a layer of grated cheese. Dot with butter and cook in a moderate oven (350°F/180°C/Mark 4) for about 1 hour, or until potatoes are cooked through. If top becomes too brown, cover with aluminium foil. Serve very hot.

Serves 4

Ingredients
1½ lb (675g) new potatoes
Butter
¼ pint (1½ dl) double cream
8 level tablespoons freshly grated Gruyère cheese
4 level tablespoons freshly grated Parmesan cheese
Salt and freshly ground black pepper

Creamed Eggs au Gratin

1 Melt 2 level tablespoons butter in a saucepan; add flour and cook until the roux just starts to turn golden. Add milk and cook, stirring constantly, until sauce is reduced to half the original quantity. Stir in double cream.

2 Add ½ pint (3 dl) of this sauce to sliced hard-boiled eggs; season to taste with a little salt and freshly ground

black pepper and pour into a heatproof *gratin* dish.

3 Combine the remaining sauce with the beaten egg; fold in whipped cream and spread over creamed egg mixture. Sprinkle with fresh breadcrumbs and freshly grated cheese; dot with butter and brown in a hot oven (450°F/230°C/Mark 8) or under the grill.

Serves 2

Ingredients
4 hard-boiled eggs, sliced
Butter
2 level tablespoons flour
¼ pint (1½ dl) milk
¼ pint (1½ dl) double cream
Salt and freshly ground black pepper
1 egg, beaten
2 level tablespoons whipped cream
Fresh breadcrumbs
Freshly grated cheese

Gratin of Scallops and Leeks

1 Remove scallops from their shells. Wash them in cold running water to rid them of sand and trim. Drain and dry carefully.

2 Separate the white section of each scallop from the orange coral and cut in half.

3 Clean leeks and plunge into boiling salted water; when water comes to the boil again, cook for 3-5 minutes, according to size of leeks. Leeks should still be firm. Drain. Press dry with a clean kitchen towel to remove excess moisture.

4 Cut leeks into 1-inch (2½ cm) pieces and arrange in the bottom of a well-buttered *gratin* dish.

5 Arrange coral and sliced scallops on top of leeks. Moisten with double cream and season generously with salt, freshly gound black pepper, cayenne pepper and grated nutmeg, to taste. Spoon over melted butter and cook in a hot oven (450°F/230°C/Mark 8) for 7-10 minutes. Serve immediately.

Serves 4-6

Ingredients
16 scallops
1¼ lb (550g) leeks
Salt
Butter
8 tablespoons double cream
Freshly ground black pepper
Cayenne pepper
Grated nutmeg

Cooking en Papillote

Cooking *en papillote* is not as difficult as it sounds. It is only half-cooking really, for when you enclose an ingredient in a *papillote* it is already half-cooked, or has at the very least been 'seized' in hot fat before being folded into the little parcel of paper, foil or parchment which gives this process its name.

There is nothing magic about this *haute cuisine* phrase: a *papillote* is just a piece of thin, strong paper or aluminium foil, about $8\frac{1}{2} \times 11$ inches ($21 \times 27\frac{1}{2}$ cm) cut into an oval or heart shape, greased with olive oil or butter and folded to enclose the ingredient to be cooked.

Cooking *en papillote* is not only colourful but gastronomic, for the ingredient cooked in this way simmers gently in its own juices, hermetically sealed, so that it loses none of its special flavour and aroma. It is almost always necessary to colour the ingredient to be cooked in butter or olive oil before enclosing it in its casing, but it is important not to cook it too much in the process or you will lose the advantages and virtues of this exciting cooking method.

Nothing adds more glamour to a meal than individual servings of trout, *rouget* or sole, veal cutlets, veal chops, or fat slices of salmon or turbot, first coloured in a little butter or olive oil and seasoned with freshly ground black pepper, salt, fresh herbs and chopped shallots and mushrooms, then enclosed in their prepared paper cases, fried for a moment in hot oil to colour and puff the cases, and cooked in the oven to succulent and savoury goodness. Serve your *papillotes* in their puffed paper shells and let your guests cut them open at the table with a knife. Aluminium foil cases are cooked in the oven only.

To cook en papillote:

1 Cut paper, parchment or foil in oval or heart shapes large enough to enclose, when folded, the food to be cooked.

2 Brush the insides of the shapes with melted butter or olive oil.

3 Sauté the food for a few minutes to colour it before placing on shapes.

4 Place food on bottom half of shape; add butter and aromatics – finely chopped onion, shallot and mushrooms – or a *julienne* of lightly poached vegetables; season to taste with salt and freshly ground black pepper.

5 If *papillote* is paper or parchment: fold shapes and crimp edges together and puff up shells by frying for a minute or two in hot oil in a frying pan. Then put shells on a baking sheet in the oven (at 375°F/190°C/Mark 5) where they will keep their puffed up appearance while the ingredients continue to cook.

If *papillote* is foil: fold shapes and seal edges well by crimping them together. Put shells on a baking sheet in the oven where the food will continue to cook.

Saumon en Papillote. Cooking en papillote *is not only colourful but gastronomic, for the ingredient cooked in this way simmers gently in its own juices, hermetically sealed, so that it loses none of its special flavour and aroma. (Recipe, page 144)*

Saumon en Papillote *(Illustration, pages 142 and 143)*

Ingredients

2 thick salmon steaks
Salt and freshly ground
  black pepper
Butter
16 thin strips of carrot,
  3 inches (7½ cm) long
16 thin strips of cucumber,
  3 inches (7½ cm) long
Groundnut oil
16 strips of spring onion
  (green parts only),
  3 inches (7½ cm) long
4-6 fresh tarragon leaves
4 tablespoons dry white wine
2 tablespoons reduced
  chicken stock (see note)
Sauce Hollandaise (see page
  63) or fresh lemon wedges

1 Season salmon steaks with salt and freshly ground black pepper and sauté steaks in 6 level tablespoons butter until seared on both sides. Remove from heat. Cool.

2 Add strips of carrot and cucumber to pan and sauté vegetables for 5–8 minutes, or until vegetables are just crisp, stirring constantly with a wooden spoon to prevent them from browning or sticking to the pan. Season with salt and freshly ground black pepper, to taste. Remove from heat. Cool.

3 Cut 4 large oval sheets of greaseproof paper, approximately 7 x 11 inches (17½ x 27½ cm). Brush paper ovals on one side with groundnut oil. Place 2 paper ovals, oiled side up, on working surface; place half the carrot and cucumber strips in the centre of each oval. Then place a salmon steak on top of vegetables. Arrange half the spring onion strips in cavity of each steak and top each steak with 2 thin slices of butter and 2–3 fresh tarragon leaves. Add 2 tablespoons dry white wine and 1 tablespoon reduced chicken stock for added flavour.

4 Close the *papillotes* by placing the remaining paper ovals, oiled side down, over the salmon and vegetables, and crimping the edges of the paper ovals together carefully, making sure that each *papillote* is well sealed.

5 Oil a baking tray with groundnut oil and put it into a moderate oven (375°F/ 190°C/Mark 5) for 5 minutes; place the *papillotes* on the heated tray; brush with groundnut oil and cook for 20 minutes.

6 To serve salmon steaks: bring *papillotes* to the table and open each *papillote* with a pair of sharp scissors or a very sharp knife. Place each salmon steak on a heated dish; surround with vegetable strips; spoon over fish juices and serve immediately. Accompany with sauce Hollandaise or fresh lemon wedges.

Note: to reduce chicken stock, cook 8 tablespoons well-flavoured chicken stock in a small saucepan until it is reduced to a quarter of the original quantity.

Serves 2

Rouget en Papillote

Ingredients

4 small rougets, 4–5 oz
  (100–150g) each
Olive oil
Salt and freshly ground black
  pepper
4 bay leaves
4 thin slices bacon, grilled
Fat or oil, for frying
4 slices lemon
4 anchovy fillets

SAUCE

4–5 egg whites
½ pint (3 dl) double cream
4–5 anchovy fillets, mashed
Salt and freshly ground black
  pepper
Freshly grated nutmeg

1 Sprinkle fish with olive oil; season to taste with salt and freshly ground black pepper; place 1 bay leaf on one side of fish and a thin slice of grilled bacon on the other side.

2 Cut 4 pieces of greaseproof paper, approximately 8½ x 11 inches (21 x 27½ cm); fold each piece in half and cut into 'heart' shape. Open; brush with olive oil and place prepared fish, bay leaf and bacon on one half. Fold paper shape over and seal edges well by crimping them together.

3 Sauté *papillotes* in deep fat or oil for about 18 minutes.

4 To make sauce: beat egg whites until stiff; whip cream; combine the two and add mashed anchovy fillets and salt and freshly ground black pepper and grated nutmeg, to taste. Cook over simmering water, stirring constantly, until sauce is just heated through. Strain and keep warm.

5 When *papillotes* are cooked, arrange them on a serving dish; open each carefully; decorate *rougets* with a slice of lemon and an anchovy fillet. Serve with sauce.

Serves 4

Caneton en Papillote

1 Cut each duck into quarters, reserving livers; place in a roasting pan; season to taste with salt and freshly ground black pepper and roast for about ½ hour in a moderate oven (375°F/190°C/Mark 5) until half cooked. Allow to cool and then bone duck pieces.

2 Put shallots, duck livers, garlic, chopped parsley, chervil and dried thyme through the finest blade of your mincer twice. Combine with Dijon mustard and dry white wine in a saucepan and bring slowly to the boil. Thicken with a little *beurre manié* (made with 1 level tablespoon each flour and butter) and 'finish' sauce by beating in 2 level tablespoons butter.

3 Cut 16 heart shapes out of sheets of white paper, each one big enough to enclose one portion of duck; place paper 'hearts' on table in pairs and brush lightly with melted butter. Place a little sauce on buttered side of one of each pair of 'hearts'; place a boned portion of duck on the sauce; cover with sauce. Top with other paper 'hearts', butter side down; roll and pinch edges together very firmly.

4 Bake *papillotes* in a preheated moderate oven (375°F/190°C/Mark 5) for about 20 minutes. Serve with remaining sauce in a sauceboat.

Serves 8

Ingredients
2 ducks (about 2¼ lb (1 kg) each)
Salt and freshly ground black pepper
8 shallots
4–6 cloves garlic
4 level tablespoons chopped parsley
4 level tablespoons chopped chervil
2 level teaspoons dried thyme
1 level tablespoon Dijon mustard
½ bottle dry white wine
1 level tablespoon flour
Butter

Vitello al Cartoccio (Italian Veal Chops in a Paper Case)

1 Sauté sliced mushrooms in 2 level tablespoons each butter and olive oil in a large heavy-bottomed frying pan for 3 minutes, stirring constantly. Add diced tomatoes, strips of ham, oregano, salt and freshly ground black pepper to taste, and cook for a minute or two more.

2 Add dry white wine; bring to the boil; lower heat and simmer for 10 minutes.

3 Season veal chops with salt and freshly ground black pepper. Heat 2 tablespoons olive oil in a large clean frying pan and sauté chops until they are brown on both sides.

4 Cut 4 pieces of parchment paper large enough to contain veal chops. Brush paper on both sides with olive oil. Place 1 veal chop in the centre of each piece of oiled paper and cover with the sauce. Sprinkle with finely chopped parsley and anchovy and grated lemon rind and fold over paper, sealing edges well.

5 Place veal packets on a baking sheet; bake in a preheated moderate oven (375°F/190°C/Mark 5) for 20 minutes, or until chops are tender.

Serves 4

Ingredients
4 veal chops, 1-inch (2½ cm) thick
8–12 button mushrooms, thinly sliced
2 level tablespoons butter
Olive oil
4–6 ripe tomatoes, peeled, seeded and diced
2 slices cooked ham, cut in matchstick-length strips
¼ level teaspoon dried oregano
Salt and freshly ground black pepper
4 tablespoons dry white wine
2 level tablespoons finely chopped parsley
2 level tablespoons finely chopped anchovies
Grated rind of ½ lemon

Success with Vegetables

Vegetables are a very important part of our diet as far as nutrition and vitamin content are concerned. In addition to tasting better, well prepared vegetables retain more of these important nutrients and vitamins than those soaked in water. The key to successful vegetable cookery is a minimum of water and cooking time in order to retain maximum flavour and texture. To me the overcooking of vegetables is the eighth deadly sin . . . and should be punished accordingly.

So, do *not* drown vegetables in water. Instead, cook them in a little butter or olive oil, with just enough water, chicken stock, white wine or even steam to bring out their delicate flavours and textures. And serve them slightly crisp, not reduced to a pulpy, colourless mass.

Of course, the care and selection of your vegetables are of the utmost importance. Cooks who have their own kitchen gardens are to be envied, for new potatoes brought in fresh from the garden, peas picked an hour before serving, tomatoes still warm from the vine, all add so much to the savour of good eating. But if this is not the case – and it rarely is today – great care must be exercised when shopping. Select vegetables that are crisp, fresh-looking and colourful. No amount of cooking and attention will revive limp, tired vegetables. They will have lost their texture and a great deal of their flavour and most of their goodness.

Don't peel vegetables unless it is absolutely necessary. It *is* true that most of the goodness is right under the skin, or in the skin itself. I usually wash vegetables with a stiff vegetable brush, or, in the case of mushrooms, tomatoes and very new potatoes, I just wipe them with a damp cloth. They are then stored in plastic bags or boxes in the refrigerator to keep them crisp and fresh until ready to be used. Parsley and other herbs will keep green and fresh in this way for weeks.

Keep a vegetable juice jar. Then if any liquid is left over, unwanted, after cooking your vegetables, strain it into the jar, kept covered and in the refrigerator for this purpose. Vegetable juices preserved in this way are wonderful flavour additives for soups, sauces and stews.

Cooks who have their own kitchen gardens are to be envied. For new potatoes and sweetcorn brought in fresh from the garden, peas picked an hour before serving, tomatoes still warm from the vine, all add so much to the savour of good eating.
Opposite page *Three Hot Vegetable Purées.*
Above *Corn and Bacon Soufflé.*
(Recipes, pages 150 and 151)

Boiled New Potatoes

Ingredients

1 lb (450g) small new
  potatoes (20–24)
Coarse salt
Butter

1 Wash potatoes and either scrape them or peel them.

2 Put potatoes in a pan. Cover with cold water; add a small handful of coarse salt and bring to the boil.

3 Simmer potatoes until they feel soft when pierced with a fork. The small ones specified in this recipe will take about 18 minutes.

4 Drain well and serve with plenty of butter and coarse salt, to taste.

Serves 3–4

Country-fried Potatoes

Ingredients

2 lb (900g) large new
  potatoes
1 medium-sized onion,
  finely chopped
4 slices bacon, finely chopped
1 level tablespoon butter
3 tablespoons olive oil
Salt and freshly ground black
  pepper
2 level tablespoons finely
  chopped parsley

1 Scrub potatoes clean. Peel them and cut them into ¼-inch (½ cm) dice.

2 Sauté finely chopped onion and bacon in butter and 1 tablespoon olive oil until onion is golden, 4–5 minutes. Put aside.

3 In a large, heavy frying pan, heat remaining olive oil and sauté diced potatoes over a high heat until they are crisp and golden on all sides. Season to taste with salt and freshly ground black pepper.

4 Return sautéed onion and bacon to the pan; toss lightly to mix thoroughly with the potatoes and sauté for 1 minute longer. Serve immediately with finely chopped parsley.

Serves 4–6

Pommes Anna

Ingredients

1 lb (450g) new potatoes
4–6 level tablespoons
  softened butter
Salt and freshly ground black
  pepper

1 Peel and slice potatoes thinly and soak in cold water for a few minutes. Drain and dry thoroughly.

2 Butter a shallow heatproof copper or enamelled iron casserole with lid (French chefs use a special thick copper 'pommes anna' pan) and place in it a layer of sliced potatoes overlapping around sides of casserole. Spread potatoes with 1 level tablespoon softened butter and season to taste with salt and freshly ground black pepper.

3 Repeat layers as above, with a final spreading of butter on top.

4 Cover casserole and cook in a fairly hot oven (425°F/220°C/Mark 7) for 45 minutes to 1 hour, or until potatoes are brown around outside edges.

5 To serve: invert golden brown potato 'cake' on to a heated serving dish.

Serves 4

Buttered Glazed Vegetables

Ingredients

1 lb (450g) small white onions,
  small carrots or small
  turnips
4 level tablespoons butter
4 tablespoons chicken stock
1 level tablespoon sugar
Salt

1 Peel onions, carrots or turnips and place them in a small saucepan; cover with cold water and cook over high heat until water boils. Remove from heat and drain.

2 Replace blanched onions, carrots or turnips in saucepan; add butter and chicken stock; season with sugar and salt, to taste, and simmer over low heat until vegetables have absorbed the liquid without burning and have taken on a little colour.

Serves 4

Steamed Carrots

1 To prepare carrots: trim tops and tails of carrots. If they are young, you need only scrub or scrape them. Old carrots should be peeled. Average-sized carrots (about 8 to the pound (450g)) can be left whole or cut into quarters. Small carrots (the finger-thick ones that come about 25 to the pound (450g)) should be left whole.

2 To steam carrots: place carrots on a rack over boiled salted water and cover steamer tightly with a lid. Steam over rapidly boiling water for about 15 minutes for average-sized carrots. If you prefer them to be softer, cook for 4–5 minutes longer.

3 To serve: toss steamed carrots with melted butter and season to taste with salt and freshly ground black pepper and add a pinch of sugar to bring out their natural sweetness. Garnish with chopped parsley and serve immediately.

Serves 4

STEAMED GREEN BEANS

Cook as above, substituting a squeeze of lemon for sugar.

STEAMED BRUSSELS SPROUTS

Cook as green beans.

Ingredients
1 lb (450g) carrots
Salt
Melted butter
Freshly ground black pepper
Pinch of sugar
2 level tablespoons chopped
   parsley

The overcooking of vegetables is the eighth deadly sin. Garden-fresh vegetables should be simmered for minutes only in clarified butter; tiny new potatoes and haricots verts should be simmered for 5 minutes in boiling salted water before being tossed in butter.

Italian Cauliflower Sauté

Ingredients

1 medium-sized cauliflower
Salt
Lemon juice
4 tablespoons olive oil
Freshly ground black pepper
2 level tablespoons finely
   chopped parsley
Lemon quarters

1 To prepare cauliflower: cut off stem and remove green leaves from a medium-sized cauliflower. Soak the head for ½ hour in cold water to which you have added ½ level teaspoon salt and the juice of ½ lemon to free it from insects. Drain, and break or cut cauliflower into flowerets.

2 To cook cauliflowerets: fill a deep saucepan with enough water to cover cauliflowerets; add ½ level teaspoon salt and bring to the boil. Put cauliflowerets in boiling water and simmer gently for 8–10 minutes. Drain.

3 Heat olive oil in a frying pan; add drained cauliflowerets and sauté until lightly coloured. Season with freshly ground black pepper and lemon juice, to taste.

4 Serve cauliflowerets immediately garnished with finely chopped parsley and lemon quarters.

Serves 4

Sautéed Tomatoes

Ingredients

4–6 ripe tomatoes
2 tablespoons olive oil
2 level tablespoons butter
Salt and freshly ground black
   pepper
Finely chopped parsley
Finely chopped spring
   onions

1 Wipe tomatoes clean and slice cross-wise into even slices.

2 Combine olive oil and butter in a large frying pan and heat until butter is melted.

3 Add sliced tomatoes and sauté for a minute or two on each side, turning tomatoes carefully with a spatula. Season generously with salt and freshly ground black pepper; sprinkle with finely chopped parsley and spring onions and serve immediately.

Three Hot Vegetable Purées *(Illustration, page 146)*

Ingredients

1½ lb (675g) frozen peas or
   1 lb (450g) frozen
   sweetcorn or 1½ lb (675g)
   fresh carrots, thinly sliced
4 tablespoons chicken stock
4 level tablespoons butter
1–2 level tablespoons instant
   potato powder
1–2 tablespoons double
   cream
Salt and freshly ground black
   pepper
Lemon juice and sugar
   (optional)

1 Place frozen peas or sweetcorn or thinly sliced raw carrots in a pan. Add chicken stock and butter.

2 Bring to the boil; push a sheet of greaseproof paper down into pan on top of vegetables; reduce heat to moderate and simmer until very tender – about 5 minutes for frozen vegetables, 10–12 minutes for carrots.

3 Pour contents of pan into a blender. Add instant potato powder. Turn to maximum speed and blend for 2 minutes, stopping occasionally to scrape down sides of goblet with a spatula. (If a blender is not available, put vegetables through a mouli or rub through a sieve. In the case of sweetcorn, return contents of sieve to purée to give it bulk and texture.)

4 Return purée to pan. Beat vigorously with a wooden spoon over a moderate heat until purée is thoroughly hot again, adding enough cream so that it just holds its shape. Season to taste with salt and freshly ground black pepper. In addition, pea purée will be improved by a squeeze of lemon juice, sweetcorn purée by ½ level teaspoon sugar. Serve immediately.

Serves 4–6

Note: if you wish, you can reserve a tablespoon or two of the cooked peas or sweetcorn kernels for garnish. Carrot purée looks well with a garnish of finely chopped parsley.

150

Corn and Bacon Soufflé *(Illustration, page 147)*

1 To prepare soufflé dish: grease base and sides of a 2-pint (1.1-litre) dish generously with butter, and coat with a mixture of freshly grated Parmesan cheese and stale white breadcrumbs, shaking out excess.

2 Preheat oven to moderate (375°F/190°C/Mark 5).

3 To prepare soufflé mixture: melt 3 level tablespoons butter in a heavy pan, blend in flour and stir over a low heat for 2–3 minutes to make a pale roux. Remove pan from heat.

4 Bring milk just to boiling point in a separate pan. Add to roux very gradually, stirring vigorously to avoid lumps. When sauce is smooth, return pan to a moderate heat; bring to the boil, stirring constantly, and simmer 3–4 minutes longer until sauce is very thick and no longer tastes of raw flour.

5 Remove pan from heat and allow to cool slightly. Beat in egg yolks, one at a time; then turn mixture into a large bowl and allow to cool to lukewarm.

6 Sauté corn niblets with finely chopped onion in 3 level tablespoons butter until onion is transparent. Add mixture to cooling sauce and stir with a wooden spoon until thoroughly blended. Then stir in crumbled cooked bacon and season with salt and freshly ground black pepper, and a pinch each of freshly grated nutmeg and cayenne pepper.

7 Add a pinch of salt to egg whites in a large bowl and whisk until stiff but not dry. Fold into lukewarm sauce as quickly and as thoroughly as possible, using a metal spoon.

8 Pour mixture into prepared soufflé dish and level off with back of spoon.

9 Place soufflé in the oven. Reduce temperature to 325°F/170°C/Mark 3 and bake for 30–35 minutes, or until soufflé is well-puffed and golden-brown. Halfway through baking time, open oven door and sprinkle top of soufflé with freshly grated Parmesan cheese without removing it from the oven. Serve immediately.

Serves 4 – 6

Ingredients

SOUFFLÉ DISH
Butter
1 level tablespoon freshly grated Parmesan cheese
1 level tablespoon stale white breadcrumbs

SOUFFLÉ MIXTURE
Butter
3 level tablespoons flour
¾ pint (4½ dl) hot milk
4 egg yolks
1 medium can corn niblets
½ Spanish onion, finely chopped
¼ lb (100g) sliced bacon, cooked until crisp, then crumbled
Salt and freshly ground black pepper
Freshly grated nutmeg
Cayenne pepper
6 egg whites

TOPPING
1-2 level tablespoons freshly grated Parmesan cheese

Corn Fritter Pancakes

1 To make fritters: mix first 6 ingredients together in a bowl, and stir lightly until well blended.

2 Melt butter in a frying pan. Drop in batter, using 2 tablespoons for each small flat fritter, and spacing them well apart to allow them to spread. Fry over a moderate heat, turning fritters once only with a spatula, for about 3 minutes, or until golden brown on both sides.

3 Drain fritters on paper towels and serve hot.

Serves 4–6

Ingredients

1 12 oz (326g) can whole-kernel corn, drained
2 eggs, lightly beaten
½ level teaspoon salt
Freshly ground black pepper
1 level teaspoon sugar
3 level tablespoons plain flour
About 2 oz (50g) butter

Marinated Mushrooms

1 Trim stems and wash mushrooms thoroughly. Drain and place in a saucepan with just enough cold water to cover them; add lemon juice and salt, to taste, and bring gently to the boil. Lower heat and simmer for 10 minutes. Pour off liquids.

2 Combine remaining ingredients in an enamelled saucepan; bring to the boil; lower heat and simmer for 20 minutes. Pour marinade over blanched mushrooms and bring gently to the boil. Correct seasoning and serve immediately.

Ingredients

1 lb (450g) small mushrooms
Juice of ½ lemon
Salt
2 tablespoons wine vinegar
8 tablespoons olive oil
1–2 cloves garlic, crushed
Sprigs of thyme and parsley
1 bay leaf
5 peppercorns
10 coriander seeds

Cooking Pasta and Rice

Pasta, *polenta*, rice and beans – according to an old Roman friend of mine – were all God's gifts created specially to give pleasure and sustenance to the Italian poor. When I lived in Italy just after the war, in the teeming, narrow streets of old Rome around the Pantheon, we used to rely on these basic foods as the delicious mainstays of living. Wonderful dishes of spaghetti and *tagliatelle* served with a hundred delicate sauces were the order of the day; or *ravioli* or *tortellini*, tossed with thick, hot cream and freshly grated Parmesan cheese.

On feast days it was a steaming hot mound of golden *polenta* (yellow cornmeal simmered in boiling water and enriched with butter and Parmesan cheese) and stuck with dozens of diminutive grilled birds on little skewers, while on more simple occasions the boiled *polenta* was cooked and then sliced and grilled until golden, and served with a wild mushroom and tomato-flavoured sauce.

Then there were *risottos,* great dishes of Italian rice simmered gently with chicken stock subtly flavoured with saffron, onion and beef marrow and spiked with wild mushrooms or diced sweetbreads. *Risotto al frutti di mare*, saffron rice tossed with tiny nuggets of fresh seafood – lobster, prawns, shrimp or tiny squid – was a favourite, too.

Finally there were the great rustic casseroles based on red kidney beans, white *haricot* beans, large flat beans from Siena or the delicate pink-coloured beans called *borlotti*, soaked overnight and then simmered with olive oil and wine, finely chopped garlic and onion, fresh herbs and dried orange peel, and enriched with every kind of pork product imaginable. I liked, too, the Italian way with dried lentils, cooked in the same way, with olive oil and aromatics, and studded with fat slices of *cotechino* or *zampone* sausage, or a fine fat partridge.

It is my firm belief that no household today should be without its Italian-inspired emergency store, well stocked with these age-old 'convenience' foods that were well known even in the time of the Caesars.

Rice

In Northern Italy, rice and *polenta* are usually served in preference to pasta – but never the pallid plain boiled rice so often served in this country. Instead the Italians toss their rice with butter and finely chopped onion, until it begins to be translucent. Then they add rich chicken stock and simmer it gently until it is wonderfully tender – neither mushily soft nor unpleasantly hard, but *al dente*, just

Pasta is primarily a dough that is made to absorb a sauce. There are over a hundred different shapes and forms of pasta – and each has its own characteristic way of absorbing the sauce with which it is served. **Above** *Spaghetti and* conchiglie *with two imaginative new sauces: Spaghetti with Black Truffles and Conchiglie con le Verdure. (Recipes, page 159)* **Right** *Tiny shapes are used in soups and* brodi *only.*

like their spaghetti. And then they flavour it with the heady taste of saffron, the earthiness of wild mushrooms, or the crisp texture of golden fried pine nuts.

For the best results, rice should be cooked in only as much liquid as it can absorb, and special care is required when serving. The grains mash very easily, so they should never be stirred with a spoon, once cooked, but tossed lightly with a fork. Always serve your rice as soon as it is cooked.

Basic Boiled Rice

Ingredients
¾ lb (350g) long-grain rice
Salt
4 tablespoons lemon juice
Butter
Freshly ground black pepper

1 Bring a large pan of salted water (at least 4 pints (2.3 litres)) to the boil with lemon juice.

2 When water is bubbling vigorously, dribble in rice gradually through your fingers so that water does not come off the boil.

3 Stir once to dislodge any grains stuck to bottom of pan and boil rice for 15-18 minutes, or until tender but not mushy.

4 Drain rice in a colander and rinse thoroughly with hot water. Shake out all excess moisture. Toss rice gently with a little butter seasoned with salt and freshly ground black pepper. Serve immediately.

Serves 4 – 6

Simple Rice Pilaff

Ingredients
¾ lb (350g) long-grain rice
½ Spanish onion, finely
    chopped
Butter
¾ pint (4½ dl) well-flavoured
    stock
Thyme
Salt and freshly ground black
    pepper

1 Wash rice; drain and dry with a cloth.

2 Sauté finely chopped onion in 4 level tablespoons butter until a light golden colour. Add rice and continue to cook, stirring constantly, until rice is translucent. Pour in hot stock, and season to taste with thyme and salt and freshly ground black pepper.

3 Cover saucepan and place in a moderate oven (350°F/180°C/Mark 4) for 15-20 minutes, or until the liquid has been absorbed and the rice is tender but not mushy. Serve with additional butter.

Serves 4 – 6

Simple Saffron Rice

Ingredients
½ level teaspoon powdered
    saffron
6 tablespoons dry white wine
1½ pints (9 dl) hot chicken
    stock
¾ lb (350g) rice
Salt and freshly ground black
    pepper
4 level tablespoons butter
Finely chopped parsley

1 Dissolve saffron in white wine; add it to hot chicken stock and combine in a large saucepan with rice and salt and freshly ground black pepper, to taste. Cover pan and simmer until all the liquid is absorbed and the rice is tender (about 30 minutes).

2 Add butter to hot saffron rice; garnish with finely chopped parsley and serve immediately.

Serves 4-6

Risotto Provençal

Heat olive oil in a thick-bottomed saucepan and sauté finely chopped onion until golden. Stir in rice and cook, stirring continuously with a wooden spoon, until rice becomes translucent. Moisten with ½ pint (3 dl) chicken stock in which you have dissolved saffron and simmer gently, stirring from time to time, adding more chicken stock as the liquid is absorbed by the rice. Season to taste with salt and freshly ground black pepper. Continue cooking in this way until rice is cooked through, but not mushy. Serve with risotto sauce.

Ingredients
¾ lb (350g) long-grain rice
4 tablespoons olive oil
1 Spanish onion, finely chopped
¾ pint (4½ dl) chicken stock
¼–½ level teaspoon saffron
Salt and freshly ground black pepper

Sauce for Risotto

1 Sauté finely chopped onion and garlic in olive oil until transparent. Stir in dry white wine and peeled, seeded and chopped tomatoes. Season to taste with salt and freshly ground black pepper; add finely chopped parsley and simmer gently for 10 minutes.

2 Add diced green pepper and simmer for a further 10 minutes.

Serves 4

SAUCE FOR RISOTTO
Ingredients
4 level tablespoons finely chopped onion
2 cloves garlic, finely chopped
4 tablespoons olive oil
¼ pint (1½ dl) dry white wine
4 ripe tomatoes, peeled, seeded and chopped
Salt and freshly ground black pepper
4 level tablespoons finely chopped parsley
1 green pepper, seeded and diced

Pasta

Pasta is really just a dough that is made to absorb a sauce. It is a serious matter in Italy, however, with its own philosophy, its own traditions and its own shapes and sauces for each area. The many shapes arise from the fact that each different form has its own characteristic way of absorbing the sauces with which it is served.

Although there are over 100 different varieties (all members of the same family), they break down roughly into these groups: (1) ropes or strings – including spaghetti, *spaghettini* and *vermicelli*. The sauce for these is usually thick, since the pasta absorbs it from the outside only. (2) Tubes – hollow shapes like macaroni and *rigatoni*. These come in all sizes, and are best with a thinner sauce that flows through the centre hollows. (3) Flats or ribbons – *fettucine, tagliatelle* and all kinds of noodles and *lasagne* (4) Envelopes – *ravioli, tortellini, manicotti* and *cannelloni*, usually stuffed first and then cooked with a sauce. (5) *Pastine* – innumerable fancy shapes. The tiny ones are used in soups only.

Properly served in the Italian way, pasta is not fattening. Always serve it in flat soup bowls, designed to keep in the heat, with only ¼ lb (100g) pasta per person, delicately sauced – almost dry in fact. Never drown it in a calorie-laden 'soup'. Pasta has an almost magic quality of being able to absorb and magnify anything it is served with. Even a simple sauce of olive oil with finely chopped flat-leafed parsley and garlic becomes a thing of beauty when warmed and tossed with a bowl of piping hot spaghetti.

To cook pasta perfectly

Pasta should be cooked in a lot of boiling water. Add a tablespoon or two of olive oil to keep the pasta from sticking together or sticking to the bottom of the pan, and 2 good handfuls of salt to flavour it. And no, that is not a lot of salt to use, because we are going to rinse the pasta in a colander to rid it of excess starch.

Pasta has an almost magic quality of being able to absorb and magnify anything with which it is served. Here, one of my childhood favourites – a steaming dish of Spaghetti with Meatballs. (Recipe, page 158)

The Italians have a wonderful expression, *al dente*, which means that the pasta is firm and resistant 'to the tooth', not mushy, but still cooked through. The best way to see whether pasta is done is to pick up a piece on a fork and bite it.

Drain pasta by putting it through a colander, then run cold water through it to get rid of excess starch. If you don't do this, the strands are apt to stick together. Then have another pot ready with some butter or olive oil in it, so that you can toss your drained pasta in it to warm up again.

Fettucine alla crema

One of the easiest pasta dishes I know – and one of the most delicious – is *fettucine alla crema*, wide ribbon noodles with a wonderful creamy sauce made with double cream and egg yolks.

Shop-bought *fettucine*, or egg noodles, will be cooked *al dente* in 12–15 minutes. Home-made *fettucine* would take only 5–8 minutes to cook. One pound of *fettucine* (450g) is enough for 4 people as a first course. For the sauce, blend 2 egg yolks in a small saucepan with 6–8 tablespoons double cream, flavoured with freshly milled salt and freshly ground black pepper.

Toss drained *fettucine* in butter until it is heated through, adding more salt and freshly ground black pepper, then add the uncooked 'sauce' of egg yolks and double cream. Stir the egg yolks and cream into the pasta, allowing the heat to cook the egg yolks so that they become a rich sauce for the pasta. All you need to complete the dish is a generous amount of freshly grated Parmesan cheese.

Pasta con le verdure

Pasta con le verdure is a new light pasta dish that is currently taking pasta lovers in Italy and America by storm. The restaurants that serve it call it *primavera* for springtime, or *verdure* for green.

The recipe is simplicity itself: chop a clove or two of garlic finely, then simmer for a moment in butter and oil. Sauté thinly sliced raw courgettes in the garlic-flavoured butter for a minute only; add lightly poached green beans, poached cauliflowerets and broccoli flowerets. Just give them a toss or two in the butter before you add frozen peas, which you have defrosted in a cup of hot water.

Toss cooked pasta over a medium heat in equal quantities of butter and olive oil. Then, add the *verdure* and its pan juices. Toss well and sprinkle generously with freshly grated Parmesan cheese, a bit more pepper, and then a big piece of butter to show that you mean business.

Pasta alla Uovo (Home-made Egg Pasta)

1 Sift 1 lb (450 g) flour and salt on to a pastry board. Make a well in the centre and into it put the eggs, the oil and 1 tablespoon cold water.

2 Work in the flour with the fingers of your right hand, until a firm dough is formed. Add a little more water if necessary to make dough hold together as you knead, but remember dough will soften quite a lot after kneading.

3 Knead the dough until very smooth and elastic. This will take 10–15 minutes.

4 Cover dough with an up-turned bowl and leave to relax at room temperature for 30 minutes to 1 hour. This makes it easier to roll.

5 Divide the dough into 3 pieces. Lightly flour a board and roll out each piece of dough as thinly as possible. The thinner the better. Roll up each sheet of thin dough into a long roll, then cut the roll crosswise into strips. The strips can then be gently unfolded and cut to the correct lengths.

This amount of dough makes 1 lb (450 g) homemade egg pasta. Tossed with a sauce or butter, it will serve 4 as a main course, 6 as a first course.

Fettucine

Sprinkle the dough lightly with sieved flour and cut into $\frac{1}{4}$-inch ($\frac{1}{2}$ cm) wide strips. Spread on a clean cloth – or hang over a broomstick suspended between the backs of two kitchen chairs – and let dry overnight. Cook in a deep pot of boiling salted water. Drain well and serve with a sauce or melted butter.

Tagliatelle

Proceed as above, but cut into $\frac{3}{4}$-inch ($1\frac{1}{2}$ cm) wide strips.

Cannelloni

Cut the dough into 4-inch (10 cm) squares. Do not dry the dough as above, but cook a few squares at a time in deep boiling salted water for 2 minutes. Remove with a perforated spoon and drop into cold water. Drain and dry on a clean kitchen towel.

Lasagne

Cut the dough into strips 6 x 2 inches (15 x 5 cm). Cook a few strips at a time in boiling salted water for 4 minutes. Drain and dry as above. Use as directed.

Ingredients

Flour
1 level teaspoon salt
4 eggs
1 tablespoon oil

Petula Clark's zest for life and youthful vitality always amaze me. Here we are putting the finishing touches to Pasta con le Verdure. (Recipe, page 159)

Tagliatelle alla Crema

Ingredients

1 lb (450g) tagliatelle
Salt
Butter
4 egg yolks
¼ pint (1½ dl) double cream
Nutmeg
Freshly grated Parmesan
    cheese

1 Bring 6-8 pints (1.7-2.3 litres) well-salted water to the boil in a large saucepan. Add *tagliatelle* and cook until tender but still firm.

2 Melt 2 oz (50g) butter in a large saucepan. Drain the pasta and, while it is still very hot, toss in the butter.

3 Beat the egg yolks with the cream and pour over the pasta; add a grating of nutmeg. Stir for a minute; remove from heat and add 2 oz (50g) more butter. The sauce and eggs should not begin to solidify. Serve with freshly grated Parmesan cheese and additional butter.

Serves 4

TAGLIATELLE ALLA CREMA CON TARTUFI BIANCHI
1 lb (450g) *tagliatelle*, cooked as above, tossed just before serving with 2 canned white truffles, thinly sliced.

TAGLIATELLE ALLA CREMA CON FUNGHI
1 lb (450g) *tagliatelle*, cooked as above, tossed just before serving with 6 oz (175g) thinly sliced button mushrooms which you have sautéed in butter.

TAGLIATELLE ALLA CREMA CON PROSCIUTTO E PISELLI
1 lb (450g) *tagliatelle*, cooked as above, tossed just before serving with 1 small packet of frozen peas, defrosted and sautéed in butter with diced *prosciutto* (Parma ham).

Italian Spaghetti with Meatballs *(Illustration, page 156)*

Ingredients

1 lb (450g) spaghetti
Salt
Freshly grated Parmesan
    cheese
Butter

MEAT BALLS

¾ lb (350g) finely chopped
    veal
½ lb (225g) finely chopped
    prosciutto (Parma ham)
2 slices bread, soaked in
    milk and shredded
1 clove garlic, finely chopped
2 tablespoons chopped parsley
Salt and fresh black pepper
1 egg, lightly beaten
Flour
4 tablespoons olive oil

SAUCE

1 Spanish onion, chopped
1 clove garlic, finely chopped
2–4 tablespoons olive oil
1 small can mushrooms,
    sliced
1 large can peeled tomatoes
6 tablespoons tomato pureé
1 bay leaf
1 small strip lemon peel
1 beef stock cube
Salt and fresh black pepper
1 tablespoon Worcestershire
    sauce

1 To make meat balls: combine meat, bread (soaked in milk and shredded), finely chopped garlic and parsley, salt and freshly ground black pepper and lightly beaten egg. Mix well and shape into small meat balls. Dredge meat balls with flour and brown on all sides in hot olive oil. Remove from pan.

2 To make sauce: sauté finely chopped onion and garlic in olive oil in a large, thick-bottomed frying pan until transparent. Add sliced mushrooms and sauté for a minute or two more. Then add peeled tomatoes, tomato purée, bay leaf, lemon peel and beef stock cube, and season to taste with salt and freshly ground black pepper. Simmer gently, covered, for 1 hour, stirring from time to time. Just before serving, stir in Worcestershire sauce.

3 Add meat balls to sauce and simmer gently for 20 minutes.

4 Cook spaghetti in boiling salted water until just tender. Drain.

5 Serve spaghetti with sauce and freshly grated Parmesan cheese and butter.

Serves 4

Spaghetti with Black Truffles *(Illustration, pages 152 and 153)*

1 Cook spaghetti in boiling salted water until just tender. Drain.

2 While spaghetti is cooking, make truffle sauce: slice canned black truffles as thinly as you can and sauté for a minute or two in butter with finely chopped garlic. This is not to 'cook' the truffles, but just to give them a little added flavour. Add truffle juice, Madeira and port and keep warm over a very low heat.

3 To serve: return drained spaghetti to a clean saucepan; add butter, and egg yolks mixed with double cream, and toss over a medium heat until spaghetti is warmed through. Add truffle sauce; season with salt and freshly ground black pepper, to taste. Sprinkle with finely chopped fresh herbs and serve immediately accompanied by freshly grated Parmesan cheese.

Serves 4

Ingredients
1 lb (450g) spaghetti
Salt
¼ lb (100g) butter
2 egg yolks
¼ pint (1½ dl) double cream
Salt and freshly ground black pepper
2–4 level tablespoons finely chopped fresh herbs
Freshly grated Parmesan cheese

TRUFFLE SAUCE
2–3 canned black truffles
4 level tablespoons butter
½ clove garlic, finely chopped
2 tablespoons truffle juice
2 tablespoons Madeira
2 tablespoons port

Pasta Con Le Verdure *(Illustration, pages 152 and 153)*

1 Wash and prepare vegetables, as below.

2 Cook broccoli and cauliflower in boiling salted water for 3–5 minutes. Drain and run under cold water. Cook asparagus and beans (or mange-touts) in boiling salted water for 3–5 minutes. Drain and run under cold water. Cook courgettes in boiling salted water for 3 minutes. Drain.

3 Melt 8 level tablespoons butter in a large saucepan; add garlic, finely chopped parsley, basil, nutmeg, freshly ground black pepper and chopped mushrooms and cook for 5 minutes.

Then add prepared vegetables and frozen peas and cook for 5 minutes longer.

4 Bring 1 large pot salted water to the boil. Add pasta of your choice and cook – *conchiglie* for 20 minutes, other pasta for 6–12 minutes, depending on the pasta. Drain.

5 Melt remaining butter and toss drained pasta in it. Add vegetables and cream and stir well, for 2–3 minutes, or until bubbling hot. Serve immediately with freshly grated Parmesan cheese and freshly ground black pepper.

Serves 6–8

Ingredients
1 small bunch broccoli
8 flowerets cauliflower
½ lb (225g) asparagus
½ lb (225g) green beans
2 medium-sized courgettes
Salt
10 level tablespoons butter
1–2 cloves garlic, finely chopped
1 level tablespoon finely chopped parsley
3–6 large fresh basil leaves, chopped (or ½ level teaspoon dried basil)
Pinch of nutmeg
Freshly ground black pepper
4 pieces dried mushroom, soaked and chopped
1 small packet frozen peas, defrosted
1½ lb (675g) very large shell macaroni (conchiglie, or pasta of your choice)
¼ pint (1½ dl) double cream
¼ lb (100g) freshly grated Parmesan cheese

To Prepare Vegetables for Pasta con le Verdure

Broccoli and Cauliflower: trim stem and remove outer leaves from broccoli and cauliflower; cut into flowerets, leaving 1-inch (2½ cm) stems. Wash and leave for half an hour in cold salted water to which you have added a little lemon juice.

Asparagus: remove stray leaf points from asparagus stems below the head. Trim stalks; scraping the lower ends with the back of a knife. If stalks are woody, break off the woody part – you will find that the stalk snaps off right at the point where the tender part begins. Trim broken edge of stalk with a knife. Cut asparagus into ½-inch (1 cm) pieces and put pieces into cold water as you prepare them.

Green Beans: top and tail beans; rinse in cold water and cut them into ½-inch (1 cm) pieces. *Courgettes:* slice thinly.

The Nine-Herb Salad of
Hintlesham is a salad in the
Elizabethan manner: sprigs of
fresh herbs and baby greens tossed in
a well-flavoured mustard
vinaigrette dressing. (Recipe,
page 163)

Salads

I know of no shop in the world other than Fauchon's in the Place de la Madeleine in Paris which has a greater variety of salads and salad herbs than I have growing in my kitchen garden at Hintlesham. I like to use as many fresh greens as I can, to ensure the utmost variety in my salads. Not just ordinary lettuce; young spinach leaves, chicory, endive, corn salad (mâche), dark Cos lettuce, Salad Bowl lettuce with its light green, crinkly leaves, and, of course, fresh herbs, all add immeasurably to the pleasure of salad-making.

For the purist, a salad evokes a beautiful vision of wonderful green leaves carefully dried, leaf by leaf, in a clean towel or in a salad basket or in one of those new machines that you just push down and the lettuce leaves dry by centrifugal force. I don't know why, but I prefer drying my salad greens by hand, perhaps because I always have since I was a very small boy. My job in the family, during the depression years, when we had no help in the house, was to dry the lettuce, leaf by leaf, with a clean kitchen towel. So easy to do.

Oscar Wilde once compared the making of a salad dressing to diplomacy. He said it really was only a question of how much oil you put with your vinegar. I like French olive oil, Italian olive oil or oil from Tunisia or Morocco. If your olive oil does not have that typical fruity olive taste, here is a trick. Just put 2 or 3 black olives in oil (not in a salt water solution) in your bottle of olive oil to give a wonderful fruity flavour to your dressing.

Making a salad dressing is really very easy: all we need is a level teaspoon Dijon mustard and 2 tablespoons wine vinegar. We don't put the olive oil in yet because mustard won't dissolve in oil; it has to dissolve first in the wine vinegar to a smooth consistency. Then we flavour the vinegar and mustard mixture with salt and freshly ground black pepper. Finally we add fruity olive oil. The perfect formula is 3 to 1 (3 parts olive oil to 1 part wine vinegar or lemon juice), or, if your vinegar

Opposite page *Valentina Cortese visited Hintlesham in a burst of Italian brio. Her glittering personality (she speaks English and French as fluently as her native Italian, and usually mixes all three in one splendid rush of words) brought great sparkle to our meals and to our filming. She proved to be as passionate about cooking as she is about everything else in life.*

is very strong, 4 parts oil to 1 part vinegar. I like to use red wine vinegar to give a nice healthy outdoors look to the vinaigrette. For a thicker dressing add an ice cube. We can add many many things to this dressing: chopped chives, or a combination of chopped basil, tarragon and chives, for example. Or we could make the dressing for Caesar's salad: just sprinkle a little freshly grated Parmesan cheese over the dressing, with garlic croûtons, finely chopped anchovies and a coddled egg (poached for 1 minute). Finely chopped anchovies, onion and fresh herbs make a very good salad dressing, too. And perhaps one of my favourite tricks is to add a bit of crumbled Roquefort cheese, chopped walnuts and fresh herbs to the dressing for a salad of spinach, watercress, corn salad and lettuce. It's really a peasant salad, which makes a very good first course.

Salads can be served as a first course – or even as a luncheon or supper dish on their own, if they are more substantial. Add sliced tomatoes, diced tuna fish, or sieved hard-boiled eggs. There's a whole world of salads, and each and every one is a delicious adjunct to good dining.

Tossed Green Salad

Ingredients
2 small heads lettuce
1 bunch watercress
Vinaigrette sauce (see below)

1 Wash lettuce leaves well in a large quantity of water.

2 Drain leaves well and dry thoroughly in a cloth or a salad basket so that there is no water on them to dilute the dressing.

3 Wash watercress and cut off stems. Shake dry. Remove any yellowed or damaged leaves.

4 To serve: pour vinaigrette sauce into salad bowl and arrange prepared lettuce leaves and watercress sprigs on top. At the table, give a toss to ensure that every leaf is glistening with dressing. Check seasoning and serve.   **Serves 4–6**

1 Add other salad greens in season – Cos lettuce, endive, chicory, *batavia*, young spinach leaves, watercress and French *mâche* (lamb's lettuce or corn salad).

2 Add finely chopped garlic and shallots to salad dressing.

3 Add orange segments and curry powder to salad dressing.

4 Add crumbled Roquefort cheese and chopped walnuts to salad dressing.

5 Add chopped peanuts, soy sauce and a dash of Tabasco to salad dressing.

6 Add 1 tablespoon each mayonnaise and double cream to salad dressing and sprinkle generously with fresh chives and fennel.

7 For crunch appeal, add diced celery, green pepper or fennel.

Eighteenth-century Dressing

Ingredients
1 small boiled potato, peeled
2 anchovy fillets
2 hard-boiled egg yolks
1 level teaspoon Dijon mustard
2 tablespoons wine vinegar
6 tablespoons olive oil
1–2 level tablespoons finely chopped onion
Salt and fresh black pepper

1 Pound boiled potato, anchovy fillets and hard-boiled egg yolks through a fine sieve into a bowl.

2 In a small bowl stir Dijon mustard into wine vinegar until well blended. Add olive oil, finely chopped onion and salt and freshly ground black pepper, to taste.

3 Pour over sieved ingredients and mix well. Add to Tossed Green Salad (see above) and toss well.

Cucumber Salad with Fresh Herbs

1 Peel and slice cucumber thinly – a mandolin cutter is best for slicing cucumber. Place cucumber slices in a glass bowl and toss with salt and freshly ground black pepper, to taste.

2 Prepare a dressing by beating half the wine vinegar and half the Dijon mustard until well mixed; add half the olive oil and salt and freshly ground black pepper, to taste, and beat again until they form an emulsion. Pour over cucumber slices; toss and chill for at least 30 minutes. Drain juices from cucumbers.

3 Make a second vinaigrette dressing with remaining wine vinegar, Dijon mustard and olive oil. Season to taste with finely chopped tarragon and chives. Pour dressing over salad and toss well.

4 Whip double cream until stiff. Add salt to taste and spoon over salad.

Serves 4–6

Ingredients
1 large cucumber
Salt and freshly ground black pepper
2 tablespoons wine vinegar
1 level tablespoon Dijon mustard
6 tablespoons olive oil
2 level tablespoons finely chopped tarragon
1 level tablespoon finely chopped chives
4–6 tablespoons double cream

Italian Tomato Salad

1 Peel tomatoes.

2 Wash Cos lettuce, discarding any yellowed or damaged leaves, and cut leaves into 1½-inch (3½ cm) strips. Shake dry and chill.

3 To make Italian dressing: combine wine vinegar, dry mustard and olive oil in a small bowl and mix well. Add finely chopped garlic and parsley, dried oregano, and salt and freshly ground black pepper, to taste.

4 When ready to serve: arrange peeled whole tomatoes and lettuce strips in a salad bowl; pour over dressing and toss well before serving.

Note: if tomatoes are too large, cut in half.

Serves 4–6

MEXICAN TOMATO SALAD
As above, but substitute guacamole dressing (see below).

Ingredients
8–12 whole small tomatoes
1 head Cos lettuce
2 tablespoons wine vinegar
½ level teaspoon dry mustard
6 tablespoons olive oil
1 clove garlic, finely chopped
2 level tablespoons finely chopped parsley
1 level teaspoon dried oregano
Salt and freshly ground black pepper

Nine Herb Salad of Hintlesham *(Illustration, page 161)*

1 Wash lettuces well. Drain well. Wash *mâche* carefully in a large quantity of water, snipping off root ends. Drain.

2 Cut fresh herbs – tarragon, basil, purple basil, *pourprier*, *roquette* and flat-leafed parsley – into tiny sprigs about 1-inch (2½ cm) long. Wash well. Drain.

3 Shake lettuces, *mâche* and herbs dry in a salad basket.

4 Arrange salad in a salad bowl. Pour over dressing; sprinkle with coarsely chopped fennel, chives and parsley and toss well.

Serves 4–6

Ingredients
1 salad bowl lettuce
1 Cos lettuce
Mâche (corn salad)
12 sprigs tarragon
12 sprigs basil
12 sprigs purple basil
12 sprigs pourprier (purslane)
12 sprigs roquette
12 sprigs flat-leafed parsley
Mustard-flavoured vinaigrette dressing (see above)
Coarsely chopped fennel
Coarsely chopped chives
Coarsely chopped parsley

Guacamole dressing

Cut in half 2 avocado pears and remove stones. Scoop out flesh with a sharp spoon; sprinkle with juice of ½ lemon and purée through a fine sieve.

Rub 1 medium-sized onion, grated, into avocado purée through the same sieve; season to taste with salt, cayenne pepper and a pinch of ground ginger, and gradually beat in 4 tablespoons of olive oil until mixture has consistency of mayonnaise. Chill before using.

Provençal Hors d'Oeuvre Salad

Ingredients

2 large green peppers
2 large sweet red peppers
6 firm ripe tomatoes
6 hard-boiled eggs
24 anchovy fillets
24 ripe olives

CAP D'AIL DRESSING

2 cloves garlic, finely
   chopped
1 level tablespoon each finely
   chopped parsley, tarragon,
   chervil and chives
6–8 tablespoons olive oil
3 tablespoons wine vinegar
Salt and freshly ground black
   pepper

1 Prepare *Cap d'Ail* dressing by combining finely chopped garlic and fresh herbs with olive oil, wine vinegar and salt and freshly ground black pepper, to taste.

2 To prepare peppers: wash and dry whole peppers; place under grill, as close to flames as possible. Cook, turning peppers continually, until skin on all sides has charred. Remove charred skin under cold water. Cut peppers into pieces lengthwise – 4–6 pieces to each pepper – and wash off seeds and excess fibre; drain on absorbent paper.

3 Slice tomatoes thickly and cover bottom of a large flat serving dish with slices. Sprinkle with a quarter of the salad dressing; add a layer of green pepper slices; sprinkle with salad dressing; add a layer of red pepper slices and sprinkle with dressing.

4 Shell eggs and slice into rings; cover red pepper slices with a layer of sliced eggs and pour over the rest of the dressing. Arrange anchovies in a latticework on top and place a ripe olive in the centre of each latticework square. Chill in the refrigerator for at least 30 minutes before serving.

Serves 4

Two fresh-tasting salads for summer : **Left** *Provençal Hors-d'Oeuvre Salad with Cap d'Ail dressing* **Right** *Spanish Appetizer Salad.*

Spanish Appetizer Salad

1 Peel tomatoes in the following manner: place each one on the end of a kitchen fork, and hold in boiling water for a minute or two (until skin of tomato begins to crack); remove from water and with a sharp knife gently peel skin from tomato. Cut in thick wedges.

2 Peel potatoes and cut into thick slices.

3 Peel and stone avocado pear and cut crosswise in thick slices. Brush slices with lemon juice to preserve colour.

4 Cut boiled pepper into thick strips.

5 Wash lettuce leaves well in a large quantity of water. They should be left whole, never cut. Drain well and dry thoroughly in a cloth or a salad basket so that there is no water left on them.

6 Line a salad bowl with lettuce leaves. Toss prepared vegetables lightly in French dressing and arrange in lettuce-lined bowl. Pour remaining dressing over salad and garnish with thinly sliced onion rings.

Serves 4–6

Ingredients
4 ripe tomatoes, peeled
4 new potatoes, boiled
1 avocado pear
Juice of 1 lemon
1 green pepper, seeded and boiled
1 head lettuce
¼ pint (1½ dl) French dressing (see page 161)
1 small onion, cut into thin rings

Pasta and Bean Salad

1 Cook macaroni in boiling salted water until tender. Drain, rinsing off excess starch with cold water.

2 Fry bacon until crisp. Crumble and set aside.

3 Make dressing by combining wine vinegar with dry mustard, salt and cracked peppercorns. Add olive oil, crumbled bacon, finely chopped onion, celery and parsley and mix well. Then add cooked, drained macaroni and drained beans. Toss until well mixed.

4 Just before serving, correct seasoning, adding a little more wine vinegar, olive oil and seasonings, if necessary.

Serves 4–6

Ingredients
1½ lb (675g) elbow macaroni
Salt
¼ lb (100g) bacon, sliced
3 tablespoons wine vinegar
1 level teaspoon dry mustard
1 level teaspoon cracked peppercorns
9 tablespoons olive oil
4 level tablespoons finely chopped onion
4 level tablespoons finely chopped celery
2 level tablespoons finely chopped parsley
1 can haricots blancs, drained

Opposite page *One salad to go. A portable picnic-hamper with everything for a super picnic salad meal—hard-boiled eggs, salad greens and vegetables, oils and vinegars and even a touch of Bordeaux mustard to give it zip. (Salad recipes begin on page 162)*

Japanese Salad

Ingredients

1 head lettuce
1 bunch watercress
1 bunch radishes
1 clove garlic, finely chopped
1 spring onion, thinly sliced

SHOYU DRESSING

2 tablespoons wine vinegar
2 tablespoons soy sauce
Dry mustard
6–8 tablespoons olive oil
Freshly ground black pepper

1 Wash and trim lettuce and watercress. Dry thoroughly. Trim radishes and slice paper-thin. Chill.

2 To assemble salad: arrange lettuce leaves in a salad bowl and spread watercress on top. Scatter thinly sliced radishes over this.

3 Make *shoyu* dressing by combining wine vinegar, soy sauce and mustard in a small bowl. Add olive oil and freshly ground black pepper, to taste.

4 Just before serving pour the dressing over the salad; sprinkle with finely chopped garlic and thinly sliced spring onion and toss until every ingredient glistens.

Serves 4–6

Provençal Salad Sandwich

Ingredients

4 rolls or 1 round loaf of
  bread
Olive oil
2 cloves garlic
8 lettuce leaves
4 large ripe tomatoes, sliced
1 small can pimento, drained
2 green peppers, seeded and
  sliced
2 hard-boiled eggs, sliced
Salt and freshly ground black
  pepper
Lemon juice
4 level tablespoons finely
  chopped parsley
16 small black olives
16 anchovy fillets

1 Slice rolls or bread in half lengthwise; pull out soft centre of rolls or bread with your fingers. Brush insides of crusts liberally with olive oil in which you have crushed garlic cloves.

2 Place 1 lettuce leaf on bottom half of each roll, or place a layer of lettuce leaves on bottom half of bread. Cover lettuce with tomato slices, canned pimento slices, green pepper slices and hard-boiled egg slices. Season with salt and freshly ground black pepper. Add lemon juice, to taste, to remaining garlic oil; add salt, freshly ground black pepper and finely chopped parsley.

3 Dribble dressing over sliced vegetables and eggs; garnish with black olives and anchovies; top with remaining lettuce leaves and cover with top half of rolls or bread.

4 Wrap rolls in foil, or cut round loaf into 4 wedges and wrap in foil; weight with a plate and chill for 1 hour before serving.

Serves 4

Mediterranean Fruit Salad

Ingredients

6–8 oranges
1 lb (450g) strawberries
1 lb (450g) white grapes
Ripe olives
Fresh mint

**HONEY AND LEMON
DRESSING**

1 tablespoon honey
2 tablespoons lemon juice
6 tablespoons olive oil
Salt and freshly ground black
  pepper

1 Peel oranges, removing all white pith, and slice into rings. Wash and hull strawberries. Wash grapes and remove stems. Combine fruits in a serving dish and chill.

2 To make honey and lemon dressing: stir honey into lemon juice and add olive oil and salt and freshly ground black pepper, to taste.

3 Just before serving, garnish fruits with ripe olives and a few sprigs of fresh mint and pour over honey and lemon dressing.

Note: this Old English salad dressing is excellent with sliced fresh fruits, or a combination of fruit and green salad, or with thickly sliced cucumbers and coarsely chopped mint.

Serves 6–8

Red Wines of Burgundy

Many of the great wines of France come from Burgundy, the area between Dijon in the north and Mâcon in the south. Just past Dijon begins the region known as the Côte d'Or – the golden slopes – divided into two rich wine-producing areas called the Côte de Nuits and the Côte de Beaune. The Côte de Nuits is made up mainly of vineyards producing red wine. As a matter of fact, Burgundy produces three times as much red wine as it does white.

Chambertin and **Gevrey-Chambertin,** like the other great wines of the Côte de Nuits, are full-bodied, round, rich red wines. Chambertin is known as the *grand seigneur* of Burgundy. First of all because of its nobility and its excellence, but also, I think, in deference to the memory of Napoleon, who loved this great wine.

The *commune* of Gevrey-Chambertin produces a range of very great red wines, of which 8 are classified as *Grands Crus* (Great Growths). The most famous of these are Chambertin, Charmes-Chambertin and Chambertin-Clos de Bèze. Apart from these *Grands Crus*, about 175,000 gallons of great red wines are entitled to be called Gevrey-Chambertin – still a marvellous wine, as it comes from right next door, but not as full-bodied and warm-textured a wine as the above.

Down the Great Wine Road from Gevrey-Chambertin we come to the village of **Morey-St-Denis,** whose most famous *Grands Crus* are Clos St-Denis and Clos de Tart. The wines are of a fine colour, full-bodied with a fine bouquet which develops with age. At **Chambolle-Musigny,** also three miles from Gevrey-Chambertin, the entire village is devoted to growing grapes. The vines are planted on all sides of the village and, indeed, on every available foot of space in between the houses. Chambolle-Musigny is a very scented wine of high flavour and fine colour. Near here too is the **Clos de Vougeot,** located in the smallest village in the Côte de Nuits, which produces a noble wine classed with those of Chambertin and Romanée as one of the finest wines in the whole of France. Clos de Vougeot, a 125-acre vineyard, is not owned by one person but by 50 to 60 different growers and smallholders, anyone of whom can call the wine they produce Clos de Vougeot. This might sound a little confusing, but all we have to remember is that Clos de Vougeot is one of the most prestigious Burgundies – a luscious and elegant red wine with a bouquet evocative of violets.

Two miles from Vougeot lies the tiny village of Vosne, where three ancient vineyards carry the name of **Romanée** to recall their ancient lineage, which goes right back to the Romans. These *Grands Crus* are La Romanée, Romanée-St-Vivant and Romanée-Conti, one of the most highly esteemed of all red Burgundies. The whole vineyard at Romanée-Conti measures only 4½ acres, producing about 500 to 600 cases of wine a year. One can see why its wines are so prized and consequently so expensive.

Perhaps my favourite wines in this region are the *Grands Crus* of Richebourg, Les Echézeaux and Les Grands Echézeaux, three noble wines of incomparable bouquet and softness of flavour which make them, to my mind, the most sumptuous and exciting wines of all Burgundy.

One of the first Burgundy wines that I enjoyed as a young man living in France, is **Nuits-Saints-Georges,** a simpler wine than the ones mentioned above, but a rich, lusty wine full of flavour, good to drink with a simple meal.

Pastries

Making pastry is child's play. After all, a good *pâte sablée* (rich shortcrust pastry) is just a combination of flour, butter, sugar and salt and a little cold water and egg yolk to hold it together. Yet the variations on this basic pastry mix – once you have acquired a little know-how – are limitless. I like to serve French savoury tarts as a perfect beginning to a special dinner, or as a main course for a summer luncheon or picnic. The basic pastry can be used for all kinds of savoury tarts and quiches – and, with a little more icing sugar added – for rich dessert tarts and flans.

The icing sugar is the 'catalyst' here – the secret ingredient that combines with all the other ingredients into a smooth, buttery, crumbly whole.

But remember: there is no guesswork when it comes to making perfect pastry. Use *scales and measuring spoons* for accurate measures; a *measuring jug* marked in fluid ounces – for all liquid measurements; a *wire pastry blender* to blend butter and flour quickly; and an *electric timer* to remind you when to take your pastry out of the oven.

Every good meal deserves a happy ending. Something just that much more exciting than a salad of fresh fruits or a fruit sorbet. Try French Raspberry Tart **(left)** *or Fresh Peaches cooked in Brouilly. (Recipes, pages 172 and 185)*

Always use French pastry tins with loose bottoms. Line with dough and bake according to instructions. Then remove fluted ring, leaving tart or flan invisibly supported on loose metal bottom. No need to serve tarts, flans and quiches in pastry tins any longer.

Fingertip pastry

My favourite kind of pastry for quiches and tarts is *pâté sablée,* a crumbly pastry which I call 'fingertip' pastry because it is so rich that you literally just press it together in the tart tin.

To make fingertip pastry you will need ½ lb (225g) sifted flour, 5 oz (180g) diced butter, 1 level tablespoon icing sugar (the secret ingredient that holds the whole thing together), a little salt to counteract the sweetness of the sugar, an egg yolk and a little iced water.

First, mix the diced butter, the sifted flour, the sugar and the salt with a pastry blender, or even more simply with two knives held scissor-fashion, so that the butter can be cut into the flour without the mix getting heavy or greasy. Cut the butter into the flour until the pieces are about pea size, then you can use your fingers to work the butter further into the flour, lifting your hands high, until the mixture resembles coarse sand.

Combine the egg yolk with an equal amount of iced water; mix well and add to the pastry in the bowl. Now, mix the dough with a spoon, as it will be a little more difficult to handle at this point. When the dough is well blended, roll into a ball; wrap it closely in a clean kitchen towel and put it in the refrigerator for 30 minutes so that it will mature and the flour will absorb the butter into one nice homogeneous mass. Fingertip pastry is as easy as that.

To roll out pastry

Flour the working surface so that the pastry will not stick to the surface, and flour the rolling pin too. Start rolling out the pastry, always rolling from the centre, turning the dough over occasionally so that the surface is always floured a bit on each side. When rolling out the pastry from the centre, try not to stretch it in any way, because if you stretch it – either in rolling it out or in fitting it into the pastry tin – you will find that when baked it pulls back again into its own original shape and leaves the sides of the pastry tin. If the pastry breaks apart or splits while you are handling it, don't worry, because fingertip pastry is so rich a mix with its icing sugar and egg yolk that you can patch it up in a second by just pressing it together with your fingers.

To line pastry tin with pastry

To line pastry tin with pastry, just roll the pastry gently over your rolling pin and lift it over the pastry tin. If you are using individual pastry tins, cut rolled out pastry into appropriately sized pieces to cover tins, leaving about 2 inches (5cm) to spare. Then ease the pastry gently over the pastry tin (or tins) and press it loosely down into the sides of tin (or tins) using a little too much pastry. Press it against the sides of the pastry tin (or tins) and up, until it is of the thickness required. Then roll your rolling pin quickly across the top of the tin (or tins) to cut off the excess pastry neatly.

Prick the base and sides of your pastry shell (or shells) all over with the prongs of a dinner fork and chill pastry for 30 minutes in the refrigerator to minimize the danger of it 'running down' the sides of the tin (or tins) when it is first put into the oven.

To bake pastry

A fairly hot oven is required for pastry. If it is not hot enough the butter will melt and run out before the starch grains in the flour have had time to burst and absorb it. If the oven is too hot, however, the pastry will burn before it has risen properly. When baking pastry, open and close the door as gently as possible and never more often than is absolutely necessary.

If pastry becomes too brown before it has cooked sufficiently, cover it over with a piece of foil or a double sheet of grease-proof paper that has been lightly sprinkled with water.

Italian Courgette and Bacon Tart

1 Preheat oven to 325°F/170°C/Mark 3.

2 Chop onion finely and sauté in olive oil with crumbled stock cube until onion is soft, stirring constantly so that it does not take on colour. Remove onion from pan with a slotted spoon and reserve.

3 Cut green bacon into ¼-inch (½ cm) slices and then cut each slice into 'fingers' about ¼-inch (½ cm) thick. Sauté in olive oil until golden. Remove from pan with slotted spoon and reserve.

4 Wash courgettes and cut off tops and bottoms. Slice courgettes as thinly as you can and sauté slices in remaining fats until lightly coloured. Season to taste with salt and freshly ground black pepper. Remove from pan with slotted spoon and reserve.

5 Combine eggs, cream and milk in a mixing bowl and mix thoroughly. Season generously with salt, freshly ground black pepper, cayenne pepper and freshly grated nutmeg.

6 Sprinkle 2 level tablespoons grated Gruyère cheese on the bottom of prepared pastry case. Combine sautéed onion, bacon and courgettes and spoon into pastry case; sprinkle with 2 level tablespoons grated Gruyère cheese and pour in egg and cream mixture.

7 Sprinkle with remaining Gruyère cheese and bake in a preheated oven (325°F/170°C/Mark 3) for 30–40 minutes or until the custard is set and golden brown.

Serves 6–8

Ingredients

1 9 or 10-inch (22½-25cm) fingertip pastry case, baked blind (see page 170)

FILLING

¼ lb (100g) green bacon
½ Spanish onion
2 tablespoons olive oil
½ chicken stock cube, crumbled
4–6 small courgettes
Salt and freshly ground black pepper
4 eggs
½ pint (3 dl) double cream
¼ pint (1½ dl) milk
Cayenne pepper
Freshly grated nutmeg
6 level tablespoons freshly grated Gruyère cheese

Curried Egg, Cheese and Onion Tart

1 Whisk egg yolks in a bowl.

2 Line a pastry tin with pastry. Prick bottom with a fork; brush with a little beaten egg and bake 'blind' in a hot oven (450°F/230°C/Mark 8) for 15 minutes.

3 Add cream to egg yolks and whisk; flavour to taste with salt and freshly ground black pepper, curry powder and grated nutmeg.

4 Sauté finely chopped onion and diced bacon in butter until onion is transparent.

5 Arrange diced cheese in pastry case. Spoon over sautéed onion and bacon and pour over the cream and egg mixture; bake in a slow oven (325°F/170°C/Mark 3) for about 30 minutes.

Serves 4 – 6

Ingredients

4 egg yolks
Fingertip pastry for 8-inch (20 cm) pastry tin (see page 170)
½ pint (3 dl) single cream
Salt and freshly ground black pepper
Curry powder
Freshly grated nutmeg
1 Spanish onion, finely chopped
¼ lb (100g) bacon, diced
2 level tablespoons butter
¼ lb (100g) Gruyère cheese, diced

Prawn and Lobster Quiche

Ingredients

PASTRY
½ lb (225g) plain flour
1 level tablespoon icing sugar
Generous pinch of salt
5 oz (150g) softened butter, diced
1–2 tablespoons iced water

QUICHE FILLING
¼ pint (1½ dl) double cream
¼ pint (1½ dl) milk
¼ pint (1½ dl) fish stock, or canned clam juice
4 eggs
½ small cooked lobster
¼ lb (100g) small Norwegian prawns
2 tablespoons Cognac
1 tablespoon lemon juice
Salt
Cayenne pepper

1 To make pastry: sieve flour, sugar and salt into a mixing bowl. Rub in softened butter a little at a time with the tips of the fingers until mixture resembles fine breadcrumbs. Do this very gently and lightly or mixture will become greasy and heavy. Add just enough iced water to make a good dough. Shape dough lightly into a flattened round, wrap in foil or plastic and put in refrigerator for at least 1 hour to ripen and become firm. If chilled dough is too firm for handling, leave at room temperature until it softens slightly. Then turn out on to a floured board and roll out in usual manner; place in a 9-inch (23 cm) pie tin and press out with fingertips.

2 Prick bottom of pastry shell with a fork; cover with a piece of foil; fill with dried beans and bake 'blind' in a pre-heated hot oven (450°F/230°C/Mark 8) for 15 minutes. Remove beans and foil. Allow pastry shell to cool.

3 Remove lobster meat from shell and dice. Place diced lobster and prawns in a dish and add Cognac, lemon juice and salt and cayenne pepper, to taste.

4 To make quiche filling: beat cream, milk, fish stock or clam juice and eggs with a whisk. Place diced lobster and prawns on the baked pastry shell. Pour the beaten egg mixture over the lobster and prawns.

5 Bake quiche in a slow oven (325°F/170°C/Mark 3) for 30 to 40 minutes, or until the custard is set and golden brown.

Serves 6–8

French Raspberry Tart
(Illustration, page 168)

Ingredients

1 9-inch (23 cm) fingertip pastry case, unbaked (see page 170)
Fresh raspberries, to cover
1 recipe crème pâtissière (see page 174)
1 recipe raspberry fruit glaze (see page 174)

1 To bake prepared pastry case: bake 'blind' in a hot oven (450°F/230°C/Mark 8) for 15 minutes. Reduce oven temperature to moderate (350°F/180°C/Mark 4) and bake for 30 minutes. If crust becomes too brown at edges, cover with a little crumpled foil.

2 Make *crème pâtissière*.

3 Make raspberry fruit glaze.

4 To assemble tart: half-fill baked pastry case with *crème pâtissière* and arrange raspberries in circles on top. Coat with raspberry fruit glaze. Serve chilled.

Serves 4–6

Orange Tart with Dates and Almonds

1 Prepare a 9-inch (22½ cm) pastry shell.

2 Bake pastry shell (see page 170).

3 Make *crème pâtissière*.

4 Peel 4 small oranges, removing all pith, and slice thinly. Arrange orange slices on top of the flan in an overlapping circle. Fill centre with finely chopped dates. Brush orange slices with a little sieved apple jelly or greengage conserve and sprinkle with slivered almonds.

Serves 4 - 6

My favourite recipes for pastry – shortcrust and fingertip – can be used for all kinds of savoury tarts and quiches, and, with a little more icing sugar added, for rich dessert tarts and flans as well. (Recipe for Fingertip Pastry, page 170)

Ingredients

1 recipe fingertip pastry (see page 170)
1 recipe crème pâtissière (see page 174)

ORANGE, ALMOND AND DATE TOPPING

4 small oranges
12 dates, pitted and chopped
Apple jelly or greengage conserve, sieved
Slivered almonds

Crème Pâtissière

Ingredients

¾ pint (4½ dl) milk
2-inch (5 cm) piece of vanilla
    pod, split
5 egg yolks
¼ lb (100g) castor sugar
2 level tablespoons plain
    flour, sifted
1 level tablespoon cornflour,
    sifted
Butter
Few drops of vanilla essence

1 Pour milk into a medium-sized pan and add split vanilla pod. Bring to boiling point over a low heat. Cover pan and put aside to infuse until needed.

2 In a bowl, whisk egg yolks with sugar until thick and light. Gradually whisk in flour and cornflour.

3 Fish vanilla pod out of milk and gradually pour milk into egg yolk mixture, whisking until well blended.

4 Pour mixture back into the pan and bring to the boil over a moderate heat, stirring constantly. Then simmer for 3 minutes longer, beating vigorously.

5 Remove pan from heat; beat in 1 level tablespoon butter and beat a little longer to cool the pastry cream slightly before adding the vanilla essence.

6 Put cream in a bowl and cover with a sheet of lightly buttered greaseproof paper to prevent a skin forming on top. Allow to become quite cold, then chill until required.

Fruit Glaze

Ingredients

½ pint (3 dl) apricot, raspberry
    or red currant jam or jelly
Kirsch

Add 4–6 tablespoons water to apricot jam and heat, stirring constantly, until liquid. Flavour to taste with kirsch.

Creamy Peach Pie

Ingredients

1 recipe fingertip pastry (see
    page 170)
2 lb (900g) peaches
Juice of ½ lemon
6 oz (175g) sugar
1 oz (25g) flour
¼ level teaspoon salt
¼–½ level teaspoon cinnamon
½ pint (3 dl) double cream

1 Prepare a 9-inch (22½ cm) unbaked pastry shell.

2 Bake 'blind' (see page 170).

3 Peel, core and thickly slice enough peaches to fill the shell. Put them in a large mixing bowl.

4 Combine lemon juice, sugar, flour, salt and cinnamon and add to peaches. Toss lightly and turn into pastry shell. Pour over double cream and bake in a hot oven (450°F/230°C/Mark 8) for 35–45 minutes, or until firm. Serve warm.

Serves 4–6

American Chocolate Tarts

Ingredients

6 individual baked pastry
    shells (see page 170)

CHOCOLATE CREAM

2 oz (50g) bitter chocolate
½ lb (225g) sugar
2 tablespoons cornflour
¼ level teaspoon salt
¾ pint (4½ dl) milk
2 eggs, well beaten
4 level tablespoons butter
½ teaspoon vanilla essence

DECORATION

½ pint (3 dl) double cream
2 oz (50g) icing sugar
½ teaspoon vanilla essence
Glacé cherries and angelica

1 To make chocolate cream: melt chocolate over hot water in the top of a double saucepan. Combine sugar, cornflour and salt in a bowl. Gradually stir in milk; then stir mixture into melted chocolate. Cook over boiling water, stirring constantly, for 10 minutes, or until thick. Pour hot mixture into well-beaten eggs, a little at a time, stirring after each addition. Return to top of double saucepan and cook, stirring occasionally, for 5 minutes. Remove from heat; add butter and ½ teaspoon vanilla essence.

2 Pour mixture into baked pastry shells.

3 Whip cream and blend in the icing sugar and vanilla essence. Decorate tarts with whipped cream, glacé cherries and angelica. Chill and serve.

Serves 6

Cakes

There is no branch of cooking where greater care and accuracy are required than in cake-making. I recommend strongly that if you are new to baking you should follow cake recipes carefully, without altering quantities or cooking times, until you have made the recipe at least twice. Then experiment as you like.

The handling of the cake has much to do with its lightness. Some cooks seem to have a knack of turning out light cakes and pastry, while others have to practise before their creations are a success.

Always preheat your oven before making your cake, especially for those cakes which include baking powder. They will spoil if they have to stand waiting for the oven to heat, and even more so if they are put into an oven that is not hot enough. You will find a moderate oven is best for most cakes; rather hotter for small and light cakes than for thicker fruit cakes.

Assemble all ingredients and cake tins before you start to make the cake. If fruit is included in the recipe, prepare it in advance.

In some cake mixtures – especially the plainer ones – the butter or fat is rubbed into the flour; in others, it is beaten to a cream before the other ingredients are mixed with it; and in still other mixtures, the eggs or egg yolks are creamed with the sugar, and the butter is added in a melted form. And in some sponges no fat at all is used.

1 When a cake rises in a cone in the centre, this indicates that your oven was too hot when you started baking. As a result, the sides of the cake hardened with a crust before the mixture had time to rise.

2 If the cake rises at one side, your oven is hotter one side than the other. Correct this by turning the cake from time to time during baking.

3 Do not open the oven door for at least 5 minutes after the cake has been put in, and then only with the greatest care. Do not slam the oven door; it can be fatal to the successful rising of the cake. Handle a cake carefully during baking. Moving or shaking it during baking is almost certain to cause it to fall.

Preparation of cake tins
Always prepare cake tins before mixing ingredients for your cake. Most cakes spoil if the mixture has to wait while you prepare tins.

To keep cakes
Do not store cakes until cold. Large cakes keep best if wrapped in paper and put in a tin box with a tight-fitting lid. Fruit cakes which have to be kept for any length of time should be wrapped in greaseproof paper and then in a sheet of ordinary paper or a clean cloth.

(A)

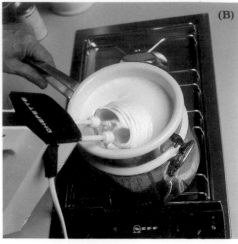

(B)

(C)

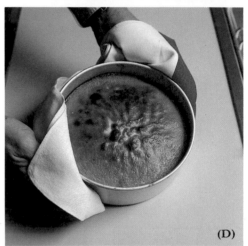

(D)

To line a round cake tin with paper

Cut a double band of paper 2 or 3 inches (5–7½ cm) deeper than the cake tin and rather longer than the circumference. Fold up an inch (2½ cm) of this band on the double fold and make a mark. Open out and make cuts along the marked off inch (2½ cm) of the paper an inch (2½ cm) or so apart. Arrange this band inside the cake tin, making the notched section of paper lie flat on the bottom of the tin. Then cut a double round of paper to fit inside the tin and lay it smoothly on the bottom.

If the tin is very shallow, the paper will not need to be shaped, but just pressed in smoothly and folded or snipped at the corners.

If the cake mixture contains a fair amount of butter, no grease is required, but if there is little or no fat in the cake ingredients, the paper in the tin should be brushed lightly with clarified butter.

4 Be sure the cake is sufficiently cooked before removing it from the oven. Small cakes are ready if they feel firm when gently touched with the finger. Larger cakes should be tested by running a warm skewer into the centre. If the skewer comes out sticky, the cake is not cooked enough; if it is dry, the baking is finished.

5 Allow cakes to stand for a minute or two before removing them from the cake tins; you will find that they turn out more easily.

6 Always cool cakes on a wire cake rack so that the air gets around the bottom and sides.

For scones or small cakes: Butter a baking sheet and sprinkle with flour. Knock edges of the sheet against table after flouring to shake off surplus flour.

For sponge cakes: Tie a double band of paper round outside of tin to project 2 or 3 inches (5–7½cm) above top edge. Coat inside of tin and paper with melted butter. Dust lightly with equal quantities of flour and sugar to give sponge cake a light, dry coating. Shake off surplus flour and sugar.

Small cake tins: Brush tins with clarified butter and dust with flour and sugar.

Sponge Cake (step-by-step)

1 Preheat oven to moderate (375°F/190°C/Mark 5).

2 Brush two 7-inch (17½ cm) sandwich tins with melted butter. Line bases with circles of greaseproof paper and brush these with melted butter as well.

3 In a large bowl, cream ¼ lb (100g) butter, castor sugar and flavouring together until light and fluffy.

4 In another, smaller bowl, whisk eggs until frothy (A). Add to creamed mixture a few tablespoons at a time, beating well between each addition. (B)

5 Sift flour with baking powder, and resift over creamed mixture. Fold in lightly with a spatula. (C)

6 Divide batter evenly between prepared tins and level off tops.

7 Bake layers (on the same shelf if possible) for 25 minutes, or until they are a rich golden colour on top, have shrunk slightly from sides of tins and spring back when pressed lightly. (D)

8 Turn layers out on to a folded cloth and peel off base papers. Turn right side up again and cool on wire rack.

9 When layers are quite cold, sandwich with good red jam, warmed to make it spread more easily, and dust with icing sugar.

Makes 6 portions

Ingredients

Butter
¼ lb (100g) plain flour
1 level teaspoon baking powder
¼ lb (100g) castor sugar
Few drops vanilla essence or finely grated lemon rind
2 eggs
Red jam
Icing sugar

The lightness of a cake has much to do with its handling. Some cooks seem to have the knack, while others have to practise before their creations are a success. (Recipe for Orange Layer Cake, page 183)

Genoese Sponge

Ingredients

3 oz (75g) plain flour
1 oz (25g) cornflour
Unsalted butter
4 eggs
4 oz (100g) castor sugar
1 teaspoon vanilla essence or finely grated rind of ½ lemon

Excellent for layer cakes, iced cakes and petits fours.

1 Preheat oven to moderate (350°F/180°C/Mark 4).

2 Sift flour with cornflour three times.

3 Take the bowl in which you intend to whisk up the cake and select a large saucepan over which it will fit firmly. Pour 2 inches (5 cm) water into the pan and bring to the boil.

4 Place about 5 oz (150g) unsalted butter in another, smaller pan; lower it into the heating water so that the butter melts without sizzling or bubbling. Remove pan from water.

5 Brush two 7½- or 8-inch (19 or 20 cm) sandwich tins with a little melted butter. Line bases with greaseproof paper and brush with butter as well.

6 Combine eggs, castor sugar and vanilla essence or grated lemon rind in the bowl. Set it over barely simmering water and whisk vigorously until very thick, light and lukewarm.

7 Remove bowl from heat. Stand bowl on a cool surface and continue to whisk until mixture leaves a distinct trail on the surface when beaters are lifted (3–5 minutes if beating with an electric mixer at high speed).

8 Gradually resift flour mixture over surface, at the same time folding it in lightly but thoroughly with a large metal spoon or spatula.

9 Add 8 tablespoons melted butter and continue with the folding motion until it has been completely absorbed. This may take slightly longer than you expect, so work as lightly as you can to avoid deflating the mixture.

10 Divide batter evenly between prepared tins.

11 Bake for 15–20 minutes, or until cakes are well risen, golden brown on top and springy to the touch.

12 Turn out on to wire racks. Peel off lining paper and allow cakes to cool completely before using.
Makes 2 7½- to 8-inch (19- to 20-cm) layers

Italian Cream Torte

Ingredients

3 oz (75g) semi-sweet chocolate
1–2 tablespoons Cognac
1 baked sponge cake layer (see page 177)
4 tablespoons maraschino liqueur
2 pints (1.1 litres) double cream
¼ lb (100g) castor sugar
¼–½ teaspoon vanilla essence
6 level teaspoons chopped glacé fruits
Swirls of whipped cream (optional) and chopped glacé fruits for decoration

1 Melt chocolate with ¼ pint (1½ dl) water in the top of a double saucepan. Remove from heat and stir in Cognac. Cool.

2 Cut sponge layer in half to make 2 thin layers; then cut each half into thin strips as high as the soufflé dish that you are going to use to mould the torte.

3 Dip each sponge strip into maraschino liqueur diluted with 4 tablespoons water. Line sides of soufflé dish with them.

4 Whip double cream until stiff. Divide into 2 portions. Sweeten the first portion with sugar and flavour with vanilla essence, to taste. Fold in chopped glacé fruits and spoon the mixture into the sponge-lined mould to form the bottom layer of torte.

5 Fold the chocolate sauce into the remaining whipped cream and mix well. Spoon chocolate cream over the glacé fruit filling. If mixture does not come to top of sponge strips, trim them level with a sharp knife. Place torte in the freezer to freeze until firm.

6 When ready to serve: unmould torte on a chilled platter and decorate top with swirls of whipped cream, if desired, and a ring of chopped glacé fruits; cut torte into wedges and serve immediately.

Serves 6–8

Almond and Hazelnut Gâteau

1 Grill almonds and hazelnuts separately in 2 trays; remove husks by rubbing in metal strainer. Combine nuts in an electric blender or a mortar, and crush very finely. Add granulated sugar and mix well.

2 Beat egg whites until they form peaks and mix with nut mixture without letting eggs fall. Spoon mixture into 4 well-buttered, shallow, rectangular cake tins and bake in a preheated moderate oven (350°F/180°C/Mark 4). Allow to cool.

3 To assemble cake: put one layer on a flat serving dish; spread with chocolate cream; top with another layer; spread thickly with prâline cream; top with another layer; spread with chocolate cream; top with final layer. Smooth sides, sprinkle top of cake with castor sugar and sides with chocolate *paillettes*. Keep for 24 hours before serving.

4 To make chocolate cream: cream cold butter well with sugar, then blend this thoroughly and slowly with cold *crème pâtissière* added little by little. Stir in melted and cooled unsweetened baking chocolate, to taste.

5 To make prâline cream: mix equal quantities of blanched almonds and sugar, and heat mixture in a thick-bottomed frying pan until well caramelized, stirring to brown it evenly. Add a few drops vanilla essence. Cool on a baking tray until it hardens. Crush to a powder by chopping and pounding with a heavy rolling pin. Cream cold butter well with 1 tablespoon castor sugar, then blend this thoroughly and slowly with cold *crème pâtissière* added little by little. Stir in powdered prâline, to taste.

Ingredients

½ lb (225g) almonds
5 oz (150g) hazelnuts
½ lb (225g) granulated sugar
8 egg whites
Butter
Castor sugar
Chocolate paillettes

CHOCOLATE CREAM

6 level tablespoons cold butter
2 level tablespoons castor sugar
¼ pint (1½ dl) cold crème pâtissière (see page 174)
Unsweetened baking chocolate, melted and cooled

PRÂLINE CREAM

Blanched almonds
Castor sugar
Vanilla essence
6 level tablespoons cold butter
¼ pint (1½ dl) cold crème pâtissière (see page 174)
Powdered prâline

Chocolate Almond Cake *(Illustration, page 180)*

1 Grind the almonds in electric blender or food processor. They should be as fine as possible.

2 Preheat oven to moderate (375°F/190°C/Mark 5).

3 Butter the sides of an 8-inch (20 cm) round cake tin. Line the bottom with kitchen paper.

4 Melt the chocolate in the top of a double saucepan over hot but not boiling water. Work ¼ lb (100g) diced butter with an electric beater until soft and light-coloured. Gradually beat in the sugar. Then add the eggs one at a time, beating with electric beater until each egg is thoroughly assimilated into the mixture. Mixture might look curdled at this point. Don't worry.

5 Stir in the melted chocolate, ground almonds, orange rind and breadcrumbs. Pour mixture into the prepared cake tin and bake for 25 minutes.

6 Remove cake from oven; invert tin and allow cake to cool on a cake rack for 30 minutes. Then remove cake from tin; strip off kitchen paper and cool cake. Leave cake overnight.

7 The following day, slice cake carefully into 2 or 3 layers. The centre of the cake should still be a little moist and soft.

8 To make chocolate icing: melt chocolate in cream with butter over hot water in a double saucepan. When smooth, add sieved icing sugar. Mix well.

9 Cool slightly before using to spread between cake layers and over top and sides of the cake.

Ingredients

5 oz (150g) almonds, skin on
Butter
¼ lb (100g) semi-sweet chocolate
5 oz (150g) sugar
3 eggs
Grated rind of 1 large orange
4 level tablespoons fine dry breadcrumbs

CHOCOLATE ICING

6 oz (175g) unsweetened or plain chocolate
8 tablespoons double cream
2 oz (50g) butter
1 lb (450g) icing sugar, sieved

Chocolate Almond Cake. (Recipe, page 179)
Savarin aux Fruits.

Savarin aux Marrons

1 If using fresh yeast, dissolve it in 4 tablespoons lukewarm water in a bowl. If using dried yeast, sprinkle granules over 4 tablespoons lukewarm water in a bowl; beat well with a fork and leave for 10 minutes, or until liquid is frothy and granules have completely dissolved.

2 Gradually sift 5 level tablespoons of the flour into dissolved yeast, mixing with a spoon to make a stiff batter. Cover bowl and leave to rise until frothy and doubled in bulk, about 20 minutes.

3 Sift remaining flour with sugar and salt into a large bowl. Make a well in the centre; add yeast mixture and lightly beaten eggs, and incorporate into flour gradually, beating vigorously with your hand or with a wooden spoon.

4 When dough is smooth, beat in softened butter. Continue to beat or work the dough by hand until butter is thoroughly incorporated. The dough should be soft and shiny.

5 Cover bowl with a cloth or plastic wrap and leave dough in a warm place to rise until doubled in bulk, about 1½ hours.

6 Grease a 2-pint (1.1-litre) ring mould with oil or melted butter. Gather dough up out of bowl and place on a floured surface; with floured hands knead lightly until smooth then break off a 2–3-inch (5–7½ cm) piece of the dough and press lightly into the bottom of the prepared mould. Continue rapidly with the rest of the dough until mould is a third to half full. Do not bother to smooth surface of dough as it will smooth out as it rises. Cover loosely with a cloth and leave to rise in a warm place (80–100°F/27–38°C), or until the dough has risen to fill the mould.

7 Preheat oven to 375° / 190°C / Mark 5.

8 Brush *savarin* lightly with egg yolk, beaten with a little water, to glaze. Place mould in the middle of the oven and bake for about 30 minutes. If top browns too much during baking, cover lightly with aluminium foil. The *savarin* is done when it is a rich golden colour and has begun to shrink a bit from the sides of the mould. Remove from oven and let cool for 5 minutes then turn out of mould and leave to cool.

9 When *savarin* is lukewarm, prick the rounded sides with a skewer or roasting fork. Place *savarin*, rounded side up, in a deep dish just large enough to hold it. Pour lukewarm syrup (½ lb (225g) sugar, cooked to syrup stage in ¾ pint (4½ dl) water with a strip of orange peel and a vanilla pod, to which you have added 6 tablespoons dark rum or kirsch) over *savarin* and allow to stand for at least ½ hour.

10 When ready to serve: pour off excess syrup and save for another use. (You'll find it very good with a fresh fruit salad.) Transfer *savarin* to a clean serving dish. Sprinkle with 2 tablespoons dark rum or kirsch. Paint with a light apricot glaze and fill centre with whipped cream or *crème pâtissière* and top cream with chestnuts in rum-flavoured syrup. **Serves 6**

Ingredients

BASIC SAVARIN

1 oz (25g) fresh yeast or ¼ oz (7g) dried yeast (1½ level teaspoons)
9 oz (250g) plain flour
2 level tablespoons castor sugar
½ level teaspoon salt
4 eggs, lightly beaten
¼ lb (100g) softened butter
Flavourless oil or melted butter, for mould
1 egg yolk beaten with a little water, to glaze

SYRUP

½ lb (225g) sugar
Strip of orange peel
Vanilla pod
6 tablespoons dark rum or kirsch

FILLING

2 tablespoons dark rum or kirsch
Apricot glaze (see page 174)
Whipped cream or crème pâtissière (see page 174)
1 tin chestnuts in syrup

Savarin aux Fruits

1 Make basic *savarin*, Steps 1–8, using a 2-pint (1 litre) cake tin instead of a ring mould.

2 Make syrup and pour over *savarin*, Step 9, and allow to stand for at least ½ hour.

3 When ready to serve: pour off excess syrup and save for another use. Transfer *savarin* to a clean serving dish. Sprinkle with 2 tablespoons dark rum or kirsch. Decorate with 'flowers' made of diced canned pineapple and glacé cherries with 'leaves' of angelica. Paint with a light apricot glaze. **Serves 6**

Ingredients

1 recipe basic savarin (see above)
Syrup (see above)
Dark rum or kirsch
Diced canned pineapple, glacé cherries and angelica
Apricot glaze (see page 174)

Little Summer Fruit Towers

Ingredients

SPONGE
Butter
3 eggs
3 oz (75g) castor sugar
3 oz (75g) plain flour, sifted

STRAWBERRY
BAVAROISE FILLING
24–30 strawberries, mashed
Finely grated rind of 1 orange
¼ pint (1½ dl) milk
1 egg yolk
2 level tablespoons castor
    sugar
1 level teaspoon powdered
    gelatine
¼ pint (1½ dl) double cream
2 tablespoons Grand
    Marnier or Cointreau
Red food colouring
2 egg whites

RASPBERRY CREAM
½ pint (3 dl) double cream
¼ teaspoon vanilla essence
1 punnet raspberries
Powdered sugar
Lemon juice or framboise
    liqueur

DECORATION
Whipped cream and ripe
    raspberries or strawberries

1 Preheat oven to moderate (350°F/ 180°C/Mark 4).

2 Grease a 12×8-inch (30×20 cm) swiss roll tin and line with buttered greaseproof paper.

3 To make sponge: whisk eggs and sugar over hot water until mixture leaves a trail on the surface. Remove from heat and fold in flour with a metal spoon. Pour into prepared tin. Bake for 15–20 minutes, or until sponge is golden and springy. Turn out on to a wire rack; peel off lining paper. Cool.

4 To make strawberry *bavaroise* filling: combine orange rind and milk and bring to the boil, stirring constantly. Remove from heat. Whisk egg yolk with half the castor sugar; then gradually whisk in hot milk. Sprinkle gelatine over 2 tablespoons cold water in a cup and leave for 10 minutes. Place cup in a bowl of hot water and stir until gelatine has completely dissolved. Blend thoroughly with milk and egg mixture. Whip cream lightly; fold into strawberry mixture. Add Grand Marnier or Cointreau, and a little red food colouring to tint mixture a rich pink. Fold in mashed strawberries. Whisk egg whites until stiff; add remaining castor sugar and continue to whisk until stiff and glossy. Fold into strawberry mixture.

5 To line six ¼-pint (1½ dl) turret moulds with sponge: carefully slice sponge cake into 2 thin layers ¼ inch (½ cm) thick, using a serrated knife. Cut a circle of sponge to fit the bottom of each mould. Then cut a strip to fit completely round inside of each mould, trimming ends so that there is no overlap.

6 Fill sponge-lined moulds with strawberry mixture and chill until firmly set.

7 To make raspberry cream: whip cream until stiff. Beat in vanilla essence. Purée raspberries with a little powdered sugar and lemon juice, or framboise liqueur, to taste. Add to whipped cream and whisk until thoroughly blended.

8 When ready to serve: turn strawberry towers out on to a wire rack over a flat dish. Mask each tower completely with raspberry cream and transfer to individual serving dishes. Top each tower with a swirl of whipped cream and garnish with a ripe raspberry or strawberry.

Serves 6

Brandy Snaps with Cream

Ingredients
¼ lb (100g) butter
4 level tablespoons fine
    brown sugar
4 level tablespoons golden
    syrup
4 level tablespoons flour
1 level teaspoon ground ginger
¼ level teaspoon grated
    nutmeg
Grated rind of ½ lemon
1 tablespoon Cognac
Whipped cream flavoured
    with Cognac

1 Melt butter, brown sugar and golden syrup; remove from heat and stir in flour, ground ginger, nutmeg and lemon rind; finally, stir in Cognac.

2 Stir mixture vigorously, off the heat, until well blended.

3 Drop mixture, 1 teaspoonful at a time, on to a greased baking sheet (the mixture will spread out during baking to about 4 inches (10 cm) across, so make sure they are at least 4 inches (10 cm) apart).

4 Bake in a moderate oven (350°F/ 180°C/Mark 4) until golden brown; leave for just a few seconds to cool, then roll each brandy snap up over the handle of a wooden spoon

5 When cool, fill with whipped cream flavoured with a little Cognac. The brandy snaps should be toffee-coloured, full of air-holes, and crisp when cold.

Makes about 24

Orange Layer Cake *(Illustration, page 177)*

1 To make cake: beat egg yolks, sugar, 2 tablespoons water, orange rind and salt until light and fluffy (5 minutes in mixer at high speed). Sift flour and cornflour, and gradually blend in egg yolk mixture. Whisk egg whites until stiff but not dry, and fold gently into yolk mixture. Place equal quantities of batter into three round 8-inch (20 cm) cake tins which have been buttered and lightly dusted with flour. Bake in a moderate oven (350°F/180°C/Mark 4) for 45 minutes, or until golden brown. Invert layers on wire racks. When cool, loosen edges and remove from pans.

2 To make topping: beat eggs, sugar and orange rind together until foamy; add sifted flour and orange juice, and cook in the top of a double saucepan, stirring all the time, until smooth and thick. Cool.

3 Fold in whipped cream, reserving some for decoration.

4 Spread two cake layers with orange topping and put cake together.

5 Cover sides of cake with topping and pat chopped toasted almonds firmly round; cover top and decorate with chocolate curls.

Makes 8–12 portions

Ingredients
CAKE
6 eggs, separated
6 oz (175g) sugar
Grated rind of 1 orange
Generous pinch of salt
3 oz (75g) flour
1 oz (25g) cornflour
Butter and flour for cake tin

ORANGE TOPPING
1 egg
5 oz (150g) sugar
Grated rind and juice of 1 orange made up to ¼ pint (1½ dl) with water
1 oz (25g) sifted flour
½ pint (3 dl) double cream, whipped
¼ lb (100g) chopped toasted almonds
Chocolate curls

Château d'Yquem

Our wine tasting tour of France took us to Sauternes – an area just a little bit bigger than the city of Manhattan – to look for the perfect dessert wine. Château d'Yquem is a wine that has no equal anywhere else in all of France. Perhaps only in some of the wines of the Rhine and Moselle region do we find this same quality of richness, glittering gold look and scented aroma of flowers and fruit.

The grapes which are used for the harvest here are the *Semillon*, the *Sauvignon* and, at times, a little *Muscatel* or *Muscadel*. In Californian Sauternes, for example, they use just one grape; they don't blend to get this fullness of body; and perhaps this is why American Sauternes are thinner, drier and less interesting.

Château d'Yquem is a wine to savour and keep for special occasions. It is a rare wine, and consequently expensive. And why is it so expensive? Because a team of a hundred and twenty women harvest the sixty acres of vines at Château d'Yquem from mid-September to December, like hordes of honey bees, from vine to vine, picking each single grape. They might return eight, twelve or thirteen times during the two to three month harvesting period. The harvesting of the grapes, one by one in this way, can be a dangerous thing, because if the winter frosts come before the harvesting is finished, the harvest is ruined; if there is not enough sun, or if too much mist comes up from the river in the early morning and does not dry out in the sun, the magic *pourriture noble*, the 'noble rot' that creates the superb flavour of this great wine, will not form. The grapes really do rot, from within, but they do not become rotten. In reality, they dry out; they dehydrate in the late sun, leaving a shrivelled, wrinkled grape which is then picked singly. It is a more fermented grape because there is less water content and more sugar, and consequently more fullness of body and flavour.

Desserts

A very good dinner deserves a happy ending. Something just that much more exciting than a salad of fresh fruits (even when doused with champagne) or a fresh fruit sorbet topped with puréed raspberries *(à la Cardinale)* or blackcurrants *(au cassis)*. Yet, to be memorable a dessert need not be elaborate or difficult to make. I often serve a large open tart of thinly sliced fresh fruit – apples, pears, peaches or pineapple – brushed with dark rum and melted butter and served piping hot with mounds of chilled whipped cream, or diminutive little chocolate 'pots' topped with a float of orange-flavoured curaçao or Grand Marnier.

For more festive occasions, I like to make the edible tulip-shaped pastry cases taught to me many years ago by René Lasserre, whose elegant restaurant *Chez Lasserre* is located just off the Champs Elysées in Paris. '*Tulipe glacée Lasserre*' combines 5 oz (150g) each flour and icing sugar with 3 egg whites and 2 egg yolks. This creamy batter is spread thinly in a saucer-sized circle on a baking sheet, baked for 5–6 minutes only in a preheated moderate oven (350°F/180°C/ Mark 4) and pressed while still hot over an orange to form a round-bottomed tulip-shaped cup. *Chez Lasserre* fills the cup with vanilla ice cream, fresh fruits and a liqueur-flavoured syrup and caps the whole confection with a gossamer-light froth of spun sugar. My version is simpler: no spun sugar, just a decorative swirl of whipped cream to finish it off (see page 189).

I find that top French restaurants often make a speciality of delicious desserts and puddings that look and, indeed, sound far more complicated than they actually are. I have chosen a series of favourite desserts, that are perfect for a special dinner party, for most of the preparatory work can be completed the day before the event, leaving just the finishing touches for the last minute.

Summer Apple Charlotte, a French baked pudding served with wine-glazed apples and chilled whipped cream is one of the few exceptions. The pudding (see page 185) can indeed be prepared the day before the party, but it must be baked for 45 minutes before guests arrive and then kept warm in the lowest of ovens until time to serve. Another exception is *Negre en Chemise,* a French steamed pudding with a topping of chilled whipped cream melting down the sides (see page 187). This too can be prepared the day before the party, but must be steamed for $1\frac{1}{2}$ hours just prior to serving.

Peaches in Brouilly *(Illustration, page 169)*

1 Put peaches in a saucepan with the sugar, ¼ pint (1½ dl) water, orange peel, cinnamon and cloves. Simmer them, covered, for about 15 minutes. Add ½ pint (3 dl) Brouilly and continue to cook, uncovered, over a low heat for 15 minutes, or until peaches are tender but have not lost their shape.

2 Holding peaches in a clean towel to keep you from burning your fingers, remove skins gently with the point of a sharp knife. Return peaches to cool in syrup.

3 When cool, transfer peaches to a deep glass serving dish and chill in the refrigerator.

4 In the meantime cook the liquid until it is reduced to the consistency of a light syrup. Add 4 tablespoons Brouilly and cool.

5 Pour syrup over the peaches and put in the refrigerator to chill. Serve very cold with whipped cream.

Serves 4

Ingredients
2½ lb (1.1 kg) small peaches
½ lb (225g) sugar
Peel of 1 orange
1 stick cinnamon
2 cloves
Brouilly
Whipped cream

Summer Apple Charlotte

1 Peel and core apples and chop coarsely. Add chopped bananas and pineapple. Cook chopped fruit in 2 oz (50g) butter with grated orange rind and lemon juice, covered, for about 10 minutes, or until the fruit is soft. Remove cover and cook, stirring continuously to prevent scorching, until mixture is quite dry. Sweeten to taste with sugar and apricot jam.

2 Butter bottom and sides of a 6-inch (15 cm) charlotte or soufflé mould and dust with sugar.

3 Trim crusts from sliced bread; cut enough triangles to cover bottom of mould.

4 Clarify remaining butter and dip triangles one by one in butter and line bottom of mould, overlapping the triangles to make an attractive pattern. Line the sides of the mould with strips of bread dipped in clarified butter, also overlapping. Fill the mould with the fruit mixture, and cover with overlapping triangles of bread dipped in clarified butter; cover with a buttered paper and bake in a moderate oven (375°F/190°C/Mark 5) for 45 minutes, or until the bread is golden. Let the mould stand for 5–10 minutes after removing from oven.

5 To serve: invert the charlotte on a heated serving dish. Surround with peeled, cored and halved apples which you have poached in red or white wine (see Peaches in Brouilly, above). Serve with chilled whipped cream.

Serves 6

Ingredients
8 eating apples
2 bananas, chopped
4 pineapple slices, chopped
6 oz (175g) butter
1 level teaspoon grated
  orange rind
Juice of ½ lemon
Sugar
2 level tablespoons apricot
  jam
1 loaf sliced bread
Poached apple halves
Chilled whipped cream

Compote of Berries in Red Wine

1 Combine ¼ pint (1½ dl) water, sugar, cinnamon stick and peel of ½ orange in a saucepan. Bring to the boil and cook until the sugar dissolves, stirring constantly. Add the red Burgundy and continue to cook until sauce comes to the boil again. Remove from heat. Cool.

2 Wash and hull or stem red currants, strawberries, raspberries and blueberries, discarding any that are not perfect.

3 Combine prepared fruits in a glass serving bowl. Pour the cooled Burgundy syrup over fruit and chill for several hours before serving.

4 Just before serving, add *julienne* of remaining ½ orange and serve with whipped cream.

Serves 4–6

Ingredients
6 level tablespoons sugar
1 stick cinnamon
Peel of 1 orange
¼ pint (1½ dl) red Burgundy
1 punnet red currants
1 punnet strawberries
1 punnet raspberries
1 punnet blueberries
Whipped cream

Ananas Givrée

Ingredients

2–3 well-ripened small
 pineapples
2–3 tablespoons dark rum
2–3 level tablespoons icing
 sugar
1 pint (6 dl) pineapple water
 ice, or sherbet
Small fresh flowers

1 Cut the pineapples in half vertically, slicing straight through the leaves, to make 4–6 'boats'.

2 With a small sharp knife cut out the flesh of the pineapple, being careful not to pierce the skin. Slice flesh of each pineapple; discard core and dice flesh into a bowl; add dark rum and icing sugar. Chill diced pineapple and pine-apple shells for 2 hours.

3 When ready to serve, drain the diced pineapple and spoon it into the shells. Top each pineapple shell with a scoop of pineapple water ice (or sher-bet). Decorate leaves of pineapple with 3 or 4 fresh flowers and serve at once.

Serves 4 – 6

Mrs Moxon's Lemon Posset

Ingredients

Grated rind and juice of
 2 lemons
1 pint (6 dl) double cream
¼ pint (1½ dl) dry white wine
Sugar
Whites of 3 eggs

1 Add the grated lemon rind to 1 pint (6 dl) of double cream and whisk until stiff.

2 Stir in lemon juice and dry white wine. Add sugar, to taste.

3 Whisk egg whites until they form peaks and fold into whipped cream mixture. Serve in a glass serving dish or in individual glasses.

Serves 4-6

Crème Caramel à l'Orange

Ingredients

½ pint (3 dl) milk
¼ pint (1½ dl) single cream
Strip of orange peel
A piece of vanilla pod, split
2 oz (50g) castor sugar
3 eggs, beaten
1 egg yolk, beaten
4 tablespoons orange juice
½ teaspoon vanilla essence

CARAMEL

¼ lb (100g) granulated sugar
1-2 tablespoons water

1 Preheat oven to moderate (350°F/180°C/Mark 4).

2 Combine milk and cream in a pan with strip of orange peel, vanilla pod and castor sugar, and bring to the boil. Remove pan from heat; cover and leave to infuse for 5–10 minutes.

3 Remove orange peel and vanilla pod from milk (pod can be wiped dry and stored in a stoppered jar for future use). Stir milk mixture into beaten eggs – do *not* beat it in; (this, together with a too-hot oven, is what usually causes the air bubbles). Flavour with orange juice and vanilla essence.

4 To prepare caramel: select a straight-sided, 1½ pint (9 dl) metal mould. Add granulated sugar and 1–2 tablespoons water, and swirl pan over a low heat until dissolved. Raise heat and boil rapidly, without stirring, until syrup turns into a rich, dark caramel. Watch it like a hawk, drawing the caramel away from the heat before it is quite ready, as it carries on cooking from the heat of the mould and will burn at the slightest provocation.

5 Holding handle of mould in a thick cloth, swirl caramel around with great care so that bottom and sides of mould are well coated. Cool slightly.

6 Pour in egg mixture; cover mould with a piece of foil and stand it in a baking tin. Pour in hot water to come halfway up sides of mould.

7 Transfer to the oven and immediately reduce temperature to 325°F/170°C/Mark 3. Bake custard for 35–40 minutes, or until set.

8 Cool mould, then turn out carefully on to a deepish serving dish to catch the caramel syrup.

Serves 4–6

Nègre en Chemise

1 Cream butter.

2 Soak bread, trimmed of crusts, in ½ pint (3 dl) double cream.

3 Shred soaked bread and add (along with cream) to butter; mix well. Add ground blanched almonds, sugar and chocolate, which you have melted over hot water and cooled.

4 Beat the mixture with electric mixer until smooth; then beat in eggs and yolks.

5 Pour the mixture into a tall mould. Cover or seal the mould and place in a large saucepan of boiling water (the water should come half-way up the mould). Cover the saucepan and steam the pudding for 1½ hours, adding more boiling water from time to time.

6 Whip remaining cream; sweeten to taste with icing sugar and serve hot pudding immediately accompanied by whipped cream.

Serves 6

Ingredients
6 oz (175g) butter
8 slices white bread
1¼ pints (7½ dl) double cream
¼ lb (100g) blanched almonds, ground
6 oz (175g) castor sugar
6 oz (175g) bitter chocolate
4 eggs
2 egg yolks
Icing sugar

Petits Pots au Chocolat

1 Break chocolate into the top of a double saucepan.

2 Finely grate the rind of 1 large orange; squeeze its juice and add both to the chocolate, together with butter.

3 Heat over simmering water, stirring occasionally, until chocolate has melted. Then remove pan from heat; add 1 tablespoon Grand Marnier or Curacao, and beat until smooth.

4 In a bowl, beat egg yolks thoroughly. Strain in chocolate mixture through a fine sieve, beating constantly. Allow to cool.

5 In another bowl, beat egg whites until stiff but not dry. Fold into chocolate mixture gently but thoroughly with a spatula.

6 Pour mixture into individual ¼ pint (1½ dl) pots or soufflé dishes. (Do not use metal pots, as chocolate may discolour.) Chill until set.

7 Just before serving, cut 2 thin slices from the centre of the remaining orange. Quarter each slice and lay a quarters, point to point, on top of each pot. Pour over a teaspoonful of Grand Marnier or Curacao; swirl around very gently so that entire surface is moistened.

Serves 4

Ingredients
¼ lb (100g) dark bitter chocolate
2 oranges (1 large, 1 medium-sized)
1 oz (25g) butter
Grand Marnier or Curacao
2 eggs, separated

Cold Chocolate Soufflé

1 Soak gelatine in a little cold water until soft.

2 Heat milk to boiling point and whisk on to the egg yolks, sugar, instant coffee and melted chocolate until well blended.

3 Place chocolate mixture in the top of a double saucepan and cook over water, stirring constantly, until mixture coats the back of a spoon. Strain if necessary; whisk in gelatine; pour into a bowl and allow to cool. Then stir over ice until the mixture begins to set.

4 Fold in whipped cream and then the stiffly beaten egg whites. Pour into a prepared 6- or 7-inch (15- or 18-cm) soufflé dish, edged with a standing collar of greaseproof paper 2 to 3 inches (5 to 8 cm) above the rim of the dish. Refrigerate to set.

5 Remove band of paper, coat sides of soufflé with grated chocolate or powdered coffee and decorate top with piped cream and chocolate *bâtons*.

Serves 4–6

Ingredients
1 oz (25g) powdered gelatine
½ pint (3 dl) milk
4 egg yolks
¼ lb (100g) castor sugar
1–2 level tablespoons instant coffee
¼ lb (100g) semi-sweet chocolate, melted
½ pint (3 dl) double cream, whipped
4 egg whites, stiffly beaten

DECORATION
Grated chocolate or powdered coffee
Whipped cream
Chocolate bâtons

Cold Vanilla Soufflé with Chopped Glacé Chestnuts

Ingredients

½ pint (3 dl) milk
1-inch (2½ cm) vanilla pod
3 egg yolks
3 level tablespoons sugar
1 level tablespoon powdered gelatine
¼ pint (1½ dl) double cream, whipped
4 marrons glacés, chopped coarsely
4 egg whites
4 marrons glacés and swirls of whipped cream, to decorate

1 Heat milk with vanilla pod. Remove pod and keep milk hot.

2 Whisk egg yolks and sugar until thick and lemon-coloured. Add hot milk and cook over hot water without allowing mixture to boil.

3 Dissolve gelatine in 3 tablespoons of warm water and add to custard; strain and cool.

4 Stir custard mixture over ice, and when it begins to set fold in whipped double cream and chopped marrons glacés followed by egg whites, beaten until stiff but not dry.

5 Tie a band of double greaseproof paper around the outside of a 5¾-inch (14½ cm) soufflé dish to stand 3 inches (7½ cm) above the rim of the dish. Pour in mixture and allow to set in refrigerator. Remove paper carefully and decorate soufflé with marrons glacés and swirls of whipped cream.

Serves 4

Individual Amaretti Soufflés Glacés

Ingredients

½ level teaspoon powdered gelatine
4 egg yolks
¼ lb (100g) granulated sugar
½ pint (3 dl) milk
3–4 tablespoons amaretti liqueur
Few drops of vanilla essence
½ pint (3 dl) double cream
6 small Italian macaroons (amaretti), crushed

1 Turn refrigerator down to lowest temperature, i.e. highest setting.

2 Select 6 individual soufflé dishes about 2½ inches (6 cm) wide across the base and tie double-thickness collars of greaseproof paper around them to come 1 inch (2½ cm) above the top.

3 In a small cup, sprinkle gelatine over 1 tablespoon cold water and leave to soften.

4 In a bowl, beat egg yolks with sugar until thick and light.

5 Pour milk into the top of a double saucepan and bring to the boil over direct heat. Then whisk into egg mixture in a thin stream.

6 Return mixture to double saucepan and stir over gently simmering water until it coats back of spoon, taking care not to let custard boil, or egg yolks will curdle. Cool slightly.

7 Dissolve softened gelatine by standing cup in hot water and stirring until liquid is clear. Blend into cooling custard, together with *amaretti* liqueur and a few drops of vanilla essence, to taste.

8 Beat double cream until soft peaks form. Fold into custard.

9 Divide mixture between prepared soufflé dishes. It should come well above the rim of each dish.

10 Freeze for about 5 hours, or until very firm. Then transfer to the main compartment of the refrigerator for about 1 hour before serving.

11 To serve: sprinkle top of each iced soufflé with finely crushed macaroons, patting the crumbs in lightly to make them stick; then carefully peel off paper collars. Serve immediately.

Serves 6

This soufflé glacé is a trompe l'oeil soufflé. Its high-rise lightness is achieved with a 'collar' made of greaseproof paper, which keeps the airy structure floating lightly above the dish.

Tulipes Glacées

1 Sift flour and icing sugar into a mixing bowl; add egg yolks and whites and mix well.

2 Grease a cold baking sheet and mark 4 circles on it with a saucer. Spread 1 dessertspoon of mixture over each circle, using back of teaspoon. Bake in a moderate oven (350°F/180°C/Mark 5) for 5–6 minutes, or until just turning brown at edges.

3 Remove each round from baking sheet; turn over and, working quickly, place each circle over the top of a greased orange. Place tea towel over pastry to prevent burning hands and mould pastry to fit orange. Remove and continue as above, baking 2–4 circles each time and shaping them over oranges as you go. Cases will keep for days in a biscuit tin. This recipe makes 12–16 *tulipes*.

4 To serve: fill 8 cases with diced fresh pineapple, which you have marinated in kirsch; add a scoop of vanilla ice cream and decorate each case with a few strawberries and raspberries and a swirl of whipped cream.

Serves 8

Ingredients
5 oz (150g) flour
5 oz (150g) icing sugar
2 egg yolks
3 egg whites
1 large orange, greased, to form pastry shapes
1 fresh pineapple, peeled, cored and diced
Kirsch
Vanilla ice cream (see page 190)
Fresh strawberries and raspberries
Double cream, whipped

Frozen Almond Creams bring a light Italian touch to summer menus.

Frozen Almond Creams

Ingredients

½ pint (3 dl) double cream
2 egg whites
Castor sugar
Salt
¼ lb (100g) chopped toasted
    almonds
Sherry, Marsala or Cognac

1 Whip cream.

2 Beat egg whites; add sugar and salt to taste, and continue beating until mixture is stiff and glossy.

3 Fold chopped almonds (reserving 2 level tablespoons for garnish) into egg mixture with whipped cream. Stir in sherry, Marsala or Cognac, to taste, and spoon mixture into 6 or 8 individual soufflé dishes or custard cups. Sprinkle with reserved almonds and freeze for 4 hours.

Serves 6 – 8

Vanilla Ice Cream

Ingredients

4 egg yolks
4 level tablespoons castor
    sugar
Salt
¾ pint (4½ dl) single cream
1 vanilla pod

1 Turn refrigerator to its lowest temperature (i.e. highest setting).

2 Combine egg yolks and castor sugar and a pinch of salt in a bowl, and whisk until light, fluffy and lemon-coloured.

3 Bring cream to the boil with a vanilla pod. Remove vanilla pod and pour vanilla-flavoured cream over egg yolk mixture in a thin stream, whisking vigorously. Add a pinch of salt and whisk again.

4 Pour mixture into the top of a double saucepan and stir over lightly simmering water until it thickens into a custard which coats the back of a spoon. Take great care not to let it boil, or egg yolks will curdle.

5 Strain custard through a fine sieve and leave to cool.

6 Pour cooled custard into a freezing tray and freeze, stirring the mixture up vigorously with a fork every ½ hour, or until half-frozen, then leaving it for a further 2 or 3 hours until frozen hard.

7 Transfer ice cream to main cabinet of refrigerator about 1 hour before serving.

Serves 4

Claret Granita Michel Guérard

1 Make a syrup by boiling 7 fl oz (2 dl) water and sugar together for 1 minute in a medium-sized saucepan. Pour the syrup obtained into a bowl and allow to cool.

2 To make *granita*: when the syrup is cold, add wine and orange and lemon juice and mix together with a small whisk. Pour the mixture into a large flat dish or container and put it in the freezer or freezing compartment of the refrigerator. The shallow depth of the liquid allows it to set more rapidly. During the course of the day, fork over the solidifying liquid regularly, scraping the crystals from the edges of the dish into the still-liquid central part. Continue until the whole is set into a mass of small light crystals.

3 Fill 6 claret glasses with the *granita*, shaping it into a dome-shape with a spoon.

4 Arrange poached fruit and a few mint leaves prettily on top of each sorbet.

Serves 6

Ingredients

Bottle of red wine, preferably St Emilion
Juice of 1 orange
Juice of 1 lemon
6 fresh mint leaves (optional)
Poached fruits for decoration
SYRUP
7 fl oz (2 dl) water
7 oz (200g) castor sugar

Michel Guérard does wonders with wine-flavoured granitas topped with poached fruits.

Emergency Store Cupboard

I
f you have friends in for drinks, it is sometimes a nice idea to invite them to stay on for an impromptu snack, a simple casserole or a home-made dish of pasta and a salad. I always have a certain number of ingredients in my emergency store cupboard or refrigerator to help on occasions like these.

First of all, I always have a few packages of Italian spaghetti, *fettucine* and *tagliatelle* on hand. Also brown rice, wild rice, short-grain rice and risotto rice; corn meal for *polenta; couscous,* and dried pulse vegetables (*haricots blancs,* red kidney beans and lentils).

Canned chicken or ham, fish and shellfish are useful for salads, or to fold into a highly flavoured sauce as a filling for crêpes. Olive oil is useful – and the other oils too: walnut oil for special salads, almond oil for sautéed fish and sesame oil for Chinese dishes.

No store cupboard can be without Italian canned tomatoes and tomato purée. And for quickly whipped up casseroles it is a good idea to have a can or two of button mushrooms, peas and button onions. I like to have a few cans of fruit on hand as well, because mixed with fresh pears and apples or perhaps a fresh pineapple and some lemon juice, or a syrup made with kirsch or Grand Marnier, even these can make a super sweet when surprise guests drop in.

Every kitchen should have a spice wardrobe: the ordinary ones like nutmeg, paprika, cayenne pepper and powdered ginger, and the more expensive ones like saffron, coriander and cumin to make our cooking more exciting.

And then there is our expensive special occasion department: first of all pickles and chutneys, mustard made with champagne, *pâté de foie gras,* white truffles from Alba (one slices them paper-thin over a very inexpensive dish of spaghetti or rice for a truly marvellous first course or luncheon or supper dish). Or combine thinly sliced white truffles and black truffles – one little can of each – and serve with spaghetti or *tagliatelle* bathed in a creamy sauce made of double cream and egg yolks and a hint of grated Parmesan cheese for a dish fit for a king (see page 159).

A well-filled store cupboard makes possible impromptu party meals.

193

But emergency store food doesn't have to be expensive. Eggs are always on hand and they are a most marvellous emergency food because we can whip up an omelette, a soufflé, or a quiche and in each of these put all the left-overs in the refrigerator. They are wonderful 'carriers', which is why store cupboard food, if you are well prepared, can make impromptu meals you can be proud of.

Pasta
Spaghetti
Macaroni
Tagliatelle
Fettucine
Pastini

Polenta and Couscous
Corn Meal
Couscous

Pulse Vegetables
Dried Haricots Blancs
Dried Red Kidney Beans
Dried Lentils
Dried Chick Peas

Rice
Short-grain Rice
Risotto Rice
Brown Rice
Wild Rice

Oils
Olive Oil
Peanut Oil
Walnut Oil
Almond Oil
Sesame Oil

Vinegars
Red Wine Vinegar
Tarragon Vinegar
Sherry Vinegar

Olives and Mustard
Bottled Stuffed Green Olives
Bottled Green Olives
Canned Black Olives

Dijon Mustard
Pommery Mustard

Canned Fish and Shellfish
Tuna
Salmon
Crab
Sardines
Anchovies
Clams
Snails

Meats and Poultry
Canned Whole Chicken
Cooked Ham

Exotics
Black Truffles
White Truffles
Pâté de Foie Gras
Pâté au Foie de Poulet
Bottled Ginger
French Dried Mushrooms
Packaged Morilles

Canned Fruits
Apricots
Pineapple
Mandarin Segments
Kadota Figs
Cherries
Plums
Peaches

Canned Soups and Vegetables
Cream of Tomato Soup
Condensed Clam Chowder
Mushroom Soup
Petits Pois
Champignons de Paris
New Potatoes
Cêpes au Naturel
Fond d'Artichauts
Red Peppers
Italian Peeled Tomatoes
Tomato Purée

Green Noodles alla Crema

1 Bring a large saucepan of well-salted water to the boil. Add green noodles and cook until *al dente* – tender but still firm.

2 While pasta is cooking, melt butter in a saucepan and stir in ¼ lb (100g) freshly grated Parmesan cheese and cream. Cook over a low heat, stirring constantly, until cheese melts and sauce is smooth.

3 Drain noodles and, while they are still very hot, toss with the sauce. Serve noodles with additional Parmesan cheese.

Serves 4

Ingredients

1 lb (450g) green noodles
Salt
¼ lb (100g) butter
Freshly grated Parmesan cheese
½ pint (3 dl) double cream

Pasta e Fagioli

1 Soak dried beans overnight in cold water.

2 Drain beans and combine with marrow bone, tomato purée and 4 pints (2 litres) water in a large saucepan. Bring to the boil; lower heat, cover, and simmer for 2 hours.

3 Chop onion and garlic finely, and sauté in olive oil until transparent. Add to soup.

4 Add finely chopped parsley, salt, freshly ground black pepper and cayenne pepper, to taste, and oregano. Simmer soup, covered, for about 20 minutes.

5 Add macaroni and continue cooking until macaroni is cooked. Serve sprinkled with Parmesan cheese.

Serves 4

Ingredients

½ lb (225g) dried kidney or haricot beans
1 beef marrow bone, about 4 inches (10 cm) long
4 level tablespoons tomato purée
1 Spanish onion
1 clove garlic
3 tablespoons olive oil
2 level tablespoons finely chopped parsley
1 level teaspoon salt
Freshly ground black pepper
Cayenne pepper
1 level tablespoon dried oregano
½ lb (225g) macaroni, broken in pieces
Freshly grated Parmesan cheese

A Venetian Variation on the Pasta e Fagioli Theme
I first enjoyed this delicious rustic bean and pasta soup in Calabria; it was a sort of poor man's spoon and fork supper, delicious and filling at the same time. Recently I came across another version in a little village just north of Venice: a highly-flavoured bean purée with cooked whole beans and macaroni stirred into it.

To make the Venetian version of *pasta e fagioli*: proceed as in Steps 1–4 above. Remove half the beans and purée the remainder in a food processor. Fifteen minutes before serving, add macaroni and continue cooking until macaroni is well done. Return reserved beans to the soup and heat through. Serve sprinkled with Parmesan cheese.

Lentils à la Provençale

1 Place lentils in a large saucepan. Fill pan with water and bring gently to the boil. Remove saucepan from heat and let lentils soak in hot water for 1 hour.

2 Drain lentils and cook with onion in salted water until tender. The length of time for cooking lentils depends on their type and their age. In any case, after ½ hour look at them from time to time to see if they are cooked. When ready, drain.

3 Heat olive oil in a saucepan; add finely chopped garlic and lentils, and continue to cook, shaking pan from time to time, until lentils are heated through.

4 Pound anchovy fillets and butter to a smooth paste, and add to lentils, stirring in well. Season to taste with salt and freshly ground black pepper. Place in serving dish and serve very hot.

Serves 4-6

Ingredients

1 lb (450g) lentils
1 Spanish onion
Salt
4–6 tablespoons olive oil
1 clove garlic, finely chopped
½ can anchovy fillets
¼ lb (100g) butter
Freshly ground black pepper

Canned Ham and Chicken Salad

Ingredients

½ lb (225g) canned ham, diced
½ lb (225g) canned chicken, diced
2 bananas, sliced
1 orange, separated into segments
1 avocado pear, peeled and sliced
¼ pint (1½ dl) double cream
¼ pint (1½ dl) mayonnaise (see page 63)
1 tablespoon tomato ketchup
1 teaspoon Worcestershire sauce
2 tablespoons lemon juice
2 tablespoons brandy
Salt and freshly ground black pepper
Lettuce leaves

1 Combine diced ham and chicken with sliced bananas, orange segments and sliced avocado in a mixing bowl.

2 Whip the cream; blend in mayonnaise; add ketchup, Worcestershire sauce, lemon juice and brandy, and pour over meat and fruit mixture. Season to taste with salt and freshly ground black pepper, and mix carefully. Serve on lettuce leaves.

Serves 4

Curried Ham and Chicken Salad with Fruits
Make curried ham and chicken salad with fruits as above. But when making the sauce, omit the tomato ketchup, Worcestershire sauce and brandy, and substitute curry powder, to taste.

Provençal Salad of Salt Cod

Ingredients

1 lb (450g) dried salt cod fillets
6 large ripe tomatoes
½ pint (3 dl) well-flavoured mayonnaise (see page 63)
1 clove garlic, finely chopped
1–2 anchovy fillets, finely chopped
1 level tablespoon finely chopped basil or tarragon
Finely chopped parsley
1 level tablespoon finely chopped capers
Lemon juice

1 Soak cod fillets overnight in a bowl under gently running water.

2 Drain salt cod and put in a saucepan; cover with cold water and bring to the boil; drain and return to saucepan; cover with cold water and bring to the boil again; turn off heat and allow to steep in hot water for 10 minutes. Strain cod, remove skin and bones and dice. Cool.

3 To prepare tomato cases: plunge tomatoes into boiling water one by one, and remove their skins. Slice cap off each and carefully scoop out all pulp and seeds. Cover loosely with foil and chill in refrigerator until ready to use.

4 Combine mayonnaise with finely chopped garlic, anchovy fillets and basil or tarragon, 2 level tablespoons finely chopped parsley, finely chopped capers and lemon juice, to taste.

5 Toss diced fish lightly in sauce until well coated; pile fish mixture into tomato cases and garnish with finely chopped parsley.

Serves 6

Canned Pineapple Romanoff

Ingredients

1 large can pineapple segments
6 level tablespoons icing sugar
3 tablespoons Cointreau
3 tablespoons rum
½ pint (3 dl) double cream
3 tablespoons kirsch
Grated rind of 1 orange

1 Drain canned pineapple and toss segments with 4 level tablespoons icing sugar.

2 Arrange segments in a bowl suitable for serving at the table, and pour over them a mixture of Cointreau and rum; chill in refrigerator.

3 One hour before serving: whip cream; add remaining icing sugar and flavour with kirsch. Spoon whipped cream into marinated pineapple pieces, tossing until every piece is coated with creamy liqueur mixture. Top with finely grated orange rind, and keep cold until time to serve.

Serves 6 - 8

Cherries Jubilee

1 Drain cherries and measure out ½ pint (3 dl) of the juice.

2 Combine sugar, cinnamon, orange juice, grated orange rind, cornflour and cherry juice, and bring slowly to the boil in blazer of chafing dish. Allow to bubble for 5 minutes, stirring from time to time, until sauce is reduced to desired consistency.

3 Add cherries to sauce and .heat through.

4 Heat Cognac and cherry brandy, and pour over cherries. Ignite, and when flames die down pour hot mixture over individual portions of vanilla ice cream.

Serves 4

Ingredients
1 large can pitted dark
    cherries
2 level tablespoons sugar
1 stick cinnamon
Juice and grated rind of
    ½ orange
1 level teaspoon cornflour
4 tablespoons Cognac
4 tablespoons cherry brandy
Vanilla ice cream (see page 190)

Canned Peach Cobbler

1 To make pastry: combine sifted flour, cornflour, salt, butter and water in a bowl. Mix well; line a deep dish with the pastry, reserving enough for top strips.

2 To make filling: combine sugar, cornflour and 2 level tablespoons butter with peach juice in a saucepan. Cook until thick – about 5 minutes. Pour over sliced peaches and add lemon juice

3 Pour filling into pastry-lined dish. Dot with butter. Top with strips of pastry and bake in a slow oven (325°F/ 170°C/Mark 3) for 30 minutes.

Serves 4 - 6

Ingredients
PASTRY
½ lb (225g) sifted plain flour
1 oz (25g) cornflour
1 level teaspoon salt
6 oz (175g) butter
4 tablespoons water

FILLING
½ lb (225g) sugar
2 level tablespoons cornflour
Butter
1 large can sliced peaches
    and juice of canned
    peaches
1 tablespoon lemon juice

Baked Bread and Butter Pudding

1 Remove crusts from bread; butter slices, and cut into thin strips. Lay bread strips in a well-buttered loaf dish. Dish should be about half full.

2 Whisk eggs in a mixing bowl; add milk, and sugar and vanilla essence, to taste. Mix well together and strain over bread strips. Allow pudding to stand until bread is well soaked.

3 Sprinkle pudding with currants or sultanas. Bake for 45-60 minutes in a moderate oven (350°F/180°C/Mark 4) until golden brown and firm to the touch. Sprinkle with sugar and serve hot.

Serves 4

Ingredients
2–4 slices bread
Softened butter
2 eggs
1 pint (6 dl) milk
Castor sugar
Vanilla essence
2 level tablespoons currants
    or sultanas

INDEXES
PART I – General

PART II – Index of Courses